MEDIA TALK

ISSUES in CULTURAL and MEDIA STUDIES

Series editor: Stuart Allan

Published titles

MEDIA TALK

Conversation Analysis and the Study of Broadcasting

Ian Hutchby

Open University Press

Open University Press
McGraw-Hill Education
McGraw-Hill House
Shoppenhangers Road
Maidenhead
Berkshire
England
SL6 2QL

email: enquiries@openup.co.uk
world wide web: www.openup.co.uk

and Two Penn Plaza, New York, NY 10121–2289, USA

First published 2006

A catalogue record of this book is available from the British Library

ISBN-10: 0 335 20995 5 (pb)   0 335 20996 3 (hb)
ISBN-13: 978 0335 20995 8 (pb)   978 0335 20996 5 (hb)

Library of Congress Cataloging-in-Publication Data
CIP data applied for

Typeset by RefineCatch Limited, Bungay, Suffolk
Printed in the UK by Bell & Bain Ltd, Glasgow

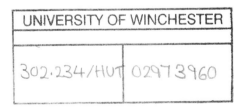

ACKNOWLEDGEMENTS

Chapter 4 originally appeared as Ian Hutchby, 'Confrontation as a spectacle: The argumentative frame of the Ricki Lake show' in Andrew Tolson (ed.), *Television Talk Shows: Discourse, Performance, Spectacle* (Lawrence Erlbaum Associates, 2001). Chapter 5 draws on material from two sources: Ian Hutchby, 'Witnessing: The use of first-hand knowledge in legitimating lay opinions on talk radio' in *Discourse Studies*, Vol. 3, pp. 481–97 (Sage, 2001) and Ian Hutchby, 'Power in discourse: The case of arguments on a British talk radio show' in *Discourse and Society*, Vol. 7, pp. 481–98 (Sage, 1996). An earlier version of Chapter 6 originally appeared as Ian Hutchby, 'Aspects of recipient design in expert advice-giving on call-in radio' in *Discourse Processes*, Vol. 19, pp. 219–38 (Ablex Publishing Corporation, 1995). Parts of Chapter 8 originally appeared as Ian Hutchby, 'Building alignments in public debate: A case study from British TV' in *Text*, Vol. 17, pp. 161–79 (Mouton de Gruyter, 1997).

CONTENTS

Case Studies Part III

Broadcasters and Politicians

Postscript

FOREWORD

Serious public discourse, the late Pierre Bourdieu declared during a passionate debate about the French media, is becoming little more than 'cultural fast-food'. He believed that it is consistently losing out to those forms of media reporting that give priority to simply entertaining members of the audience. In-depth current affairs interviews on French television, for example, are routinely being transformed into 'mindless talk show chatter' between 'approved' (that is to say, 'safe') speakers willing to participate in what are largely staged 'exchanges'. This relentless search for the sensational and the spectacular, he argued, ensures that an undue emphasis is placed on certain types of dramatic events, namely those that are simple to discuss. Moreover, Bourdieu maintained, because media people are 'so afraid of being boring, they opt for confrontations over debates, prefer polemics over rigorous argument, and in general, do whatever they can to promote conflict'. In other words, he lamented, 'the focus is on those things which are apt to arouse curiosity but require no analysis, especially in the political sphere.'

In privileging for investigation 'media talk' as a conceptual problematic on its own terms, Ian Hutchby offers a different perspective on the relationship between media and public discourse. *Media Talk* begins with the deceptively simple observation that radio and television broadcasting involves talk in all its genres, before explaining why both 'serious' and 'entertaining' talk are more complicated – and, indeed, more deserving of our attention – than might first appear. From there, Chapter 1 describes and assesses the emergence of an empirical interest in broadcast talk as a key development in media sociology. Chapter 2 provides an accessible introduction to the methods of conversation analysis, and proceeds to highlight the contribution made by this approach to exploring relevant concerns – such as the relationship between broadcasters and audiences, and the public role of media output in civic life. Subsequent chapters focus on a range of talk-based media genres, including radio phone-ins, controversial talk shows, news interviews, advice programmes and current affairs debates. Across a series of case studies, Hutchby not only describes the communicative imperatives of talk on radio and television, but offers ongoing illustrations of how the analysis of media talk can be carried out in practical terms. Overall, this book makes a compelling case for the study of broadcast talk as a significant contribution to media and cultural studies, demonstrating why media conversations need to be prioritized for examination. Indeed, as Hutchby shows, such conversations are both involved in – and, crucially, are partly constitutive of – an everyday awareness of the social realities around us.

The *Issues in Cultural and Media Studies* series aims to facilitate a diverse range of critical investigations into pressing questions considered to be central to current thinking and research. In light of the remarkable speed at which the conceptual agendas of cultural and media studies are changing, the series is committed to contributing to what is an ongoing process of re-evaluation and critique. Each of the books is intended to provide a lively, innovative and comprehensive introduction to a specific topical issue from a fresh perspective. The reader is offered a thorough grounding in the most salient debates indicative of the book's subject, as well as important insights into how new modes of enquiry may be established for future explorations. Taken as a whole, then, the series is designed to cover the core components of cultural and media studies courses in an imaginatively distinctive and engaging manner.

Stuart Allan

NOTE ON DATA AND TRANSCRIPTION

The data used in this book comprise transcripts of television and radio programmes recorded off air. The transcription and presentation of actual examples of broadcast media talk is key to the approach being described in the book. Therefore the reader should treat the transcripts as a central part of each chapter. Even though I comment in detail on most transcripts, it is important that they are read closely in their own right. Initially, due to the technical nature of the transcripts, this may not be easy. It is therefore important to read and, where necessary, refer back to the following glossary of transcription symbols used in the book. The main aim of these symbols is to provide a sense, in written transcription, of how a stretch of talk 'sounds' on the tape. Therefore the main things to look out for are symbols indicating stress or emphasis, pauses, loudness or quietness, and overlapping or interruptive talk. (For more detailed information on data and transcription the reader should consult Chapter 3 of Hutchby and Wooffitt, 1998.)

Transcription conventions

(0.5)	Numbers in brackets indicate a gap timed in tenths of a second.
(.)	A dot enclosed in brackets indicates a 'micropause' of less than one tenth of a second.
=	Equals signs are used to indicate 'latching' or absolutely no discernible gap between utterances; or to show the continuation of a speaker's utterance across intervening lines of transcript.
[ ]	Square brackets indicate the points where overlapping talk starts (left bracket) and ends (right bracket). Although the start of an overlap is always marked, the end is only sometimes marked.

[[	Double left square brackets indicate turns that start simultaneously.
(())	Double brackets are used to describe a non-verbal activity: for example ((banging sound)). They are also used to enclose the transcriber's comments on contextual or other relevant features.
( )	Empty brackets indicate the presence of an unclear utterance or other sound on the tape.
.hhh	h's preceded by a dot are used to represent audible inward breathing. The more h's, the longer the breath.
hhhh	h's with no preceding dot are used in the same way to represent outward breathing.
huh	Laughter is transcribed using 'laugh tokens' which, as far as the
heh	transcriber is able, represent the individual sounds that speakers make
hih	while laughing.
XXX	Rows of X's are used to indicate audience applause. Upper-case X's signify loud applause, while lower-case x's are used to show quiet or fading applause.
sou:::nd	Colons indicate the stretching of a sound or a word. The more colons the greater the extent of the stretching.
sou-	A dash indicates a word suddenly cut off during an utterance.
.	Punctuation marks are not used grammatically, but to indicate prosodic
,	aspects of the talk. A full stop indicates a falling tone; commas indicate
?	fall-rise or rise-fall (i.e. a 'continuing' tone); question marks indicate a marked rising tone.
↑↓	Upward and downward arrows are used to mark an overall rise or fall in pitch across a phrase.
a:	Underlining of a letter before a colon indicates a small drop in pitch during a word.
a:	Underlining of a colon after a letter indicates a small rise in pitch at that point in the word.
Underline	Other underlining indicates speaker emphasis. Words may be underlined either in part or in full, depending on the enunciation.
CAPITALS	Capitals mark a section of speech markedly louder than that surrounding it.
→	Arrows in the left margin point to specific parts of the transcript discussed in the text.
° °	Degree signs are used to indicate that the talk between them is noticeably quieter than surrounding talk.
< >	Outward chevrons are used to indicate that the talk between them is noticeably slower than surrounding talk.
> <	Inner chevrons are used to indicate that the talk between them is noticeably quicker than surrounding talk.

ABOUT THE AUTHOR

Ian Hutchby is Professor of Communication at Brunel University. He is the author of *Confrontation Talk* (Erlbaum, 1996), *Conversation Analysis* (with Robin Wooffitt, Polity, 1998) and *Conversation and Technology* (Polity, 2001); and editor (with Jo Moran-Ellis) of *Children and Social Competence* (Routledge, 1998) and *Children, Technology and Culture* (Routledge, 2001).

1 | DISCOVERING MEDIA TALK

This book is about the forms of talk used by broadcasters, both on radio and on television, as their means of communicating with audiences – whether the co-present bodies of which a studio audience is comprised, or the altogether more amorphous, distributed population making up the 'absent' audience of viewers and listeners. It is also about the forms of talk used by audience members themselves when they are given the opportunity, through broadcast **genres** such as audience participation debates, phone-ins and the like, to take up their own role in the production of broadcast talk. Drawing upon a range of media forms and genres, I argue that a focus on talk can provide insights into the very nature of '**mass communication**' in the specific arena of radio and television broadcasting.

The forms of talk I examine are various, and include televised audience debates (Chapter 3), confrontational TV talk shows (Chapter 4), open-line talk radio shows (Chapter 5), advice-giving broadcasts (Chapter 6), news interviews (Chapter 7) and political panel discussions (Chapter 8). These are not, of course, the only types of broadcast talk that radio and television audiences can encounter. But they do have a number of things in common. First, each of them involves, in different ways, a large proportion of *unscripted* talk, or what Erving Goffman (1981), writing about radio continuity announcers, called 'fresh talk'. By that, Goffman meant talk that does not involve the speaker reading aloud from a text or recalling memorized lines. Much of the talk that radio and television audiences encounter is pre-scripted: for instance in news bulletins, in documentaries, in drama or in situation comedy. But in phone-ins, talk shows, interviews and the like, while there may well have been some planning and preparation prior to the broadcast, the talk as it unfolds in the real time of the show is not scripted, meaning that the participants have to be creative in reacting and responding to one another's talk in the course of its production.

A second thing these forms have in common is that they all involve *live* talk: that is, the talk is either broadcast live (as in the majority of news interviews or phone-ins), or else the show as broadcast effectively preserves a sense of liveness in its very editing. In other words, although it has been prerecorded, the edit seeks to sustain the viewer's experience of the event as a 'single take'. In this sense, the book addresses a specific type of media talk: communicative interaction 'live on air'.

A third common feature is that these forms of talk do not just involve professional broadcasters. Rather, in talk shows, interviews, debates and the rest we find broadcasters in interaction with speakers from outside the broadcasting profession: politicians, representatives of social organizations and institutions, eyewitnesses at newsworthy events, sportspeople, and, perhaps most significantly, ordinary members of the public. In this sense, the talk is of particular interest because it crosses between key sociological categories such as 'private' and 'public', 'lay' and 'professional', in complex ways. For instance, news interviews may involve politicians – public figures who seek to represent the interests of ordinary people – talking to broadcast journalists – a different type of public figure also seeking to represent ordinary interests – in the context of broadcasting, which is a public form of talk received in the private domains of people's homes. In audience participation shows, there may be experts or institutional representatives involved along with professional broadcasters, and in addition the voices of private individuals or laypersons from the mundane sphere of everyday life are given a central place.

In each of these ways, the study of talk on radio and television invites us into further consideration of a range of important issues such as the relationship between broadcasters and audiences and the public role of media output. Far from being a trivial or secondary aspect of the pervasive phenomenon of mass communication, media talk is central to a whole raft of concerns at the heart of contemporary media studies.

Broadcasting and the centrality of talk

The starting point for an interest in media talk lies in one very central fact: the activity of talking is key to each of the main genres of broadcast media output, whether news and current affairs, advertising, documentary, drama or entertainment. While the technological infrastructures of broadcasting may be evolving (from terrestrial to satellite; from restricted channel output to expandable 24-hour multi-channel availability), one thing remains constant – the audiences for radio and television programming are bombarded with talk in a rich variety of forms.

To take just a few commonplace examples: Radio and television journalists read out news items, interview politicians and others in the news, and talk to correspondents on the scene at newsworthy events. Chat show hosts interview their celebrity guests. Radio disc jockeys talk, briefly or at length, in the spaces between playing records. Talk radio hosts talk to those members of the audience who have called in to have their say on a topical issue. Quiz show hosts direct prize-winning questions to their contestants. Sports commentators talk the audience through what is happening during a sporting event. Meanwhile pundits talk about what either is about to happen or has just happened at that same event. Even the actors in soap operas and other dramas speak lines that simulate ordinary conversation in various settings.

The centrality of talk to radio and television broadcasting is particularly well demonstrated by the power of its noticeable absence during unplanned lapses in the stream of broadcast sound. Broadcasting itself often makes an issue out of this. Humorous out-take ('blooper') compilation shows regularly contain excerpts from news broadcasts showing cutaways to outside correspondents who are not yet ready to deliver their piece to camera, or interviewees in remote studios who have not been told that they are about to go on camera, resulting in silences which have to be 'filled' by extempore talk from the studio anchor. Indeed, on radio in particular, there is a general injunction against allowing any silence of more than a few seconds for fear that the listener will assume something is wrong with the signal and change channels.

Radio broadcasting even has automated mechanisms designed to guard against the possibility of so-called 'dead air' (that is, silence) by switching on music if any stretch of broadcast silence goes on for more than a few seconds. In the UK, this was recently brought to the fore when the BBC planned a broadcast of avant garde composer John Cage's notorious silent composition *4′33″*, in which the orchestra is instructed to make 'no intentional sounds' for four minutes and thirty-three seconds (Cage, 1960 [1952]). To facilitate the broadcast, the station had to be doubly sure that all the automatic anti-dead air mechanisms had been disabled.

Perhaps because of its ubiquity, talk as a broadcasting activity in its own right has largely been ignored, or more strictly, taken for granted by media analysts. No doubt this is also due to the fact that the activity of talking is often seen as a trivial phenomenon, one which has nothing much to do with more pressing issues such as the nature of media bias, persuasion, or the portrayal of violence. But my starting point in this book is that whatever aspect of broadcasting we think about, at some level we are inevitably thinking about the use of spoken language.

For example, any study of media bias, such as in the news reporting of strikes, politics or war, is based on accounts of the relevant events that the media produce. Those accounts are necessarily linguistic: they use language to describe events in a particular way. Sometimes that language is written rather than spoken, as in the case of newspapers; but even then the written accounts themselves rely heavily on talk, in interviews, phone calls or other information-gathering activities involving reporters and their sources (Clayman, 1990). Similarly, any study of how the media persuade, such as through adverts, necessarily relies on a description of the persuasive language that is used, and the relationship between that and the persuasive images that adverts give us. Even studies of media as entertainment rely to a large extent on the fact that certain forms of language are used to 'cue' audiences into the sense that what they are encountering is, in fact, entertainment. The language of innuendo, confession and confrontation that is characteristic of many popular talk shows, game shows and 'reality' shows is recognizably different from the 'serious' language that we hear during a documentary.

We can broaden the argument still further. Television and radio talk has to be seen as key to the nature of the relationship between the media, public opinion and public knowledge. The media not only play a central role in defining particular issues as newsworthy and therefore 'opinionable', but also provide the broadest and most accessible public spaces in which ordinary members of the populace can express their opinions on such issues. These range from radio phone-ins (Hutchby, 1996) to audience participation shows such as *Donahue* (Carbaugh, 1988) or *Oprah* (Livingstone and Lunt, 1994), to the increasingly pervasive use of e-mail and text messaging by which audiences can contribute in all sorts of broadcast events (Thornborrow and Fitzgerald, 2002). The media have developed specific forms of interviewing, and have in the process made the interview one of our principal sources of information about anything ranging from major world events to the lifestyles of the rich and famous (Schudson, 1994). Broadcast interviews are carried out entirely through a specialized form of talk, in which broadcaster and interviewee normatively restrict themselves to the exchange of questions and answers (Clayman and Heritage, 2002). The interview is thus a particular type of social interaction that has become very widely used in the media. Indeed Atkinson and Silverman (1997) have argued that partly due to the prevalence of interviews as a form of broadcast talk (not just in news programming but in light entertainment too), we live in an 'interview culture' where more and more we expect the interview to be our anchor to world events and the lives of celebrities.

It is surprising, therefore, that only comparatively recently has media talk begun to be studied as a phenomenon in its own right. The last few years have seen the appearance of a small number of studies which each focus on detailed analysis of one particular genre or aspect of broadcasting: for instance, news interviews (Clayman and Heritage, 2002), audience participation debates (Carbaugh, 1988), or talk radio shows (Hutchby, 1996). There have also been a number of collected editions addressing a wider range of programme types (Scannell, 1991a; Bell and Garrett, 1998; Haarman, 2000; Tolson, 2001) and books that argue for the centrality of a focus on discourse for the critical analysis of the relationship between media and society (Fairclough, 1995; Scannell, 1996; Matheson, 2005).

In this book I both draw upon and develop ideas and methods found in this small but growing body of research. Using a selection of case studies based on the particular genres of media talk I mentioned at the start, and subjecting them to analysis using methods that I will outline in Chapter 2, the following chapters show how we can find, in the small details of talk, interesting phenomena that cast light on the work that broadcasters do, consciously or tacitly, to produce effective communication in the particular contexts of radio and television. In this sense, the book does not simply argue that media talk is a worthwhile object of analytic attention for media researchers. It also seeks to demonstrate *how* that is the case, by illustrating how the application of specific methods can be used to yield insights into the practices by which broadcasters and audiences communicate.

In this opening chapter, I will trace out some of the background against which an analytical interest in media talk itself developed. Central to that interest is a key question for media research: that of the relationship between the products of broadcasting and the understandings and practices of its audience. Among a small collection of media researchers in Britain during the 1980s and 90s, there developed a critique of what had become the accepted approach to this question – an alternative perspective which sought to argue that talk, as a central practice within broadcasting, was nevertheless rendered systematically invisible by conventional conceptual and methodological approaches to media analysis. The following sections sketch out the main lines of this critique.

Broadcasters and audiences (1): From effects to texts

From the 1970s onwards, media sociology has given a great deal of attention to the question of how audiences 'consume' or 'make sense of' what radio and television broadcasters present to them. One strand of this interest lies in a research tradition which focused on the 'uses and gratifications' that audiences derive from different kinds of media output (Blumler and Katz, 1974). Uses and gratifications research itself began as a critical response to some of the earliest forms of media research which were concerned with the power of the mass media to influence audiences, or more specifically, to produce negative effects in terms of social behaviour and social consciousness, usually without audiences having any real awareness of this power. For instance, in the mid-twentieth century the sociologists Paul Lazarsfeld and Robert Merton (1948) developed their argument that one of the central functions of the mass media was to produce a 'narcotizing effect' by virtue of which the populace suffered a dulling of social consciousness and critical awareness, essentially as a result of the simplified stories that were offered to them. This idea, which was also developed from a different theoretical angle by the Frankfurt School (Adorno and Horkheimer, 1972), can still be traced today in ongoing debates about the 'dumbing down' of culture in the mass media.

A more recent example of effects research is a study by two psychologists, Hans Eysenck and D.K.B. Nias (1978), in which they used experimental techniques to support the general proposition that the more violence people watch on television the more 'desensitized' they become to violence. Using measures of viewers' galvanic skin responses (the amount that they sweat) Eysenck and Nias (1978) claimed to provide evidence that groups of people who have just watched a violent episode on television reacted less strongly to being shown other violent scenes than a comparative group who had not previously watched the violent film. Their conclusion is one that can easily be recognized from much media commentary on the amount of violence shown on television today: 'desensitization, by reducing anxiety, may make people more likely to carry out acts of aggression in the future' (Eysenck and Nias, 1978: 184). Eysenck and Nias thus argued in favour of the judicious use of censorship in order to reduce this apparent threat (for critical discussions of the logic of this argument, see the papers collected in Barker and Petley, 1997).

One of the key problems that can be identified with effects research is the implicit model of the audience that it relies upon. To put it very simply, audience members are typically treated as **cultural dopes** who are conditioned or acted upon by the media outside of their own active awareness. The uses and gratifications approach sought to develop an alternative view of audiences as active consumers of media output. Far from it being the case that the mass media produced unconscious effects that changed audience behaviour, it was argued, audience members actively and critically selected those aspects of media output which most suited their various everyday needs; be it a desire for entertainment, for escapism, for information about events in the world, or whatever. Thus, people *use* the media, and they experience or derive certain *gratifications* from the media.

Uses and gratifications research has also been criticized for its particular implied model of the audience member. Like effects research, though in a slightly different way, this approach tends to adopt a behaviouristic standpoint. But while effects research often takes a basic stimulus-response position, uses and gratifications research favours a more complex model. It sees people as having innate 'needs' which are then 'gratified' by certain kinds of media output. In other words, its overall aim is to get at the psychological mechanisms by which media output is related to the aims and objectives that people formulate in their heads. This actually makes it in some ways very similar to the kinds of research media organizations themselves do in order to monitor audience 'tastes': it asks what audiences 'want', what they 'get out of' certain programmes, and it has a particular interest in how programmes satisfy individual 'needs'. In order to discover this, the methods deployed in uses and gratifications research tend to be interviews, focus groups, the use of 'viewer diaries', and questionnaires. These are the kinds of techniques often used by media organizations themselves when they want to determine something about the popularity of programmes. Later in the book we will come to a critique of such methods seen as offering a 'window' on to people's inner thought processes.

A third, and particularly significant approach to the understanding of audiences developed in part out of a critique of the assumptions underpinning both of these earlier perspectives. A group of researchers at the Centre for Contemporary Cultural Studies (CCCS) at the University of Birmingham, UK, during the 1970s and 80s argued that both traditional effects research *and* uses and gratifications research tended to see the relationship between media and audience in a one-dimensional way: for effects research the question was how the media affect the audience, whereas for uses and gratifications, the question was how the audience puts the media to use in satisfying needs. The CCCS group wanted to show that the whole thing is far more fluid and complex than is implied in either of these research programmes (for a collection of relevant papers see Hall *et al.*, 1980).

In this pursuit the CCCS group drew on an approach that had developed within film studies and was associated primarily with the influential journal *Screen*. For this reason, it is often referred to as 'Screen theory'. Drawing on the study of literature, Screen theory argued that media products could be seen as 'texts' the meanings of which the audience 'read' or interpret, much the same as we do with books or other literary artefacts (see MacCabe, 1985). But whereas anything we encounter in the media presents us with meanings which we have to interpret, their argument was that we are not free to make whatever interpretations we like. The meanings of a text are 'written' in the process of production in such a way as to make only certain 'subject-positions' available to the viewer, or 'reader'. The most well-known example of this idea is the view that 'realist' films – that is, films that present audiences with people and events that are supposed to represent reality in a natural and therefore believable manner – are inevitably 'bourgeois', in the sense that they serve to support the established social order. For Screen theory, this is so because such films do not challenge our view of the 'natural order' of things, the way things are 'supposed to be'. Rather, they reinforce it by allowing us to interpret the films only in certain ways: as representations of 'real life' (however dramatized and romanticized). By contrast, *avant garde* films such as those of French director Jean-Luc Godard, which dispense with conventional narrative and do not aim to represent events in any kind of naturalistic way, are progressive precisely because they do *not* present an easy set of interpretations but function to challenge our everyday perceptions of how things should be or should happen.

The complexities of this argument are many, and the interested reader should turn to MacCabe (1985) for greater detail (see also Moores, 1993; Nightingale, 1996; Ross and Nightingale, 2003). For now, the key point is that Stuart Hall (1980) and others at the CCCS utilized the 'textual' idea developed by Screen theory while at the same time arguing that, in its original form, there were numerous things wrong with this approach. For one thing, studies tended to centre upon the interpretive work of the researcher, who in a God's-eye kind of way, would attempt to delineate the possible meanings and associated subject-positions embedded in a given media text, thereby, it was claimed, revealing its hidden ideological content. The audience's interpretations themselves were therefore sidelined. Relatedly, Screen theory involved a form of textual determinism, in that it was assumed that there are specific meanings embedded in any media text which function to 'situate' the reader (the audience) in particular subject-positions and disenable them from taking up certain other positions.

Hall (1980) argued that the meanings that any given media text makes available are not fixed and there may be considerable sociological variation in the readings that different audience constituents produce. It thus became much more important to attend to the *variable* readings that any media product made possible. More than that, it became important to look empirically at the variable readings that were actually *made* by given audiences in concrete situations. Clearly, audiences encounter and make sense of the media within the contexts of everyday life; thus there may be a sense in which the frameworks of meaning found in other spheres of everyday life have an impact on the frameworks of meaning developed in relation to the media. Finally, it was recognized that at this stage little was known of what people *really* do with the media outside the context of a questionnaire, focus group or interview where, for instance, they are being asked questions by a uses and gratifications researcher as to how certain programmes satisfy their needs.

The key theory at the heart of this work became known as the *encoding/decoding* model, after the title of Hall's (1980) paper. Hall argued that the mass media – primarily, radio and television – should be understood in terms of a *circuit* of communication. At one part of the circuit are the producers, who encode, or 'write', the meanings of their programmes in particular ways and with particular kinds of audience understandings in mind. At another part of the circuit are the audience, or consumers, who decode, 'read' or interpret that programme in particular ways. These two parts of the circuit are linked by the processes of distribution (broadcasting, advertising, etc.), on the one hand, and feedback (viewing statistics, market research, etc.) on the other. Within this circuit, 'preferred' meanings may be built into certain media texts by their producers: that is, the structure and organization of a programme and its mode of representation may be designed to encourage the viewer to accept its version of 'truth' or 'reality'. Crucially, however, audiences – and it is important to note that they are now being described in the plural, as disparate, fragmentary collections of individuals, rather than the homogeneous mass often envisaged by earlier approaches – are not automatically tied to such 'subject-positions' by ideological elements written into the media text. Rather, they are actively involved in defining their own positions in relation to that text, and so may adopt readings that question, challenge or reject elements of the text's 'message'.

One key significance of Hall's theory, therefore, is the recognition that there may not be any necessary symmetry between the frameworks of meaning involved in *encoding* a particular text and those involved in *decoding* it. Indeed, whether there can in fact be said to be any kind of stable or definite meanings embedded in media texts is systematically problematized by this model. A second significance is the implication that either 'end' of the encoding/decoding circuit can be subject to empirical enquiry: we could go and do a study of how media producers encode their products just as much as we could look at how audiences actually decode them.

The main analytical interest taken up by researchers using this model in the CCCS and elsewhere tended to be in the 'decoding' side. Drawing on the work of political sociologist Frank Parkin (1972), Hall (1980) suggested three basic types of reading that could be discerned in audience decoding: *dominant, oppositional* and *negotiated* readings. Briefly, a 'dominant' reading would be one that accorded with the preferred interpretation encoded within the programme. For Hall, this also implied an acceptance of the worldview and political ideals of contemporary capitalist society, which it was assumed underpinned most popular broadcast output, especially soap operas and news programmes. An 'oppositional' reading would be one that overtly challenged that implied worldview, and that potentially also criticized either the programme as a whole or its underlying ideological assumptions (Parkin (1972) originally preferred the term 'radical' as this position often involves a heightened level of class consciousness). A 'negotiated' reading would be one that took some kind of middle line between these two extremes, for instance, by agreeing with the programme's overall 'message' but taking issue with certain individual parts. (The term 'negotiated' is perhaps unfortunate in this context, since, as noted above, all three types of reading can in fact be considered as negotiated positions.)

Some of the earliest and still most influential empirical studies of audience sense-making were undertaken by David Morley in an attempt to find some evidence for Hall's theories. Morley's most well-known work, in collaboration with Charlotte Brundson, was based on a study of the British TV magazine show *Nationwide*, examining how it encoded the meanings of the events it reported on and, more importantly, how different categories of audience decoded or made sense of those meanings (Brundson and Morley, 1978; Morley, 1980). Their procedure was first to produce their own 'analytic reading' of the *Nationwide* programme, then to find out what different 'socially situated clusters of viewers' made of it, by means of loosely structured group interviews (the audience study used around 30 groupings with differing mixes of ethnic, gender and occupational backgrounds).

The initial assumption was that there would be dominant, negotiated and oppositional readings, and these would broadly correspond with the class position of their subjects and the kinds of discourses about social processes to which they had access in their daily lives. However, the findings of this study were complex, and crucially, showed no direct correlation between social situation and decoding strategies. Rather, it became clear that while socioeconomic status may serve to limit the range of interpretive resources available to different groups, nevertheless groups occupying the same class or occupational position were internally differentiated in terms of whether they produced dominant, negotiated or oppositional types of reading. While this may not have supported the original hypothesis, it remained a significant conclusion; one which has substantially influenced subsequent research in the field of audience reception.

A number of criticisms have been levelled at the encoding/decoding model and the empirical research it inspired. First, it is overtly political. Hall was drawing not only from the work mentioned above, but also, and possibly more directly, from the Marxist theory of hegemony associated with Antonio Gramsci (Gramsci, 1971). Because of this, like the *Screen* theorists, he was explicitly concerned with the *ideological* functions of the media. Indeed it is only within this framework, in which the media are seen as a powerful ideological force closely bound up with the establishment and mainte-nance of hegemony for capitalist structures of social order, that the three types of potential audience readings can in fact make sense. Parkin (1972) had developed his original dominant, negotiated and radical categories in an attempt to explain the political anomaly of why certain types of working-class voters voted Conservative rather than, as might be predicted from their class and occupational background, Labour. The upshot of this was that research tended to *assume* that certain things can be found in audience accounts before the research was actually carried out. The clearest example is the *Nationwide* study itself, in which assumptions about the relationship between class position and 'dominant', 'negotiated' or 'oppositional' readings were nothing like as clear cut as the theory predicted.

A related criticism focused on the way that Hall and Morley were working with *class* as the key sociological variable. In a study of the use of video-recorders in the home published at about the same time, Dorothy Hobson (1980) drew on feminist theory to show how the appropriation of media within the domestic sphere is quite severely differentiated along *gender* lines. The housewives in her study had a very clear idea of the kind of TV programmes they saw as 'women's shows' (soap opera, light entertainment, quiz shows, American drama) and those they categorized as 'men's shows' (news, current affairs, documentaries, war movies). The women still seemed to think that what they categorized as men's programmes were somehow more 'important' than the ones they liked. In this sense, Hobson argued, women may have had a very active role as interpreters of media output, but those interpretations tended to reinforce a particular, dominant conception of gender roles in media consumption.

Despite these criticisms, much contemporary empirical research into audience sense-making owes a great deal to the original models and methodological techniques developed by the CCCS group. There is an ongoing programme of research which has become known as 'reception research', the central characteristic of which is to find ways of gaining closer access to the interpretive work of audience members (see Moores, 1993; Nightingale, 1996; Ross and Nightingale, 2003). For instance, reception researchers may ask groups of people to watch a recording of a television programme, and then interview them about the range of meanings that the 'text' has for them (see Barbour and Kitzinger, 1999). Although these researchers do not tend to begin, like Brundson and Morley (1978) did, with their own analytical reading of the programme, nevertheless one danger of this approach is that audience understandings are subsequently reinterpreted within the framework of the researcher's own reading of the programme, thereby ironicizing the whole process. The opposite danger is that the endless variety of audience sense-making practices is uncritically celebrated, resulting in a rather empty, 'populist' festival of diversity (Cobley, 1994; Seaman, 1992).

Broadcasters and audiences (2): From texts to talk

Early research on broadcast talk within media studies developed in part out of a critique of the whole textual approach to the relationship between media output and audiences. For instance, in a series of publications, media historian Paddy Scannell (1988a, 1989, 1991b) criticized the conventional procedures of media analysis for their focus on the mediation of 'messages' between the 'encoding' institutions of broadcasting and the 'decoding' or receiving audience at home. As remarked earlier, analysis therefore tended to focus either on the ideological assumptions underpinning the production of programmes ('texts'), or on the understandings of audience members upon watching or listening to that programme ('readings'). For Scannell, this text-reader model meant that the discourse practices of broadcasting themselves tended to vanish. His historical explorations of the development of early broadcasting (Scannell and Cardiff, 1991) had come to focus on shifts in forms of talk utilized by broadcasters to address their absent audiences with progressively more sociability and communicative ease. It was this side of broadcasting – the formal structures of discourse that constituted programmes themselves, as encountered by audiences in the actual activity of viewing and listening – that was radically missing from conventional media studies; and it was this that was to become the central object of attention for broadcast talk studies.

Drawing on a range of influences in linguistics, philosophy and sociology (discussed further in Chapter 2), researchers began to sketch out a novel approach to the question of the relationship between radio and television and their audiences. Through working with detailed transcriptions of the talk that occurred in radio and television broadcasts, based on recordings of shows as they were put out on air, these researchers began to reveal how talk itself could be treated as a legitimate object of study in relation to broadcasting – a factor that traditional approaches had ignored.

Some of the earliest studies were collected in two significant volumes: a special edition of the journal *Media Culture and Society* (Scannell, 1986) and a collection of studies with the title *Broadcast Talk* (Scannell, 1991a). The contributors to these publications sought to understand broadcast talk as a phenomenon that is worthy of analysis in its own right, rather than the mere carrier of media 'messages'. They started from the position that since broadcast talk is, at the most basic level, a form of talk like any other, its specific properties could be revealed by subjecting it to analysis in the way that other forms of talk have been analysed and comparing its features with those other forms of talk. In relation to conventional procedures of media research, therefore, it was argued that it is 'increasingly unrealistic to analyse the structure and content of [mass media] messages independent of the interactional medium within which they are generated' (Heritage, Clayman and Zimmerman, 1988: 79–80). The key aim of broadcast talk studies was, and remains today, to reveal the frameworks and dynamics of that interactional medium.

In addressing that aim, two major questions are: (1) What are the ways in which **mass communication** is accomplished as a *public form of discourse*; and (2) How do broadcasters design their talk so as to *relate to their audiences* in specific, inclusive, and cooperative ways? These questions go to the core of what is distinctive about this form of talk. It is a form of talk that is hearably, designedly, public, a part of the so-called 'mass communication circuit'; while at the same time it is talk that, to its audiences, comes across as somehow intimate, direct: addressed, if not specifically 'to them' then at least 'for them'. We only have to compare our experience of, say, watching a celebrity interview show or listening to a wildlife documentary with that of listening to a politician addressing a public meeting, a lecturer addressing a large class or a church minister giving a sermon to get a sense of how we can feel more 'personally' addressed, or at least more comfortable, in the first kind of case than in the latter. Nevertheless, each of these forms of talk can be described as talk 'in public' and 'for the public'. Where does the difference lie? Crucially, unlike forms of public speech-making (see Atkinson, 1984a), broadcast talk is a form of talk in public that is oriented towards an approximation of the conditions of interpersonal communication in everyday face-to-face conversation.

Scannell (1988a, 1989) crystallized this in his important concept of the **communicative ethos** of broadcasting. The talk of radio and television broadcasters, he argued, can be characterized by a distinctive communicative ethos which seeks to instill a sense of familiarity and, hence, inclusiveness and sociability in the audience. This communicative ethos is something that broadcasters can be understood as *working* to produce. In other words, it is not a 'natural' practice or way of talking but a performance; one in which certain aspects of everyday casual conversation are imported into the broadcaster's discourse and modified according to the distinctive institutional contexts of broadcasting – primarily, as we come to below, the fact that the main **recipients** of a broadcaster's talk, the audience, are not present at the time that talk is being produced. Forms of talk that embody this ethos did not emerge at the very beginning of radio and television but evolved, along with increasing sophistication in programming, in a process that has been traced through historical archives (Scannell and Cardiff, 1991).

Donald Horton and Richard Wohl (1956), in an early psychological study of broadcasting's relationship with its audiences, captured something of this emerging communicative ethos in their concepts of '**parasocial interaction**' and 'intimacy at a distance'. These terms were coined in an attempt to comprehend some of the peculiar social phenomena that were emerging around early television watching. Intrigued by how, or indeed why, some people could become fans of television personalities to such an extent that they would imaginarily involve their heroes in intimate aspects of their everyday lives such as, in extreme cases, sexual fantasies, Horton and Wohl proposed that techniques of address used by these personalities, such as direct address to the camera lens, promoted a form of 'non-reciprocal' intimacy in which the viewer could come to feel that they were being personally addressed, whereas the personality's talk was specifically *im*personal.

Parasocial interaction therefore refers to a form of talk that is possibly quite particular to broadcasting: talk that is hearably personal while being, at the same time, specifically impersonal. It is talk that crosses the boundaries between the 'private' and the 'public' in unique ways. Yet, as Scannell and Cardiff (1991) show in their excavation of the foundational years of British broadcasting (from the 1920s to the 1940s), the earliest forms of broadcast talk did not display any natural mastery of these techniques; rather, the production of talk that was hearably personal while being specifically impersonal was something that had to be learned.

The initial practice seems to have been to use the radio as a medium to talk *at* the listener rather than *to* him or her. Broadcasters saw the radio merely as another means of mass public address, and the early days of the BBC radio service were characterized by unpopular practices such as broadcasting sermons or official 'talks' on matters of the public good. It was mainly in gradual recognition of the unique conditions of reception characteristic of broadcasting that such practices were abandoned in favour of more 'conversational' styles: initially rudimentary and often clumsy, but gradually developing a sense of communicative ease in an evolving process that is still underway today. One can think, for example, of the stylistic changes currently taking place in news broadcasting, where the static newsreader seated behind a desk in front of the camera is gradually being replaced by newsreaders in full view, either standing, seated on the edge of their desks or walking up and down a platform in front of a large-scale 'media screen' on which facts, figures and satellite-linked images of remote interviewees appear.

Scannell and Cardiff's (1991) historical account was explicitly restricted to the case of British broadcasting, but Camporesi (1994) later showed how large a part was played in the evolution of a more informal style in British broadcasting by its relationship with the practices and products of American broadcasting. Although there was a certain degree of entrenched resistance to the importation of American stylistic innovations, at the same time there was a recognition among early British broadcasters that Americans had more quickly developed a sense of ease in their ways of relating to audiences, and there was, consequently, a great deal of subtle borrowing in the development of British broadcast talk.

The key point in all of this is that the conditions of reception for radio and television give the audience a wholly different shape to that in traditional forms of mass address. It is not understandable as a 'captive' audience in the sense of a church congregation; nor even a 'mass' audience in the sense of those gathered to hear a piece of oratory or political rhetoric in some civic space (see Atkinson, 1984a). In the early days of radio and television, broadcasters came to recognize that their talk was being heard in the ordinary spaces of everyday domestic life, and that their programmes were received in the interstices of existing domestic routines. However it was not just the structure of their schedules (Scannell, 1988b), but the very design of their utterances, that had to acknowledge that context of hearing.

The communicative ethos of broadcasting revolves around producing forms of public talk that are nevertheless hearably ordinary, routine and familiar. As Scannell put it: 'All programmes have an audience-oriented communicative intentionality which is embodied in the organization of their setting . . . down to the smallest detail. . . . Most importantly, all broadcast output is knowingly, wittingly *public*' (1991b: 11). And at least partly by virtue of this, if broadcast talk 'seems both ordinary and trivial it is also relaxed and sociable, shareable and accessible, non-exclusive, equally talkable about in principle and in practice by everyone' (Scannell, 1989: 156).

Part of the way in which this is achieved consists in broadcast talk drawing on, while at the same time systematically transforming, the routines and conventions of everyday face-to-face conversation. This is equally to suggest that methods that have been used to study ordinary conversation can be deployed in the analysis of the communicative practices of broadcasting, an issue I return to in Chapter 2. However, broadcasting's communicative ethos has also to be understood as a response to the fact that broadcast talk is actually, and inevitably, very different from ordinary conversation by virtue of being a **form of institutional discourse**.

The nature of this institutionality derives from another circumstance that is unique to broadcasting: 'Broadcasters, while they control the discourse, do not control the communicative context. The places from which broadcasting speaks and in which it is heard are completely separate from each other' (Scannell, 1991b: 3). Broadcast talk may be received, in large part, in the home, and consumed within the interstices of ordinary everyday domestic routines and activities; but it is produced, mainly, in the distinctive institutional setting of the studio. Yet while studios can, and often do, contain audiences who are co-present with the broadcasters (especially in genres such as game shows, celebrity talk shows and comedies), it is equally common for the only other parties co-present in the studio to be the production crew. And even when a show is produced in the presence of a studio audience, the audience of viewers and listeners remains a principal recipient toward whom the talk is oriented. A key question, therefore, is that of how broadcast talk is designed for recipiency by an *absent* audience: an audience of 'overhearers' (Heritage, 1985).

In summary, studies of broadcast talk initiated a shift in the focus of media analysis from *text* to *talk*. Whereas 'texts' imply 'readers', 'talk' implies 'recipients'. It is more accurate to refer to 'recipients' rather than 'hearers' or 'readers' because radio and television audiences do not just hear the language that is broadcast, nor do they simply 'interpret' it in the way implied by the text-reader model. Rather, in ways often similar to everyday conversation, they are *addressed* by it, invited into forms of parasocial interaction and attentive listenership, even though they remain absent from the site of its production. For this reason, the term '**overhearing audience**', while convenient, is somewhat inaccurate. A better term to refer to the audience for broadcast talk might be '**distributed recipients**'. This seems to capture the sense in which the audience is addressed, albeit often indirectly, and situated as a ratified (though non-co-present) hearer rather than an eavesdropper. (Nevertheless, 'overhearing audience' is so common in the existing literature that I will sometimes use that term, though the quote-marks should indicate that it is not necessarily to be taken literally.)

The relationship between talk and recipiency that is striven for in broadcasting is embodied in its *communicative ethos*, which emphasizes inclusiveness and sociability. The communicative ethos of broadcasting means that the talk itself can be defined in terms of three major features. First, it is a form of talk in public that, nevertheless, is oriented towards an approximation of the conditions of interpersonal communication in everyday face-to-face situations. Second, it is talk that effects certain systematic variations on the structures and patterns of ordinary conversation by virtue of being an institutional form of discourse. Third, it is a specific kind of institutional talk by virtue of being produced for the benefit of an 'overhearing' audience; or, put slightly differently, it is oriented towards the fact that it should be hearable by non co-present persons as somehow addressed to them.

Outline of the book

In this opening chapter I have traced out the development of an empirical interest in media talk as a phenomenon of analysis in its own right. I began by noting the centrality of talk to the vast majority of radio and television programme genres. Then, by means of a focus on the relationship between broadcasters and their audiences, showed how research foregrounding talk emerged in part out of a critique of the dominant text-reader models adopted in analysis of mass communication processes. Text-reader models tend either to take broadcast talk for granted, or place it in the background in favour of theoretical interests in issues such as the ideological under-pinnings of programmes. By contrast, research on broadcast talk aims to unfold the structures of discourse and patterns of social interaction that serve as the actual make-up of programmes.

Chapter 2 addresses the question of how such unfolding of discourse structures and patterns can be undertaken. Although there are a wide variety of analytical approaches available, each of which direct their focus in slightly different ways (for overviews see Bell and Garrett, 1998; Matheson, 2005), the approach I take in this book derives from a single method, known as **conversation analysis**. As we see in the next chapter, the name itself is misleading since conversation analysis has been used to study a whole range of different forms of talk, especially those that are related to institutional or organizational interactions. Given the defining characteristics of broadcast talk outlined above, I argue that conversation analysis is in fact the most appropriate method for analysing that form of talk because it explicitly uses the structures and patterns of ordinary conversation as a comparative basis for understanding other, more specialized or institutional forms of talk. I provide an accessible introduction to the main tenets of the conversation analytic approach, and also offer an illustrative comparison between conversation analysis and another widely adopted perspective in the study of broadcast talk, critical discourse analysis.

The remainder of the book consists of case studies of different broadcast talk genres, divided into three parts. Part I considers aspects of the audience participation television talk show. The issues addressed here include the relationship between 'lay' and 'expert' discourses in televised debates about topical issues, where in Chapter 3 I argue that such identity categories, key as they are to the nature of audience participation broadcasting, have to be seen as bound up with particular ways of talking and also with the different participation 'spaces' opened up by the hosts of such shows.

A related issue is the styles and structures of rhetorical performance engaged in as ordinary people 'have their say' in audience participation shows. I show that there are similarities between such lay performances and the rhetorical techniques used by more seasoned public speakers such as politicians. In Chapter 4, I turn to examine the discourse of staged confrontations in the largely American 'trash television' genre associated with *Ricki Lake* and *Jerry Springer*.

Part II turns our attention towards radio talk. Chapters 5 and 6 look at different types of radio phone-in show that raise a range of issues for the analysis of media talk. First of all I focus on open-line talk radio where two particular questions are addressed. First, how do lay speakers seek to legitimate their viewpoints in this mediated context for discussion of controversial issues of the day; and second, how do the hosts of such shows construct disputes with callers, as many of them are notorious for doing? This leads into a consideration of power as a discourse phenomenon related to the structural characteristics of participation on talk radio. Chapter 6 examines a different type of radio phone-in, the advice-giving show, and here a key issue becomes that of how advice talk in this particular mediated context is designed to take account of the 'overhearing' audience as well as the caller.

Part III moves on to look at mediated political discourse, focusing on the talk of politicians in two principal types of broadcast. Chapter 7 takes as its topic the news interview. I examine how the relatively formal turn-taking structure of interviews (based as they are on the exchange of questions and answers – or attempts to evade answering) can, on closer examination, reveal a complex interplay of competing agendas as journalists and politicians vie with one another to place their version of events 'on the record'. Finally, in Chapter 8, I turn to the venerable political panel debate format, in which a range of political representatives are quizzed by members of an audience of lay people on topical issues. My concern in that chapter is with how members of the panel, again, vie with one another over whose version of events wins out, with the added complexity here of the presence of a studio audience, whose affiliations themselves can be brought into play as politicians take sides in matters under debate.

Further reading

Barker, M. and Petley, J. (eds) (1997) *Ill Effects: The Media/Violence Debate*. London: Routledge.

Bell, A. and Garrett, P. (eds) (1998) *Approaches to Media Discourse*. Oxford: Blackwell.

Hall, S., Hobson, D., Lowe A. and Willis, P. (eds) (1980) *Culture, Media, Language*. London: Hutchison.

Scannell, P. (ed.) (1991) *Broadcast Talk*. London: Sage.

Scannell, P. and Cardiff, D. (1991) *A Social History of British Broadcasting* (Vol. 1). Oxford: Blackwell.

2 | ANALYSING MEDIA TALK

As I remarked in Chapter 1, broadcast talk can be subjected to analysis in terms of methods that have also been applied to other forms of talk, including, principally, everyday conversation. Although it was originally developed in American sociology in the 1960s, conversation analysis (or CA) is an approach that has been successfully applied to the study of media talk. From the mid-1980s, conversation analysts have made a central contribution to the general field of broadcast talk studies. Their focus has mainly been on interactional forms of talk such as those found in interviews, talk shows, debates, phone-ins and the like: in short the main genres of media talk that are covered in these pages.

It might, on the face of it, seem strange to apply methods that were originally developed in the study of everyday conversation to the analysis of mass communication. But as we will see, CA studies have the potential to transcend the common distinction between 'mass' communication and 'interpersonal' communication. It is not so much that interpersonal communication represents a completely different domain of study to that of mass communication. Rather, utilizing what we know about how humans communicate on the interpersonal level can reveal much about how communication occurs at a 'mass' level, at least in the context of radio and television. The case studies discussed in subsequent chapters use this as a starting point to demonstrate how key questions developed within the broader field of media studies can be approached from a different angle, shown in a new light, and in many respects reshaped by the application of conversation analysis.

In this chapter I provide a basic introduction to CA, focusing on its background, underlying assumptions about language and social life, and analytical techniques. Beginning with a broad overview, I then turn to a more detailed consideration of the relevant application of CA to the study of talk in media settings. Finally, CA is compared to another major approach to media discourse, critical discourse analysis (CDA).

Part of my intention will be to show how what have often been characterized as fundamental differences between these two approaches may not be that at all. Primarily, while it has been claimed that CA, unlike CDA, is 'resistant to linking properties of talk with higher-level features of society and culture – relations of power, ideologies, cultural values' (Fairclough, 1995: 23), I show that there is a good deal of evidence that such linkages are indeed central to many CA studies.

Throughout the chapter, it will be useful to bear in mind the three key distinguishing features of talk on radio and television that I identified in Chapter 1:

- Broadcast talk adopts elements of everyday conversation as part of its overarching communicative ethos;
- Broadcast talk is nevertheless different from ordinary conversation by virtue of being an institutional form of discourse that exists at the interface between public and private domains of life (e.g. the studio settings in which the talk is produced and the domestic settings in which it is received);
- Broadcast talk is a specific type of **institutional discourse** because it is directed at an 'overhearing' audience separated from the talk's site of production by space and also, frequently, by time.

Conversation analysis: An overview

Conversation analysis originated in the work of American sociologist Harvey Sacks in the 1960s. Sacks, who worked at the University of California from 1962 until his untimely death in a road accident in 1975, was similar to two other great innovators in the study of language, Ferdinand de Saussure (1984 [1915]) and Ludwig Wittgenstein (1953) in that he produced his most original ideas in the form of his lectures to students. Sacks's practice of tape-recording these lectures and having them transcribed meant that his work could nonetheless be distributed to a wider audience; and indeed, in 1992, a posthumous edition of the collected *Lectures on Conversation* was finally published (Sacks, 1992).

Sacks also published some articles in the traditional academic style (e.g. Sacks, 1972a, 1972b, 1975) and many of the classical studies in early CA were co-authored between Sacks and two other important figures, Emanuel Schegloff and Gail Jefferson (e.g. Schegloff and Sacks, 1973; Sacks, Schegloff and Jefferson, 1974; Schegloff, Jefferson and Sacks, 1977; Sacks and Schegloff, 1979; Jefferson, Sacks and Schegloff, 1987). These and other studies have had an enormous influence among researchers investigating the practices of human communication, first of all at the interpersonal level but also, and increasingly, in the context of institutional dialogue and mass communication.

CA can be understood as part of a broader movement within both linguistics and sociology that sought to challenge ideas about everyday language, or more specifically, talk, that were predominant in the mid-twentieth century. The main thrust of this challenge was to argue that human language has to be seen as a form of social practice and that meaning is inevitably bound to specific social contexts of use. This was pitched against ideas in linguistics that saw language as an abstract descriptive device; and the belief in sociology that language use was a fairly transparent phenomenon that was of relevance only in the sense that it offered a window on to people's thoughts, beliefs and attitudes.

In linguistics, the central tendency at that time was to find ways of describing words, sentences and their meaning in as abstract and generalized terms as possible. This ultimately meant removing language from its actual contexts of use. For instance, Noam Chomsky (1965) made a highly influential argument that language should be understood in terms of two analytically distinct elements: linguistic *competence* and linguistic *performance*. Competence Chomsky thought of as the abstract knowledge of grammatical structure that humans acquire as they learn language, and that enables them to produce meaningful sentences. Performance, on the other hand, is the actual use of language in concrete utterances. He argued that while competence (tacit knowledge of syntactic structure) could be described scientifically, performance could not because it is too disordered. Performance, in other words, is an essentially degenerate realization of linguistic competence (Chomsky, 1965). The upshot was that linguistic analysis in this mode tended to focus on invented sentences rather than those taken from the everyday contexts of language use, because the analyst could thereby ensure that the grammar and syntax to be analysed would be free of the 'imperfections' that almost inevitably occurred in natural speech.

An alternative view came from 'ordinary language philosophers' such as Ludwig Wittgenstein (1953) and J.L. Austin (1962), along with other linguists working in the field of *pragmatics* (Levinson, 1983). These argued that the meaning of any sentence or utterance simply could not be fully grasped if it were removed from the context of social interaction in which it was produced. Wittgenstein (1953) developed the viewpoint that language is a tool which humans put to use in pursuit of specific aims in concrete circumstances of social life. The meaning of words does not reside in the accuracy with which they describe things in the world, but in the things they are used to *do* by their speaker. One of Wittgenstein's famous arguments is that the verb 'to understand' does not refer to any concrete mental state within a person's brain, but to that person's ability to *display* that they understand by carrying on with the relevant activity. For example, saying that 'G' is the letter that follows 'F' displays one type of understanding of letter sequencing in the alphabet; being able to recite the whole series from A to Z is how one displays that one understands 'the alphabet'. The meaning of a phrase such as 'I understand the alphabet' is therefore squarely tied to its actual context of use.

At around the same time, Austin (1962) developed an approach known as speech-act theory. He started off by noting that there is a whole class of utterances that are primarily important because of what they do, rather than what they describe. Some examples are 'I sentence you to life imprisonment', when uttered by a judge, or 'I pronounce you husband and wife' when uttered by a priest, or 'Keep out' when uttered by a guard. Austin referred to these as speech-acts. In each of them, the speaker is not simply describing a state of affairs, but performing an action which has consequences for others to whom the utterance is directed.

Austin then generalized his theory to argue that all utterances can be described as having three elements, which he called *locution* (the words that a sentence is made up of), *illocution* (the intended meaning that the speaker wishes to convey) and *perlocution* (the consequences or effect that the utterance has on its hearer). He developed this view in a series of lectures originally delivered at Harvard University in 1955, and subsequently published as the book *How To Do Things With Words* (Austin, 1962). Like Wittgenstein's work, this was a radical departure from most philosophical work on language which treated it as abstract, something which could be looked at in the same way as mathematics or pure logic. Both thinkers, in slightly different ways, took it out of this realm and showed how in fact language is not simply about describing the world, it is also about action in the world.

Conversation analysis is also in favour of the view that language use is a form of social action, and that the study of everyday talk cannot properly be undertaken outside of the interactional contexts in which the talk takes place. But CA needs to be understood not just in relation to linguistic ideas but also in terms of a critique of prevailing sociological notions. Conventional sociological thinking sees talk – especially ordinary conversation – as essentially trivial, treating it merely as a tool for finding out about larger-scale social phenomena such as class, gender or deviancy, through responses to interview questions, for example. Although sociologists accept that our capacity to use language is a major factor distinguishing humans and human society from the animal world, that capacity is not treated as a topic of analysis in its own right. Rather, sociologists *rely* on language as a resource that provides them with access to the other phenomena they are interested in – whether these are 'external' phenomena such as class, gender, ethnicity and so on; or 'internal' phenomena such as people's beliefs and attitudes about such factors. Conversation analysis argued that sociology should instead treat talk and its interactional organization as a *topic* of analysis in its own right, rather than a resource for the pursuit of other questions.

Crucially, CA's founder Harvey Sacks also took a completely opposite line to Chomsky's argument that linguistic performance was too disordered to be scientifically analysed. Sacks's principal idea was that ordinary talk, though it sometimes appears chaotic and is grammatically imperfect, is nevertheless a highly ordered, socially organized phenomenon. This idea emerged from Sacks's observations of transcripts he had begun to make of naturally occurring telephone conversations.

His engagement with recorded conversations led Sacks to argue against the prevailing policy in linguistics – especially among the followers of Chomsky but also among ordinary language philosophers and pragmaticians – to use *invented* sentences as their data. For Sacks, this could provide only strictly limited information about how actual humans use language because utterances generally occur not as isolated sentences but in the context of conversational sequences. And as he pointed out, there is a major difference between inventing a sentence that would make sense as an utterance, and inventing a sequence of turns that one could confidently predict the occurrence of:

> One can invent new sentences and feel comfortable with them. One cannot invent new sequences of conversation and feel comfortable about them. You may be able to take 'a question and an answer', but if we have to extend it very far, then the issue of whether somebody would really say that, after, say, the fifth utterance, is one which we could not confidently argue. One doesn't have a strong intuition for sequencing in conversation.
>
> (Sacks, 1992, Vol. 2: 5)

Thus, CA represented a radical departure from the analytical procedures of almost all linguistics in the 1960s by insisting that analysis should concentrate on *recorded* talk in natural settings of social interaction, rather than invented sentences or versions of exchanges jotted down in the form of field notes.

The focus on sequences is key to the conversation analytic approach. By concentrating on how utterances are produced as *turns* in interactional sequences, conversation analysts argue that it is possible to observe and analyse participants' own understandings of one another's actions, and of what is going on in any given social context. This is because turn-taking requires people to display, in any 'next turn', their understanding of what was being said or done in the *prior* turn. If that displayed understanding is accurate, then the first speaker's next turn in the sequence will reveal that (for instance by carrying on with the conversational thread). Similarly, if it happens to be incorrect, that too will be displayed in the following turns (for instance by the first speaker seeking to correct, or 'repair', the faulty understanding). The point here is that because these understandings are displayed by the coparticipants for each other, they are available also to the analyst looking at a recording or a transcript of their talk.

This can be illustrated by looking at some conversational data (I will later turn to data derived from media sources). The following utterance occurred during an exchange at breakfast between a mother and her school-age son:

(1) KR:2
1 Mother: Do you know who's going to that meeting?

Taken in the abstract, this can be seen as an example of what pragmaticians would call an indirect speech-act (Levinson, 1983). These are utterances that are not necessarily meant to be understood literally. For example, the sentence 'Can you pass me the salt?' is not usually taken to be a literal question requiring a literal answer such as 'Yes, I can' or 'No, I can't'. Rather, to use Austin's (1962) terms, its illocutionary function is as a request for the salt to be passed, and its perlocutionary function is to get the recipient to pass the salt. The speaker's intention is not communicated directly in the words that are spoken (as they might be, for instance, in the sentence 'Pass me the salt!') but by means of implication.

In terms of extract (1) above, Mother's utterance could in fact be interpreted as doing one of at least two different types of indirect action. It could represent a genuine request for information about who is attending the meeting; or it could be a 'pre-announcement' (Terasaki, 2004): a preliminary to some information Mother wishes to announce about who is going. In the first case, the required response would be an answer which informs Mother about the meeting's attenders ('Yes, Mr So-and-so and Mrs So-and-so'); whereas in the second case, the response would be something like, 'No, who?', which would provide the opportunity for her to announce what she knows about the attenders.

But seeing this simply as an example of the abstract category 'indirect speech-act' does not tell us about the kind of utterance it actually was in the unfolding sequence in which it occurred. In speech-act theory and pragmatics, the emphasis tends to be on the analyst's interpretation of what utterances could potentially mean in certain inter-actional contexts. However, for CA the crucial issue is how the *participants* in that interaction understand, or make sense of, any given utterance. Therefore, what we have to do is look to see how the recipient(s) of such utterances interpreted them. When we do that, this is what we find:

(1) **KR:2 [Continued]**

```
1   Mother:   Do you know who's going to that meeting?
2   Russ:     Who?
3   Mother:   I don't know!
4   Russ:     Ouh:: pro'bly: Mr Murphy an' Dad said
5             prob'ly Mrs Timpte an' some o' the teachers.
```

Russ's first response, 'Who?', clearly shows that he initially interprets Mother's utterance as a pre-announcement. However, Mother's next turn, 'I don't know!', displays that Russ's inference was in fact incorrect: she was actually asking an information-seeking question. Following this turn, Russ backtracks and reinterprets the first turn as a genuine request for information, and produces (in lines 4–5) the small amount of information that he has available.

This sequence demonstrates a number of things. First, that people's understandings of one another's actions can actually unfold as sequences themselves unfold. This in turn makes it possible to analyse the co-production of mutual understanding using what conversation analysts call the **next turn proof procedure**: namely that any 'next' turn in a sequence displays its producer's understanding of the 'prior' turn, and if that understanding happens to be incorrect, that in itself can be displayed in the following turn in the sequence. The sequence above also demonstrates that people's utterances in conversation are not necessarily determined by their individual beliefs, preferences or mental states but can be determined instead by their orientations to the structural organization of conversation. The fact that Russ displays in his final turn that he does possess knowledge about who is going to the meeting shows that in initially responding with 'Who?', it was not that he did not know but that he was orienting (incorrectly as it turned out) to Mother's first turn as doing a particular kind of action (a pre-announcement) requiring a particular kind of response. (For more detailed discussion of these points, see Schegloff, 1988; Terasaki, 2004.)

On a more general level, this shows how conversation analysts approach their data (naturalistic recordings of talk and interaction) with two distinctive aims: to describe the structural organization that informs the local production of a stretch of talk; and to describe the methods used by participants to engage in mutually intelligible, orderly courses of social interaction. CA views members of society as knowledgeable agents actively involved in the intersubjective construction and maintenance of their shared social worlds.

CA also emphasizes the fact that utterances do not occur as isolated actions but as actions situated in an ongoing context of social interaction. In fact, all such actions are described as both 'context-shaped' and 'context-renewing':

Actions are context-shaped in that they are understood, and produced to be understood, in relation to the context of prior utterances and understandings in which they are embedded and to which they contribute. They are context-renewing because every current action forms the immediate context for a next action and will thus tend to renew (i.e. maintain, alter or adjust) any more generally prevailing sense of context which is the object of the participants' orientations and actions.

(Heritage and Greatbatch, 1991: 95)

Thus, contexts for action can be analysed by investigating the ways that participants, in their means of organizing their turns at talk, display for one another (and hence for the analyst too) their understanding and sense of what is going on at any given moment.

The preceding discussion illustrates a number of basic principles in CA, and these are summarized in Table 2.1. Since its inception in the 1960s, these principles have been applied to a wide range of different forms of talk, from ordinary telephone conversations to consultations in doctors' surgeries, from family dinnertime talk to communication between airline pilots and ground crew, from job interviews to television interviews with celebrities or politicians, to speeches given at political rallies. While some conversation analysts have focused mainly on the investigation of ordinary conversation, examining talk as a social institution in its own right with its own structures (Atkinson and Heritage, 1984; Lerner, 2004), others have concerned themselves with the analysis of 'institutional' interaction, applying the findings of CA to the study of how talk plays a role in the management of other social institutions (Boden and Zimmerman, 1991; Drew and Heritage, 1992a). It is in the latter type of work that we find a linkage with the analysis of media talk.

Table 2.1 Methodological principles of CA

Conversation Analysis: Five Principles

1. Talk is a principal means for *accomplishing social actions*.
2. Talk is produced in specific *interactional contexts*, and how people talk is highly *sensitive* to that context.
3. Talk and interaction are *orderly*; that is, we can find systematic *patterns and structures* in the ways that people use talk to interact.
4. Talk is organized *sequentially*; that is, by focusing on how people take turns at talking we can understand how they interpret the immediate interactional context, since turns are *related together*.
5. The best way to analyse this is by looking at *recordings* of naturally-occurring interaction, rather than using fieldnotes, as in ethnography, or intuition, as in many kinds of linguistics.

CA and media talk: Broadcast talk as institutional interaction

I have already mentioned the three defining characteristics of broadcast talk: (i) it displays a close relationship with the structures and patterns of ordinary conversation; (ii) it should however be understood as an institutional form of discourse; and (iii) it is talk that is produced for the benefit of an overhearing audience. A particularly important role in revealing these features is played by the comparative analysis of **speech exchange systems** developed within conversation analysis.

As we have seen, a central feature of CA is a focus on the turn by turn unfolding of **talk-in-interaction**. This approach is linked to the view that participants themselves use that sequential development as an interpretive resource in order to make sense of one another's actions. In analysing talk-in-interaction, then, CA places great emphasis on the immediate sequential context in which a turn is produced.

But there is a broader sense of 'context' which can be invoked. Talk does not occur in a vacuum. It is always situated somewhere. These situational contexts range from chance meetings in the street, through conversations with friends and family members, to larger-scale organizational settings such as workplaces, schools, and various kinds of service institutions, including even more specialized settings such as doctors' consulting rooms, courts of law, or TV and radio studios. The question is, what can CA's essentially local idea of context tell us about these wider social contexts?

To answer this question we need to understand what characterizes institutional interaction itself. As Erving Goffman (1961) once pointed out, institutions are things that social scientists spend a great deal of time trying to describe and explain, but which they have not found a very apt way of classifying. CA has found one way round this problem. As far as CA is concerned, what characterizes interaction as institutional is to do not with theories of social structure, as in most sociology, but with the special character of speech exchange systems to which participants can be found to orient themselves.

This idea has its roots in a seminal paper on turn-taking by Sacks, Schegloff and Jefferson (1974). There, the authors proposed that different forms of talk could be viewed as a continuum ranging from the relatively unconstrained turn-taking of mundane conversation, through various levels of formality, to ceremonial occasions in which not only who speaks and in what sequential order, but also what they will say, are pre-arranged (for instance, in wedding ceremonies). By selectively reducing or otherwise transforming the full scope of conversational practices, concentrating on some and withholding others, participants can be seen to display an orientation to specialized, non-conversational or 'institutional' contexts.

This involves moving beyond a commonplace conception of context, in which the contexts of interaction are thought of as 'containers', which people enter into and which, at the same time, exert causal influences on the behaviour of participants within them. This is an assumption that underlies a good deal of work in sociology and sociolinguistics (Coulter, 1982; Schegloff, 1991). However, it raises the problem of the 'cultural dope' (Garfinkel, 1967; Heritage, 1984). Basically, the container view of context fails to pay sufficient attention to the active knowledge that participants have of the production of their behaviour. Rather than seeing contexts as external social forces which impose themselves on participants, conversation analysts argue that we need to begin from the other direction, and see participants as knowledgeable social agents who actively display for one another (and hence, also, for observers and analysts) their orientation to the relevance of contexts.

This is not to deny that the wider social contexts of interaction may have an over-arching relevance for the participants. Intuitively, we know that a lively sense of context routinely informs our actions in the various social scenes of everyday life. For instance, if we were to call a radio phone-in programme, it is unlikely that in the midst of that activity we would suddenly be under the impression that we were calling a friend about a dinner invitation. In general, it seems, we 'know what we are doing', and are aware of the social settings for our actions.

But for conversation analysis, this intuitive view is inadequate. By relying on the private realm of individual awareness, it fails to account for the essentially *public* means by which participants display for one another their orientation to context and their understanding of each other's actions. As in mundane conversation, CA looks for a proof procedure that will show how participants make available for each other (and hence for the analyst too) the relevance of an institutional setting. That proof procedure is found in the observable details of talk-in-interaction.

CA has developed a distinctive means of locating participants' displayed orientations to institutional contexts. This is done by adopting a comparative perspective in which the turn-taking system for conversation is treated as a benchmark against which other forms of talk-in-interaction can be distinguished. Ordinary conversation is defined by a **turn-taking system** in which the order, size and type of turns are free to vary. By contrast, other, non-conversational forms of talk-in-interaction involve either the reduction or the systematic specialization of the range of practices available in ordinary conversation.

Media talk should be understood in these terms as a non-conversational or institutional form of talk. Utilizing the comparative perspective sketched out above, we can begin to see how conversation analysis enables broadcast talk researchers to draw out the unique features of broadcast talk, and to understand the active role played by participants themselves in establishing and maintaining the forms of talk (or speech exchange systems) that are characteristic of radio and television broadcasting.

In an account of broadcast news interviews from a CA perspective, John Heritage and David Greatbatch (1991) identified two basic categories of speech exchange system that describe institutional forms of talk. They referred to these as 'formal' and 'non-formal' systems. Both of these involve the use of specialized forms of turn-taking which involve either the reduction or the systematic specialization of the range of practices available in ordinary conversation. Formal systems are those in which 'the institutional character of the interaction is embodied first and foremost in its *form* – most notably in turn-taking systems which depart substantially from the way in which turn-taking is managed in conversation' (Heritage and Greatbatch, 1991: 95). Primarily, in broadcasting, this refers to the interview – particularly the news interview – where the range of turn types available to participants is drastically reduced. In order to maintain their talk within the normative conventions of the 'interview', participants have to restrict themselves for the most part to one of two types of activity: asking questions (the role of the interviewer) and giving answers (the role of the interviewee).

This does not mean that the speech exchange system determines the actions of participants in a causal way. Clearly, at any point an interviewee could choose not to answer the interviewer's questions, or could choose to put questions to the interviewer instead (and we see some examples of this in Chapter 7). The point is that by doing so the interviewee would be open to sanction for no longer acting appropriately as an interviewee; and in fact, in extreme circumstances the interview itself may no longer be recognizable as an 'interview' at all. But by displaying their orientation to the normative speech exchange system, restricting themselves to either asking questions or giving answers, interviewer and interviewee collaboratively work to maintain the context of 'news interview' as relevant for themselves and for their audience.

Formalized speech exchange systems can also impact on the management of specific activities such as disputes over opposing viewpoints, as detailed in David Greatbatch's (1992) study of the panel set-up in some broadcast news programmes, where a number of participants with varying stances on an issue act jointly as interviewees with the interviewer as chair. In this environment, disagreement is an intrinsic feature of the encounter. Greatbatch notes that in panel interviews, interviewees are selected precisely on the basis of their differing standpoints on issues. Panel formats thus 'allow interviewers to facilitate combative interaction through the airing of disagreements between the interviewees themselves' (Greatbatch, 1992: 272).

However, the specialized speech exchange system of the setting leads to disputes taking distinctive forms. The interviewer is accorded a central mediating role, with two main consequences. First, he or she is allotted the task of eliciting, through questions, the position or version of events supported by each antagonist. Consequently, oppositional turns are generally not adjacently positioned, since each side's opportunity to put forward its case needs to follow an intervening question from the mediator.

A result of this structural feature is that opposing sides in the dispute tend not to address their disagreements directly to each other, but instead to direct their talk at the interviewer as a third party. This leads to disputes being generally less confrontational than when disputes are conducted in unmediated person-to-person exchange. For example, panel participants who take issue with other participants' statements will not refer to their adversary in the first person (as in 'You say (X)') but in the third person (as in 'I disagree with what Professor So-and-so says'). In the panel interview setting, disputants who shift into direct person-to-person opposition may be required by the interviewer to redirect their utterances to him or her, and return to referring to codisputants in the third person. However, in the interests of ensuring a lively and entertaining debate, interviewers may equally allow interviewees to argue with each other directly for short periods of time. As Greatbatch (1992) shows, there are nevertheless various ways in which the interviewer retains overall control of the course of the dispute, and at any point he or she may re-establish the mediated format.

We thus get a sense of how formal institutional interaction involves 'specific and significant narrowings and respecifications of the range of options that are operative in conversational interaction' (Heritage, 1989: 34). The specialized turn-taking systems found in formal types of institutional setting show how participants orient to the relevance of an institutional context. But formalized speech exchange systems also have an impact on the ways in which social activities such as disputing or generating controversy are accomplished in formal settings for media talk.

In non-formal systems, things are less straightforward because there is no **turn-type pre-allocation** system to constrain the participation options open to speakers in different institutional roles. In many types of media talk, participants are able to produce a far wider range of turn types than simply question and answer. Talk shows and phone-ins, for instance, often have a hearable quality that is much closer to everyday conversation than the formalized patterns of the interview. If we are to find how participants themselves display their orientation to the context of broadcast talk, this must therefore be located in other aspects of talk. Drew and Heritage (1992b: 28) suggested that it might have to do with the ways in which particular, contextually relevant activities are organized within sequences; as they put it, 'systematic aspects of the organisation of sequences (and of turn design within sequences) having to do with such matters as the opening and closing of encounters, and with the ways in which information is requested, delivered, and received'. One way in which this can be done is to compare how one particular interactional task is accomplished in the broadcast setting with how the same task is done in ordinary conversation.

Radio phone-ins (or talk radio) represent a form of interactive broadcast talk that is not organized according to any strict turn-type distribution rules (Hutchby, 1991). Yet, as in everyday telephone conversation (Hopper, 1992), the most routinely structured segment of calls to a talk radio show is the opening sequence: the first few seconds of each broadcast colloquy. Comparing the opening sequences of calls to a talk radio show with opening sequences in everyday telephone calls, we can find evidence of systematic orientations to the phone-in context as displayed in the details of talk (Hutchby, 1999).

In conventional telephone interaction, participants generally do not have visual access to one another. Therefore, in order to be sure with whom they are interacting they need to engage in verbal forms of identification and recognition (Schegloff, 1979; but see also Hutchby and Barnett [2005] on calls to mobile phones). Thus, the way speakers design their first utterances will begin to reveal how they categorize themselves in relation to the other. For instance, in the following extract, it seems clear that the two participants in this telephone conversation rapidly establish their identities as friends who are well known to each other:

(2) **HG:1**

```
1              ((phone rings))
2    Nancy:    H'llo?
3    Hyla:     Hi:,
4    Nancy:    HI::.
5    Hyla:     How are yuhh=
6    Nancy:    =Fi:ne how er you,
7    Hyla:     Oka:[y,
8    Nancy:        [Goo:d,
9              (0.4)
10   Hyla:     .mkhhh[hh
11   Nancy:          [What's doin',
```

This opening sequence can be described in terms of the four 'core sequences' that Emanuel Schegloff (1986) found to be characteristic of mundane telephone call openings. In general, before the first topic of the call is introduced, four sets of preliminary activities tend to be accomplished: (i) the answering of the telephone caller's 'summons'; (ii) a mutual identification and/or recognition sequence; (iii) a greeting sequence; and (iv) a routine enquiries ('How are you') sequence. Of course, this can be done in widely varying ways (see Schegloff, 1979). One thing to notice in the above extract is that the two speakers establish one another's identity, and start chatting about 'What's doin',' (line 11) without exchanging names at all. Hyla (the caller) recognizes Nancy's voice as Nancy answers the phone's summons in line 2. Hyla's first utterance, 'Hi:,' in line 3, exhibits that recognition; and at the same time, invites Nancy to recognize her own voice (note that she does not self-identify by saying, 'Hi, it's Hyla'). After Nancy's return greeting (line 4), they move into a 'How are you' exchange without needing to check their mutual recognition in any way. Following that, Nancy invites Hyla to introduce a first topic by saying 'What's doin' '.

Turning to the institutional setting of the talk radio show, we find a strong contrast in the form of opening sequences. Rather than passing through a set of four relatively standard sequences, calls on talk radio are opened by means of a single, standard two-turn sequence, which is exemplified by the following extract:

(3) **H:21.11.88:6:1** [H = Host, C = Caller]
1 H: Kath calling from Clapham now. Good morning.
2 C: Good morning Brian. Erm:, I:: I also agree that
3   thee .hh telethons a:re a form of psychological
4   blackmail now. .hhh Because the majority of
5   people I think do know . . . ((continues))

Here, identification and recognition, greetings, and topic initiation are accomplished in rapid succession in two turns occupying lines 1 and 2. In line 1, the host announces the caller, and then provides a first greeting which invites her into the speaker role for the next turn. In line 2, after returning the greeting, the caller moves without ado into introducing her 'reason for the call'. Typically for this setting, that reason consists of her expressing an opinion on some issue: 'I also agree that thee .hh telethons a:re a form of psychological blackmail.'

Clearly, the kinds of tasks and issues around identification and first topic that are involved in calls on talk radio are different from those arising in mundane conversational calls. One of the main differences is that in mundane telephone talk, participants need to select from among an array of *possible* relevant identities and a range of possible things that the call may be about. The structure of the opening in extract (2) allows those tasks to be done. In the institutional setting of the talk radio show, the opening is designed in such a way that the participants can align themselves in terms of *given* institutional speaker identities ('host' and 'caller'), and move rapidly into the specific topical agenda of the call.

If we look more closely at the construction of the opening turns, however, we find more detailed evidence of the participants' orientations to the specialized features of their interaction. Here are some further examples:

(4) **H:23.1.89:2:1**
1 H: Bob is calling from Ilford. Good morning.
2 C: .hh Good morning Brian. (0.4) .hh What I'm phoning
3   up is about the cricket . . .

(5) H:30.11.88:10:1

```
1   H:   Mill Hill:: i:s where Belinda calls from. Good
2        morning.
3   C:   Good morning Brian. .hh Erm, re the Sunday
4        o:pening I'm just phoning from the point of
5        vie:w, .hh as a:n assistant . . .
```

(6) H:21.11.88:11:1

```
1   H:   On to Philip in Camden Town. Good morning.
2   C:   Yeh guh morning Brian. Erm (.) Really what I
3        wanted to say was that I'm fascinated by watching
4        these telethons by the anuh- amount'v
5        contradictions that're thrown up by them . . .
```

In these opening sequences, the design of each turn exhibits clearly the speaker's orientation to the specialized nature of the interaction. For instance, the host's first turns already have an institutional quality to them in that they are constructed as *announcements*. In most types of telephone call, the answerer's first turn is an answer to the summons represented by the telephone's ring. We thus find typical responses such as a simple 'Hello?' (see extract [2]); or, more commonly in Continental countries (Houtkoop-Steenstra, 1991; Lindstrom, 1994), self-identifications in which the answerer recites their name. In institutional settings, once again answerers self-identify, but this time usually in organizational terms: e.g., 'Police Department', 'Sociology', or 'Simpson's car hire, how can I help?'

However, in the talk radio data, the host begins by identifying not himself but the *caller*: e.g., 'Kath calling from Clapham'. These first turns, in which the caller's name and geographical location are announced, display that the host's talk is designed principally for reception by the overhearing audience. By constructing his turn as an announcement, the host exhibits an orientation to the broadcast nature of the interaction.

Callers' turns too are designed to fit the institutional properties of the talk radio show. In each case, callers introduce topics on which they propose to offer opinions: 'What I'm phoning up is about the cricket'; 're the Sunday o:pening'; or 'Really what I wanted to say was that I'm fascinated by watching these telethons'. But there is a sense in which those topics get introduced not just as topics but as *issues*. One way this is done is by referring to them using the definite article: '*the* cricket', '*the* Sunday o:pening', and so on. Using this form of reference, callers can provide their topics with a sense of being generally recognizable. This is because to refer to a topic with the definite article is to invoke some degree of shared knowledge between speaker and recipient(s) (Clark and Haviland, 1977). This way of introducing topics constructs them as given themes in the public domain. In this sense, callers specifically introduce topics that are the 'right' kind of thing to be discussing in the public sphere of a talk radio show.

This point is illustrated further by the fact that callers do not phone in about personal or private problems and complaints; not, at least, unless these can be explicitly related to an identifiable public concern. For instance, consider the following extract:

(7) H:2.2.89:4:1
1   H: And good morning to Ma:ndy from Ruislip. Good
2   morni[ng.
3   C: [Good mor:ning Brian. .hhh We've got a real
4   problem he:re with dogs fouling our footway,

Although the caller begins by formulating the topic in quite personal terms, 'We've got a real problem he:re', the issue itself is one that potentially affects not just this caller but anyone living in a modern urban neighbourhood. This way of constructing topics as themes in the public domain serves as an indication of the ways in which speakers display, in the design details of their talk, an orientation to the particular kinds of public space for talk that broadcasting involves. In various ways, therefore, the design of turns and sequences allows us to locate the participants' orientations to context even in non-formal institutional settings such as talk radio, where the type and order of turns are not pre-allocated.

The critical agenda: conversation analysis and critical discourse analysis

Despite its success in developing and applying a coherent methodological programme for the analysis of media talk, CA has been the subject of criticism from media discourse researchers propounding what can be described as a 'critical agenda'. These criticisms focus on two related issues. First, there is a claim that CA lacks an adequate sense of the contextualization of utterances within a wider set of social relations. Second, conversation analysts in general are thought to be unwilling to make links between the 'micro' details of talk-in-interaction and the 'macro' levels of sociological variables – class, gender, and so forth. These two points inform the position of those working in the field known as *critical discourse analysis* (CDA), which is probably the most widely adopted approach to the study of media talk other than CA. For instance Norman Fairclough, a leading proponent of CDA, argues in his work on media discourse that the CA approach is flawed by being 'resistant to linking properties of talk with higher-level features of society and culture – relations of power, ideologies, cultural values' (Fairclough, 1995: 23).

This statement reflects a common, though inaccurate, conception of the kind of work that CA produces. Such a conception is based in the fact that CA often comes across as reluctant to engage explicitly with sociological concepts such as power, gender, class, and so on. Partly this has to do with its theoretical lineage. As mentioned earlier in the chapter, CA emerged in the context of a critique of conventional sociological thinking which sees talk merely as a resource for demonstrating the existence of macro-level phenomena (power, gender, class, etc.) that the sociologist assumes affect people's behaviour. While the proponents of CDA are quite comfortable with an approach to discourse that is, as Fairclough puts it, 'informed by . . . social theory insights' (1995: 54), many conversation analysts remain suspicious of what they see as the preconceptions built into such 'insights'.

However, I argue that a good deal of work in CA does indeed link the properties of talk with 'higher-level' features of society. In particular, as I will suggest, there is a tacit idea of power to be located in much CA work on institutional discourse. Making this idea more explicit is important, not least for challenging the view that CA is a 'microlevel' approach with little or nothing to say about the relationship between language use and wider social issues.

Fairclough's (1995) position, and that of CDA in general, is that the analysis of media talk must be undertaken not just in terms of the local construction and exchange of turns between participants, but must be related to external structures – historical, social, and ideological – which impact upon the meaning of actions undertaken within the talk. As Fairclough (1995: 54) puts it: 'calling the approach "critical" is a recognition that our social practice in general and our use of language in particular are bound up with causes and effects which we may not be at all aware of under normal conditions.' He goes on:

> Connections between the use of language and the exercise of power are often not clear to people, yet appear on closer examination to be vitally important. . . . For instance, the ways in which a conventional consultation between a doctor and a patient is organised, or a conventional interview between a reporter and a politician, take for granted a whole range of ideologically potent assumptions about rights, relationships, knowledge and identities. For example, the assumption that the doctor is the sole source of medically legitimate knowledge about illness, or that it is legitimate for the reporter – as one who 'speaks for' the public – to challenge the politician. Such practices are shaped, with their common-sense assumptions, according to prevailing notions of power between groups of people. The normal opacity of these practices to those involved in them – the invisibility of their ideological assumptions, and of the power relations which underlie the practices – helps to sustain these power relations.
>
> (Fairclough, 1995: 54)

In CDA, this stance tends to lead to an analytic assumption that power relations and other sociological variables are pre-established features of the context, in a way akin to what I earlier described as the 'container' theory of context. For instance, it may be claimed that institutions 'are characterised by . . . hierarchical relations of power between the occupants of institutional positions' and, consequently, in their actions institutional agents 'exercise the power which is *institutionally endowed upon them*' (Thompson, 1984: 165, my emphasis).

This points to a key difference between the two approaches: while CA aims to describe the ways that participants display that they *are* aware of specific contextual factors (by observably modifying the ways that they talk, for instance), CDA maintains that there are other factors, external to the situation the speakers are in, and of which the speakers may *not* be aware, that impact on the production of their talk.

However, for proponents of conversation analysis, this stance leads to a crucial problem. Clearly, since these factors are said to operate outside the awareness of the participants themselves, it falls to the analyst to demonstrate where and how they affect the talk. The problem with this is that such a policy can end up giving too much licence to the analyst to 'read in' the relevance of external factors where there may be no other evidence to support the claim beyond the analyst's assertion. By assuming the relevance of these factors before the analysis of data actually starts, the analysis is in danger of becoming a self-fulfilling prophecy.

But we do not need to start from the assumption that factors such as power and ideology operate outside the immediate awareness of participants. CA is not in favour of the view that power relations somehow pre-exist and determine the course of actual concrete encounters; but by focusing on the local management of talk-in-interaction this approach can in fact provide compelling accounts of how power comes to operate as a feature of, and is used as a resource in, institutional interaction. Indeed, even though the issue is usually left entirely implicit, a good deal of CA can be seen as dealing with a possible analysis of power, where power is viewed in terms of differential distributions of discursive resources. These resources enable certain participants to achieve interactional effects that are not available (or are differentially available) to others in the setting.

An important phenomenon here (though by no means the only one, as we see in later chapters) is the question-answer sequence that is central to much of the institutional interaction that CA researchers have analysed (Drew and Heritage, 1992b). In many forms of institutional interaction, questions do indeed get asked primarily by institutional figures, such as attorneys, doctors, and news interviewers. Questions are a powerful interactional resource for the simple reason that the asking of a question places constraints on the discourse options available to its recipient. And while individual questions constrain, sequences of questions can constrain more strongly. For example, in Atkinson and Drew's (1979) courtroom studies, the fact that the attorney is able to ask sequences of questions that the witness is restricted to answering gives particular powers to the attorney. One of these is what Drew (1992) later described as the 'power of summary'. The questioner 'has "first rights" to pull together evidence and "draw conclusions" '; in other words, to define the meaning and the terms of a particular set of answers, which is something that the witness cannot do. 'The witness is left in a position of addressing and trying to deal with the attorney's selection of which items to pull together: she has no control over the connections which are made ... nor over the inferences which may be drawn from such juxtapositioning' (Drew, 1992: 507).

However, saying this does not draw us back towards the idea that power relations are pre-established and external to actual concrete practices, because the characteristic question-answer sequence is not a natural but an *oriented-to* feature of such types of interaction. In other words, institutional figures do not simply have 'rights' to ask the questions; they, along with other participants in the setting actively collaborate in *accomplishing* the question-answer form of the interaction (Thornborrow, 2002). This in itself can have distinctive consequences for relations of power within institutional encounters. For instance, studies of doctor–patient interaction have shown how patients may be complicit in the construction and maintenance of a power situation in which the doctor not only determines the topics that will be talked about, but also defines the upshots and outcomes of their discussions (Frankel, 1984, 1990; Heath, 1992).

Richard Frankel (1984, 1990) observes that while there is no institutional constraint against patients asking questions and initiating new topics, these activities are overwhelmingly undertaken by doctors and not by patients. He argues that this asymmetry arises out of a tacitly negotiated state of affairs in which there are two significant features. The first is that doctors routinely open up restricted participation options for patients by asking information-seeking questions which require strictly factual responses. The second is that patients themselves orient to and reproduce this asymmetrical distribution of participation rights by choosing to offer new information to the doctor mainly in the form of additional components tagged onto a response to the doctor's question. In this way, they preserve the doctor's role as questioner and their own role as answerer, even when they are introducing new information on their own initiative.

In a similar vein, Christian Heath (1992) shows how asymmetries are oriented to by patients during the consultation, as patients systematically withhold responses to doctors' announcements of a diagnosis, other than brief acknowledgement tokens such as 'yeh' or 'mm'. Given that the diagnosis represents a piece of 'expert' knowledge which the doctor passes on to the patient, by withholding responses patients display their orientation to preserving the expert status of the doctor. Heath even shows that this withholding is done when the patient is given an opportunity to respond through the doctor leaving a pause following the announcement of diagnosis.

Unlike many studies using CDA, these CA accounts focus on the existence of asymmetries without going on to make explicit claims about power in institutional discourse. But that is not to say that those kinds of claims cannot be made. By showing how participants display an orientation to institutional settings by engaging in certain activities and refraining from others, and illustrating how activities such as questioning are used to constrain the options of a coparticipant, CA can also be used to demonstrate how power can be a feature of those activities. What is implied by these studies is that oriented-to activity patterns, such as differences in questioning and answering moves, may themselves be intrinsic to the play of power in institutional interactions.

Thus, while CDA claims CA is 'resistant to linking properties of talk with higher-level features of society and culture – relations of power, ideologies, cultural values' (Fairclough, 1995: 23), that in fact is not the case. Rather, CA is resistant to *assuming* linkages between the properties of talk and higher-level features of society and culture. The debate between CA and CDA is not about the *existence* of factors such as power in interaction. Rather, it is an argument about the nature of claims that can legitimately be made about the data we gather to analyse language use in social interaction. This brief discussion about the different approaches to 'critical' issues taken by CDA and by CA therefore illustrates a central methodological policy that distinguishes CA from many other perspectives within linguistics, sociology and media studies (including CDA): an insistence that it is more important to try and explicate the ways in which the participants in any interaction display their understanding of what they are doing than to begin from theoretically driven assumptions about what might be going on (Schegloff, 1991).

Like many aspects of CA, that methodological policy is best understood through illustration using actual examples of data. In the following chapters I therefore turn to case studies of specific genres of media talk-in-interaction. Here, we will see how the principles and analytical practices outlined in the present chapter come to be applied to the organization of talk on radio and television. We will also see how the application of those principles and practices enables us to view the forms of talk found in broadcasting, and the kinds of questions posed about that talk, in new ways. I begin by considering the distinctive type of 'public discourse' produced on audience participation talk shows, including how the relationship between 'experts' and 'laypersons' is constructed through aspects of turn-taking and turn-design.

Further reading

Atkinson, J.M. and Heritage, J. (eds) (1984) *Structures of Social Action: Studies in Conversation Analysis*. Cambridge: Cambridge University Press.

Drew, P. and Heritage, J. (eds) (1992a) *Talk At Work: Interaction in Institutional Settings*. Cambridge: Cambridge University Press.

Fairclough, N. (1995) *Media Discourse*. London: Edward Arnold.

Hutchby, I. and Wooffitt, R. (1998) *Conversation Analysis*. Cambridge: Polity.

Sacks, H. (1992) *Lectures on Conversation* (2 Vols. ed. G. Jefferson). Oxford: Blackwell.

Sacks, H., Schegloff, E.A. and Jefferson, G. (1974) A simplest systematics for the organisation of turn-taking for conversation. *Language*, 50: 696–735.

CASE STUDIES PART I:
TELEVISION TALK AND AUDIENCE PARTICIPATION

AUDIENCE PARTICIPATION TELEVISION AND PUBLIC DISCOURSE

From the earliest days of radio and television, broadcasters have developed numerous forms of audience participation show. David Cardiff and Paddy Scannell (1986) describe how some of the earliest forms of audience participation show in the context of British broadcasting were actually designed as morale-boosting media events during the Second World War. In those years, shows would tour the regions of England as carnivalesque occasions in which ordinary people took the stage to tell stories about their abilities to carry on in the face of adversity and send out messages of support for the troops. These radio shows were hugely popular among audiences.

In more recent times the audience participation debate show has become increasingly popular. This genre of media talk includes a range of different types of show, both in terms of style and content. Three main types can be identified: first, the *issues-based* show which focuses on broadcasting audience participation debates about topical social issues, and usually involves some participation by 'experts' or, occasionally, celebrities. Second, the *confrontation-based* show which focuses on the staged production of confrontations between friends, relations and family members, with 'expert' comment often provided at the end of each show in the form of a summary of moral issues either by a pop psychologist, a magazine columnist, or even the host himself. A third type within the genre is the audience participation political debate in which politicians and members of the public are brought together in the television studio to debate topical issues in response to questions set by audience members.

One important aspect of audience participation broadcasts is that they represent a different conception of the relationship between media producers (programme makers) and media consumers (audiences) than the one that underpins a large proportion of news and current affairs broadcasting. In news programming and documentary making, the media have traditionally sought to limit the access of 'ordinary' people, and have concentrated on allowing a voice for representatives of elite groups such as politicians (Livingstone and Lunt, 1994). In news interviews, for instance, it has long been accepted that it is the interviewer's role to quiz the elite representative purportedly on behalf of, and for the benefit of, the audience at home (Schudson, 1994).

By contrast, in shows such as *Kilroy* and *Oprah*, as in talk radio shows, there is a quite different entitlement to speak. Members of the public themselves are allowed and encouraged to express their views and to establish agendas. Furthermore, in shows such as *Jerry Springer, Ricki Lake, Trisha* or *Queen Latifah*, ordinary people's own 'private' issues, such as family rows, come to be played out and argued over, if not resolved, on the public stage.

One upshot of the trend towards (different kinds of) audience involvement has been that analysts have considered such shows not just in terms of the distinctive communicative ethos of broadcasting, but also in terms of the distinctive type of 'public discourse' they create. That discourse is 'public' in two important senses: first in the ordinary sense of involving an audience in **co-presence** with the debators; second, in the historically novel sense of being broadcast and hence accessible by a further, 'absent', geographically and temporally distributed audience. The question thus becomes, what if anything is distinctive about the public discourse of audience participation broadcasts?

Audience participation talk: From themes to structures

While there are numerous books that seek to comment on the nature of public discourse in audience participation TV (Carbaugh, 1988; Ferrara, 1994; Livingstone and Lunt, 1994; Munson, 1993; Priest, 1995; Shattuc, 1997; Tolson, 2001), only a small proportion of them actually focus in any detail on the organization of *talk* in such shows. Two early studies that are worth mentioning are those by Donal Carbaugh (1988) and Sonia Livingstone and Peter Lunt (1994), each of which take different approaches to the public discourse of audience participation TV. Carbaugh looks at how these shows *reflect* cultural ways of thinking and making sense of social issues; while Livingstone and Lunt are more concerned with how the shows actually *create* a new kind of public discourse which challenges traditional ways of producing expert knowledge about social issues.

Carbaugh (1988) is interested in how the long-running US show *Donahue*[1] provides a forum in which ordinary people talk about cultural themes in late modernity such as 'being an individual', 'sharing', and 'communicating'. In a sense, this is to treat the discourse of a *Donahue* show as a microcosm of contemporary US society at large. As Carbaugh (1988: 4) puts it: 'Just as we have learned about Roman society by studying orations in the Assembly, and Colonial society by studying negotiations in the town hall, so we should learn much about contemporary American society by studying the kind of talk that is heard on *Donahue*.'

In other words, Carbaugh looks at the ways of speaking on that particular show to discover what that tells us about how US culture treats the relationship between individual and society. The main themes he draws out are:

(i) The symbols of 'personhood' that are used in *Donahue* discourse; and
(ii) Genres of 'speaking' – what it means to 'communicate' about personhood.

Under (i), *personhood*, audience contributors were found repeatedly to talk about things such as 'the individual', 'self', 'rights' and 'choice'. In terms of (ii), *speaking*, contributors tended to talk about 'being honest', 'sharing feelings', and 'communicating'. One interesting upshot of this is that the combination of these two modalities generates a picture of North American cultural discourses that often appears deeply contradictory.

This is illustrated clearly by comparing the following two extracts, in the first of which the show's host, Phil Donahue, addresses a wife who is having problems with her husband:

(1) Carbaugh, 1988: 66

1	Host:	Do you talk to your husband about this?
2	Woman:	We try.
3→	Host:	We have no remedy here except to say your husband
4→		has a responsibility to be more verbal

Note here, in the arrowed lines, the emphasis placed on the 'responsibility' to be communicative. By contrast, in extract (2), where a woman has 'asked what she could do to help her father "face the situation" ' (Carbaugh, 1988: 66), the emphasis turns to the other side of the coin: the right of individuals to *avoid* 'expressing themselves' if they so choose:

(2) Carbaugh, 1988: 67

1	Host:	Talk to him.
2	Woman:	I've tried but he is constantly evading the
3		subject. He will change the subject constantly.
4		He just avoids it.
5→	Host:	I assume that you have to respect that, huh. You
6→		can't force feed someone the opportunity to
7→		express themselves.

What we see here is that although 'being honest' and 'sharing feelings' are preferred, still it seems that the 'choice' or 'rights' of the 'individual' *not* to talk must be respected. In fact it appears in these extracts that the latter, individual side of the coin gets priority. In Donahue's phrase, 'You can't force feed someone the opportunity to express themselves.'

Carbaugh argues that the public discourse of *Donahue* can tell us a lot about the symbolic patterns and structures of meaning circulating in civil society. Particular discourse genres are used by speakers which act as a trace for the cultural categories that symbolize contemporary US culture as a whole, instantiating complex cultural models of the self, responsibility and rights. Thus, the discourse of *Donahue* interfaces the public and the private in two ways: on the one hand it is the public talk of private citizens, while on the other it illustrates the reflection of wider social patterns of reasoning in the speech of individual participants.

Although Carbaugh (1988) places primary emphasis on the actual speech of audience contributors, the actual amount of talk that is analysed throughout the book remains very small. In fact, Carbaugh's principal analytical interest is not in the organization of the talk itself, but in the 'wider' issue of what the public discourse of *Donahue* can tell us about the symbolic patterns and structures of meaning circulating in civil society. He thus tends to focus on talk in terms of 'cultural resources' at the expense of any real concern with the interactional organization of the talk as constitutive of the show's discursive arena. In other words, to return to a theme deriving from conversation analysis, Carbaugh is more interested in the 'symbol system' of *Donahue* discourse than its speech-exchange system.

Coming from a different angle, and addressing a different type of talk show, Livingstone and Lunt (1994) are more interested in the differential epistemological grounding of 'lay' and 'expert' discourse. Among other things, they trace the way in which audience participation shows prioritize the lay and subordinate the expert perspectives, thus transforming the conventional preference among radio and television programme-makers. They suggest that in many broadcasting genres which involve both expertise and ordinary experience (such as documentaries) the expert perspective is valorized through the operation of the following binary oppositions:

Lay:	Expert:
subjective	objective
ungrounded	grounded in data
emotional	rational
unique	replicable
concrete	abstract

(From Livingstone and Lunt, 1994: 102)

Audience participation debate shows, by contrast, tend to valorize the lay perspective, through the operation of the following quite different set of oppositions:

Lay:	Expert:
authentic	alienated
narrative	fragmented

hot	cold
relevant	irrelevant
in depth	superficial

(From Livingstone and Lunt, 1994: 102)

Through these oppositions, expert opinion is often fundamentally challenged. This is especially so in British shows, where experts are not separated from audience members but sit together with them, with the host roaming among them carrying the microphone. Thus, while there is an observable spatial equality between lay people, who talk about their *experience* of the issue (such as homelessness), and professionals, who often try and *explain* issues, ordinary experience is almost always prioritized over the experts' supposedly 'objective' view. Livingstone and Lunt argue that these shows represent significant cultural spaces in which democracy is exercised and the thoughts and opinions of experts and professionals are challenged and made accountable.

Pursuing this argument, Livingstone and Lunt (1994) describe TV debate shows as an 'intergeneric' discourse form. Principally, they see the talk as shifting between three main generic forms: the 'debate', the 'romantic narrative' and the 'therapy session'. On the level of 'debate', they argue that audience discussion programmes represent a forum for public debate between 'experts', in the shape of public figures or representatives of professions, and lay members of the public. The shows represent a particular kind of debate forum, in which the lay perspective is systematically prioritized over the expert viewpoint. On another level, the debate show can be compared to the romance genre, or fairy tale, where the host takes the role of the popular or romantic hero, with a mission to resolve particular social problems through talking to the other characters in the 'story', often with their own individual narrative to offer which will support or undermine the hero as he or she journeys through the 'quest' of a particular programme. The third generic form they identify in TV debates is that of therapeutic discourse, where a sense of private interaction and self-disclosure is produced through members of the audience talking about their individual stories and troubles, and being supported by expressions of intimacy and sympathy from the host, who may also make suggestions for solving these problems by taking on the role of 'therapist'. More recently, Lunt and Stenner (2005) have pursued this approach in relation to the more controversial audience participation shows exemplified by *Ricki Lake* and *Jerry Springer*, as discussed in Chapter 4.

But whereas it may be possible abstractly to characterize the discourse of audience participation debates in this way, it turns out that Livingstone and Lunt (1994) are basing their claims largely on what participants and television audiences say *about* these programmes, rather than on an analysis of the interactional dynamics of the talk produced during the broadcast itself. Much of their data derives from interviews with audience participants who have appeared on the show, or with the show's host and producers, rather than from transcripts of the broadcast talk itself.

Thus, while this study, like Carbaugh's (1988), aims to describe the characteristic discourse genres of this distinctive form of broadcast talk, in neither book is much attention paid to the specific interactional and sequential contexts in which different forms of talk come into play, and in which the different participants get to speak. This is crucially important because, as research in conversation analysis has shown, 'turn-taking in its various forms constitutes a fundamental dimension of spoken interaction that may structure both its form and its substance' (Heritage *et al.*, 1988: 81).

Since the publication of these two books, a number of collections have appeared which take a more conversation-analytic approach to the question of how audience participation shows comprise specific forms of broadcast talk-in-interaction (Haarman, 2000; Thornborrow, 1997a; Thornborrow and van Leeuwen, 2001; Tolson, 2001). The argument these authors make is that simply identifying the various forms of discourse that make up the broadcast is not enough. The interactional structures through which the debate is constructed, in live talk within the studio, represent a crucial shaping element which any properly adequate analysis must take into account. In the remainder of this chapter, therefore, I use a case study of one audience participation debate show to illustrate the application of CA methods to the question of how structures of talk-in-interaction are closely related to the precise nature of the 'public discourse' produced by these shows.

From discourse genres to forms of talk

The data that follows is an extract from an episode of the *Oprah Winfrey Show* in which there occurs a debate between members of the public in Chicago, USA, and representatives of the Chicago police department. It is important to point out that the show was broadcast at a particularly sensitive time in the recent history of American policing. The debate within the show was focused around the case of Rodney King, a black motorist who had been secretly filmed by a member of the public being intimidated and severely beaten by white police officers after his car had been stopped under suspicion on a Los Angeles street. The footage was subsequently broadcast on national television news, and led first to a series of riots in Los Angeles and, later, to a controversial court case involving members of the Los Angeles police department. However, the discussion itself transcends the issue of the Rodney King beating to draw in issues that are still highly relevant today: for example, questions of police racism and brutality, public perceptions of and reactions to police tactics and the official responses of police organizations to such concerns.

The extract can be conveniently split into four phases. In the first phase, which comes from the opening of the show, the host begins by introducing the show's theme, and there follows a segment in which her commentary over video playbacks of relevant scenes is interspersed with studio monologues:

(3) Oprah Winfrey Show

1   ((Opening jingle))

2   ((Applause))

3   Host: The pol<u>i</u>ce. (0.4) Are they our fr<u>ie</u>nd or our foe.

4   ((Applause dies down))

[Video]:

5   Film cop: Whaddaya think of traffic work Steve? Like it?

6   Film kid: <u>Oh</u> sure!

[Voice over VT]:

7   Host: When we grew up we were taught the policeman was

8   our fr<u>ie</u>nd. .hh Remember Officer Friendly? .hh

9   Remember seeing a police officer in <u>y</u>our

10   neighbourhood and feeling .hh safer because he

11   was the:re? .h and the tr<u>a</u>ffic cop who sm<u>i</u>led at

12   you as you passed him.

13   (1.8)

[Studio]:

14   Host: But tod<u>a</u>:y one out of three people <u>sa::y</u>, .h

15   they distr<u>u</u>st the police that's according to a

16   recent .h Gallup poll. .hh Could seeing police

17   beatin:g on home <u>v</u>ideos, .h have made people

18   more afraid?

19   (2.0)

[Voice over VT]:

20   Host: .hh The ruthless beating of motorist Rodney King

21   by Los Angeles police officers in M<u>a</u>rch of this

22   year .h was played <u>over</u> and <u>over</u> on newscasts

23   from coast to coast. .hhh In Fort Worth Texas a

24   woman videotaped a patrolman .h clubbing a man

25   by the side of an Interstate. .hh Her camera

26   recorded the officer .h taking twenty four

27   p<u>ow</u>erful swings .h at the <u>hand</u>cuffed suspect.

28   .hh and last year in: Tarns California .h two

29   officers were taped as they ch<u>o</u>ked a twenty year

30   old man, .hh and beat him <u>eight</u> times with a

31   nightstick, .h until <u>he</u> was kno:cked

32   <u>un</u>conscious. The officers were not ch<u>ar</u>:ged with

33   the crime, .h and s<u>e</u>ttled out of court.

[Studio]:

34   Host: Euchh. (.) .hhh Today we've g<u>a</u>thered police

35   officers, <u>a</u>:nd citizens. .hh to vent their

36   frustrations and uh, h<u>o</u>pefully better underst<u>and</u>

| 37 | | one another. .hh What do you think of the |
| 38 | | police, that's the question we're asking today. |

The second phase begins here. In this phase, the host addresses members of the studio audience, asking them for their views on her question in lines 37–38 above, 'What do you think of the police':

39	Host:	What do you say.
40		(1.5)
41	Man 1:	I think that uh, all police think black people
42		look alike.
43	Host:	Mm h<u>m</u>m.
44		(1.1)
45	Host:	And [what do <u>you</u> think
46	Audience:	[x-xx-xxx-x-xxx-
47	Man 2:	I think u:h when they got their <u>ba</u>:dges (.) uhm
48		(.) they were here to serve and prot<u>ec</u>t but (.)
49		uh f- widda widda gun an a ba:dge, they- they
50		believe that they're above the <u>law</u> that's:
51	Audience:	[((Applause))
52	Man 2:	[that's how most (people) (believe)
53	Audience:	((Applause))
54	Host:	And what do <u>you</u> think.
55	Woman 1:	My son and two other white guys, and a black
56		friend were driving along the <u>cops</u> stopped them,
57		.h <u>pul</u>led the black guy out, .hh <u>push</u>ed 'im
58		against the hood <u>threw</u> 'im on the floor, .hhh
59		(.) r- ff- <u>roughed</u> 'im up (.) a::nd, didn't do
60		anything to my so:n and his friends but pat them
61		down so it was cl<u>ear</u>ly a racist incident.
62		.hhh It made my son so angry that he'd
63		like to become, .hh a l<u>aw</u>yer, to fight
64		this kind of racism in the police
65		department.
66	Audience:	((Applause))

In the third phase of the extract, the host introduces, and then asks questions of, two 'expert' guests who are presented as representing (albeit in different ways) the police perspective:

| 67 | Host: | Well, (.) we have some specially invited guests |
| 68 | | here Tony Bouza who's the former chief of police |

69		of Minneapolis and author of the book called .hh
70		the Police Mystique, .hh and Commander Hugh
71		Holton who's the current commander, .h of the
72		thi<u>r</u>d district, of uh police here in Chicago. .h
73		Commander, Holton? (1.2) Are police racist?
74	Holton:	.hh I think we have as much racim- <u>i</u>sm in the
75		Chicago police department as we have in America
76		as a whole. .hh The police officers are taken
77		from American society in the city of Chicago,
78		.hh it is required that (0.5) before you can
79		app<u>ly</u> to be a police officer you have to be a
80		resident.
81	Host:	Uh h<u>uh</u>.
82	Holton:	So: I think that it's as much reflected with
83		<u>u</u>:s, .h but the thing is we can't t<u>o</u>lerate it.
84	Host:	Okay. .h So when you say it <u>is</u> as much
85		reflected, .h we <u>do</u> live in a racist society you
86		would admit that.
87	Holton:	Ye [s I do.
88	Host:	[So it means, the answer to that question is,
89		then police, are r<u>a</u>cist.
90		(0.2)
91	Holton:	I s<u>a</u>y that we have as much <u>in</u> the police
92		department as we would have in society but, .h
93		we won't we cannot t<u>o</u>lerate racism in the pol<u>ice</u>
94		department. .h If we fi:nd d-if we find like,
95		the lady said as far as that being a racist
96		incident, .hh an investigation of the incident
97		sh<u>ou</u>ld get someone disciplined if not fired.
98	Host:	[[What about-
99	Holton:	[[.hh We-
100	(Man)	[[[((inaudible))
101	Host:	Uh [what if-
102	Holton:	[If we- We h<u>ire</u>- if <u>we</u>- [did not hire-
103	Host:	((to audience member)) [Please if you're
104		gonna speak go to the mike please if you're
105		gonna speak.
106	Holton:	If we didn't h<u>ir</u>:e (0.2) if we didn't hire
107		police officers who eventually have problems we
108		wouldn't have to f<u>ire</u> as many.
109	Host:	.hh Okay. .h Tony? Is that true or not. Are
110		police officers racist?

```
111   Bouza:   Yes. (.) Uh they are racist uhm ours is a
112            racist society, .h uh police do ver- many
113            heroic and beautiful thin:gs, uh it's funny
114            in those videotapes that it's little brother
115            watching big brother, .h which I think is a
116            kind of turn around of George Orwell's
117            vision, .hh
118   Host:    Right.
119   Bouza:   but w- the reality is that we live in a racist
120            society, that the police are the instruments of
121            the overclass trying to keep the underclass
122            under control the underclass, .hh is homeless
123            and poor and black, .h and and the police as
124            instruments of the overclass uh practice many
125            racist .hh er pr- u:h policies, a:nd uh
126            stereotype, .h and- but they also do heroic and
127            beautiful things and we will hear about some of
128            those today as well.
```

Finally, in the fourth phase, the host turns again to the opinions of audience participants. During the contributions of audience members in this phase, the separation
between audience and 'specially invited guests' becomes broken down. Note, for
instance, how the earlier audience contributions took a generalized form and did not
focus on the particular police officers in the studio; note also the way in which the host,
in lines 103–105 above, refused to allow an audience member to interrupt Commander
Holton. In what follows, we see that audience members begin to focus more centrally on
Holton himself, as the Chief of Chicago police; and also that the host now facilitates
some form of interaction between audience members and guests:

```
129   Host:    Okay. What do you say sir?
130   Man 3:   .hhh It's not just a question of individual cops
131            being racist or not. .hh The police department
132            as itself, is a racist institution. (0.5) An'
133            I'll give you an example. In December of this
134            year, (0.5) the London office of Amnesty
135            International issued the first time ever, (.) an
136            accusation against the Sh- uh police department
137            in the US, (.) for using torture against
138            suspects right here the Chicago police
139            department.
140   Host:    Mm hm.
141   Man 3:   Has been doing this since nineteen seventy two.
```

142	Host:	Has been doing what.
143	Man 3:	Using electro sh<u>ock</u>, (0.4) burns, (0.2)
144		suffocation .hhh and threatened execution on
145		black prisoners <u>a</u>ll black prisoners it's
146		a [racist-
147	Host:	[How do you know that.
148		(0.3)
149	Man 3:	.hhh Cuz there are affidavits, OPS complaints,
150		(0.8) .hh testimony and depositions (.) in civil
151		cases going back. The Chicago police department
152		.hh has promoted him from the r<u>a</u>nks, .hhh until
153		today he's one of the highest ranking officers
154		in the Chicago police department. .hhh That
155		sends a message to every cop in the department
156		that the way to get ahead in Chicago, .hh is to
157		be racist, v<u>i</u>olent, an' even to use <u>torture</u>. .h=
158	Audience:	=x[x-XXXXXXXXXXXXXX[XXXXXXXX]XXXXXXXXX=
159	Audience:	[<u>WOOO</u> [<u>OOOOOO</u>! [ ]
160	Audience:	[WOOOoo! [Woo [hoo!]
161	Audience:	[<u>WOOO</u>!]
162	Audience:	=XXXXXXXXX=
163	Man 3:	=That's the report from London. Right there.
164	Host:	D'you wanna respond to that?
165	Holton:	Yes. (.) This was just handed to me I haven't
166		<u>re</u>ad the report.
167	Host:	Uh huh.
168	Holton:	B<u>ut</u>, as far as (0.6) <u>ra</u>cism, brutality and
169		violence being criteria for promotion to the- in
170		the Chicago police department I don't believe
171		that's true. .hh <u>I</u> was not promoted in that way,
172		(.) there is no <u>e</u>vidence that <u>I</u> can see n-not
173		(.) withstanding this report, .h to sh<u>ow</u>
174		anything like that.
175	Host:	Well you all real- recognise that there is a
176		problem right that's <u>one</u> of the reasons why
177		we're doing this show [.hh] what <u>happened</u> to=
178	Holton:	[Yes]
179	Host:	=Officer Fri<u>end</u>ly.
180	Holton:	Well,
181	Audience:	((Laughter))
182	Holton:	when we t<u>a</u>lk about, when we- when we t<u>a</u>lk about
183		the public <u>lo</u>sing co:nfidence in the police

```
184              (0.6) our ca:ll volumes are tremendously up. We
185              are receiving more calls than we ever have in
186              history so .hh the people need us. And I feel
187              that they wouldn't be calling us unless they had
188              some confidence in us that we would be able to
189              get the job done when we get there.
190   Host:     Uh huh. You say what ma'am?
191   Woman 2:  I say that the, uh report that's sitting on
192              Superintendent Martin's desk which is, he's the
193              head of the oaf- Officer Professional Standards
194              which is the internal police investigative body,
195              .hh only goes, .h to his desk, .h when an u- s-
196              a:: complaint against an officer has been
197              sustained. .h There's been forty documented
198              cases of torture against .h him and other police
199              detectives underneath him, .h and twenny of them
200              have named him personally. .hh Now, there's been
201              medical testimony, court testimony, .h u::m,
202              there's the Cook County deputy medical examiner
203              has looked at burns on people's bodies, .hhh and
204              have said, yes, these are consistet- consistent
205              with black men's allegations against this man..h
206              Not only that, if they were white suspects this
207              would n::ever, allowed- be [allowed to con [tinue.
208   Audience:                            [x – x – x –   [XXXXXXXX
209              XXXXXXXXXXXXXXXXXXXXXX[XXXXXXXXX
210   Host:                                        [The personal
211              feelings a:re about police officers the fact is that
212              they do put their lives on the li:ne, .hh every day.
```

Having run through the extract, we can begin with some preliminary observations. In the most basic sense, most of this extract consists of a series of sequences initiated by the host, in which she asks some type of question and members of the audience or experts on the panel provide a response (not necessarily an answer). Both the questions and their responses take a wide range of forms. For instance, looking at the responses, it is relatively easy to identify the following: clichés ('all police think black people look alike'); opinions ('I think we have as much racism in the Chicago police department as we have in America as a whole'); stories/anecdotes ('My son and two other white guys and a black friend were driving along . . .'); accounts/justifications ('If we didn't hire police officers who eventually have problems we wouldn't have to fire as many'); factual descriptions ('There's been forty documented cases of torture against him and other police detectives under him'); accusations ('the police department as itself is a racist institution'); rebuttals ('as far as racism, brutality and violence being criteria for promotion in the Chicago police department I don't believe that's true'); commentaries ('The ruthless beating of motorist Rodney King by Los Angeles police officers in March of this year was played over and over on newscasts from coast to coast . . .'); and many more. The questions themselves also take different forms, with some being invitations to speak and others being requests for an answer on a specific point. The significance of these differences is an issue to which I return presently.

Immediately, then, it is possible to say that even in this seven-minute extract from one episode, the range of discursive 'genres' or forms of talk that are used is very wide. Yet the forms I have mentioned are very different from the generic conventions described by Livingstone and Lunt (1994), in two senses. First, there are many more forms than the three they focus on (those of therapy, romance and debate). More importantly, the forms I have listed come from a different source to those they identify. The forms of discourse I describe have their roots in ordinary conversation, rather than being literary or metaphorical.

How, then, are these different forms of talk actually used? What are the sequential contexts in which participants speak, and how do they practically manage their participation in those contexts? By focusing on these questions, we gain a better under-standing of the ongoing, situated production of the 'public sphere' of audience par-ticipation broadcasting. This understanding begins from the viewpoint that the show does not create a public domain of discourse just by virtue of existing. Such a domain is created and sustained in and through the interactional matrix within which partici-pants take their turns at speaking. That interactional matrix draws attention towards a range of key issues. I will focus on a particular sequential aspect of the way that talk-in-interaction, carried out within the speech exchange system of the show, is tied up with the nature of participation in this highly public discourse arena: the role of questions and their responses.

Questions and participation structures

Questions are central discursive devices in this show, as they are in interview and talk shows generally. There are many different types of question forms which occur in this extract alone. Different types of questions have different interactional functions. For instance, consider the series of questions in the opening sequence of the show, where the host establishes the issues to be discussed during the programme. These are addressed to both the studio and the viewing audience and are embedded within a voice-over commentary describing the content of video clips shown on screen:

The police. Are they our friend or our foe? (line 2)
Remember Officer Friendly? (line 8)
Remember seeing a police officer in your neighbourhood and feeling safer because he was there? (lines 9–11)

Could seeing police beating on home videos have made people more afraid? (lines 16–18)

What do you think of the police, that's the question we're asking today. (lines 37–38)

It seems clear that the function of these questions is to focus the debate on two contrasting representations of the police (as 'friend' or 'foe'), and to open up the discursive forum to participants for 'saying what you think' about them. More than that, however, one of the central effects of this sequence, in which questions and reports are juxtaposed, is to establish a tension between factual accounts (with video-taped evidence) and personal opinions. This is one of the key tensions which Livingstone and Lunt (1994) identified as characteristic of the discourse of audience participation TV. The question that remains to be addressed is: How exactly is that tension played out in the turn designs and sequential structures of the ensuing dialogue?

In order to address that issue, we can draw on another of the key tensions identified in the Livingstone and Lunt study: the relationship between 'expert' and 'lay' discourse. They argue that audience participation debates tend to prioritize the discourse of ordinary experience over that of expertise and authority. Lay perspectives on events are treated as 'authentic', 'relevant' and 'in depth' whereas expert viewpoints come across as 'alienated', 'fragmented' and 'superficial'. Again, though, the issue of precisely how lay and expert speakers actually participate within the interactional structures of the live show are not really addressed. It is not just a question of how individual participants are officially categorized, nor even of the kinds of discourse they typically employ. Audience participation debates have a distinctive sequential structure in which the host plays a central mediating role, moving from speaker to speaker with the microphone, inviting their contributions. Thus, a significant element is the way in which different participants are actually invited to speak by the host.

In the above data extract, looking at this element gives us a much closer view of the situated, interactional constitution of 'lay' and 'expert' viewpoints in the unfolding course of the talk. Immediately following the introductory sequence, the host shifts from directing her talk at the combined audience of viewers and collective studio participants to addressing individual participants. Beginning in line 39, she initiates a series of question-response sequences which accomplish two things. First, they enable different participants, from both the audience and the expert panel, to speak on the topic. Second, however, these questions construct distinctive participation spaces into which those speakers are invited to move. These participation spaces are systematically different for lay speakers from the audience and expert speakers from the panel, respectively.

The host's question in line 39 is characteristic of the way she invites the talk of audience participants. It takes the form of an 'open' question: 'What do you say?' or 'You say what?' which invites the participant to produce an opinion on the issue at hand:

39   Host: What do you say.
40   (1.5)
41   Man 1:   I think that uh, all police think black people
42   look alike.
43   Host: Mm h<u>m</u>m.

And indeed, in this case, the response is duly framed by the words 'I think that . . .', thereby marking the utterance as a personal opinion.

This open question form recurs throughout the extract whenever the host addresses audience participants:

45   Host: And what do you think

54   Host: And what do you think.

129 Host: Okay. What do you say sir?

190 Host: Uh <u>hu</u>h. You say what ma'am?

The point about these invitations is that, formally, they enable the respondent to construct their utterance in whatever way they choose. Subject only to the general constraints of the discussion topic (set by the host in the opening sequence), audience participants are invited to 'speak their minds' on the issue. However, the types of responses provided by audience members after this opener are by no means always opinions, neither are they always overtly marked in the same way. In the next question-response sequence, at line 55, the speaker produces not an opinion but a personal anecdote as her response to the host's question. She tells a story about an event involving her son and some friends (one black) being stopped by the police. Her opinion is only provided in the form of an entailed proposition embedded in the coda to this story (lines 62–65): '. . . to fight this kind of racism in the police department' (i.e., 'in my opinion [and as my story demonstrates], there is racism in the police department').

A further answer-type produced in response to the host's 'You say what?' invitation is found in the later account (lines 130–157) of police racism based on an Amnesty International report (Man 3). This participant shifts the talk between the personal and the factual by producing documentary evidence, in the form of the report's description of police torture of black prisoners, to support his assertion that the police department is itself a racist institution. At line 163 the speaker actually indicates the presence in the studio of the Amnesty report as proof of the facts of his account:

163 Man 3:   That's the report from London. Right there.

I will say more about the structures and functions of these audience contributions in the next section. The main feature to which I want to draw attention at present is the stark contrast between the 'You say what?' device and the way the host invites the contributions of the two professional representatives, Commander Holton and Tony Bouza. The host's opening questions to Holton and Bouza (lines 73, and 109–10) are both polar interrogative (yes/no) forms:

73   Host: Commander, Holton? (1.2) Are police racist?

109   Host: .hh Okay. .h Tony? Is that true or not. Are
110   police officers racist?

These are not invitations to produce an opinion as such, in the same way as she uses 'You say what?', but rather to provide some kind of *answer* based on what they 'know' from their status as 'experts'. This difference in question form and associated participatory status for the respondent leads to a different dynamic between facts and opinions to that which is observable in the host's interactions with audience participants.

We can see this by picking up on the markedly different ways in which Holton and Bouza respond to what is essentially the same question: 'Are police racist?' Holton, who appears on the show as the current chief of the Chicago police department and whose talk therefore is open to being treated as the official representation of the views and policy of the police department, attempts to avoid giving a 'straight' answer. Holton begins by framing his answer, like some of the audience participants, as an opinion:

73   Host: Commander, Holton? (1.2) Are police racist?
74   Holton: .hh I think we have as much racim- ism in the
75   Chicago police department as we have in America
76   as a whole

In other words, the 'Yes' or 'No' answer projected by the question does not appear as such: instead, an opinion-framed account is offered which *implies* an affirmative answer at the same time as offering an account, or reason, for that answer (that American society contains racism so therefore it is inevitable that certain police officers will be racist in as much as they are Americans). While this may be a clever way of appearing to answer the question without going 'on record' as saying 'Yes, police are racist', it is noticeable that the host is concerned to pursue that unequivocal response (see the turns beginning at lines 84 and 88):

81   Host: Uh h<u>uh</u>.
82   Holton: So: I think that it's as much reflected with
83   <u>u</u>:s, .h but the thing is we can't t<u>o</u>lerate it.
84   Host: Okay. .h So when you say it <u>is</u> as much
85   reflected, .h we <u>do</u> live in a racist society you
86   would admit that.

```
87  Holton:   Ye[s I do.
88  Host:        [So it means, the answer to that question is,
89                then police, are racist.
90      (0.2)
91  Holton:   I say that we have as much in the police
92                department as we would have in society but, .h
93                we won't we cannot tolerate racism in the police
94                department.
```

She pursues a 'straight' response using a neat strategy, manoeuvring Holton into admitting that 'we do live in a racist society' (line 85) and that therefore, by his own logic, 'police are racist' (line 89). Nevertheless, Holton still declines to provide a straight answer even given this apparently logical conclusion, instead returning in lines 91–94 to his original, qualified response.

By contrast, Bouza, who appears on the show as an ex-police officer, and therefore as an 'independent' expert, offers a response which matches the polar interrogative form of the question, before going on to offer an account which defends police officers' heroism:

```
109  Host:     .hh Okay. .h Tony? Is that true or not. Are
110                police officers racist?
111  Bouza:    Yes. (.) Uh they are racist uhm ours is a
112                racist society, .h uh police do ver- many
113                heroic and beautiful thin:gs, ((continues))
```

Bouza's account overall is ambivalent in its attitude towards the police, describing them both as 'instruments of the overclass' (line 120/1) and as doing 'heroic and beautiful things' (line 126/7). However, unlike Holton, the host responds to him only with a single utterance, 'Right' (line 118). This may well be because the account itself is prefaced by a straight affirmative answer which appears to acknowledge the police's racism, even though that acknowledgement, when we look closely, is tempered by the phrase, 'ours is a racist society'. In other words, Bouza uses exactly the same account as Holton, which is to acknowledge that the police are racist in as much as society itself is racist. Whereas Bouza's use of this account is framed within the participatory space which the host's question opens up for him – that of a knowledge-based answerer – Holton's use of the same account was framed within the different participatory space of an opinion-giver. The host's challenge, and pursuit of a straight answer, indicates her orientation to the different categories of speakership that are being constructed in the show's discursive space in and through the production of differently formatted questions.

We thus see how, in the design of her question turns, the host constructs systematically different participation spaces for differently categorized speakers. 'You say what?' situates its recipient as the repository of an opinion. 'Are police racist?', on the other hand, situates its recipient as the repository of an answer. The relationship between expert and lay participation in this form of broadcast discourse is not simply a matter of the categorization of speakers, nor of the discourse genres they can be found to employ. As these extracts show, there is an important sense in which that relationship is rooted in the ways different participants are enabled to speak in response to the mediating talk of the show's host and in the participation structures that talk sets up.

Rhetorical arguments and the presentation of opinions

A further interesting feature of our data can now be mentioned. It is noticeable that the studio audience tends to affiliate with opinion presentations from lay speakers, but not those of 'experts', by applauding. This may chime in with Livingstone and Lunt's (1994) idea that shows such as this tend to prioritize the discourse of lay participants – who are treated as speaking with relevance and authenticity – over that of professionals or experts – who speak in the abstract terms of institutions, bureaucracy and the like. But from the point of view of an interest in media talk, the question becomes one of *how* lay speakers construct their talk so as to enable it to be responded to with applause. It may be that the audience in this show, antagonistic towards the police and the 'official' response to accusations of racism, systematically *withhold* applause after both Holton and Bouza's turns. But the fact that they do applaud following certain contributions from among their own number (although interestingly not *all* such contributions) raises the question of how 'successful' applause-generating turns are constructed by their speakers. This becomes a question of how speakers mark the conclusion of their opinion presentations: what rhetorical devices are used to indicate that their point is now made, their argument now complete?

The content of audience contributions tends to be, in a broad sense, 'opinionated'. In general in these shows, people use their turns in order to take up positions, or argue with others' positions, on the issue. Joanna Thornborrow (1997b) has shown that lay speakers' turns can take a variety of forms, from single sentence aphorisms such as 'I think all police think black people look alike', to extended stories recounting some personal experience. However, whatever form they take, Thornborrow argues that the turns function as position-taking contributions in the debate. Thus, even stories that appear simply to recount a set of events without overtly making a point can be treated by other participants as *implicating* a point and situating the speaker in relation to the issue under discussion.

In fact it seems that successfully presenting an opinion in this discursive context means more than simply stating what your opinion is. As in the case of the host's 'Yes/No' questions put to the experts, which were oriented to as actually requiring somewhat more than a 'Yes' or 'No' response, the opinion-generating question 'You say what?' is typically oriented to as requiring more than a simple statement of a viewpoint. On those occasions where opinion presentations do consist of single phrases or sentences, such brief turns can prove problematic for either the speaker or the potential respondent (or both). As we see in more detail below, there are rhetorical devices available by which speakers may manage the occurrence of audience applause in the studio. However, in single sentence opinion presentations, there may prove to be problems for those who want to react to the speaker's view, as we see in this detail from the *Oprah Winfrey* extract:

```
39   Host:       What do you say.
40         (1.5)
41   Man 1:      I think that uh, all police think black people
42               look alike.
43   Host:       Mm hmm.
44         (1.1)
45   Host:       And [what do you think
46   Audience:       [x–xx–xxx–x–xxx–
```

In the above extract, the host responds simply by saying 'Mm hmm'. Subsequently there is a 1.1-second gap during which the audience member says nothing more, and the host moves on to address another contributor. The audience in fact applauds the first speaker's opinion, but only after the pause, once it is clear that the host has treated the man's contribution as complete by moving on. The applause itself is only weak and sporadic.

By contrast, consider the following detail from later in the debate:

```
190  Host:       Uh huh. You say what ma'am?
191  Woman 2:    I say that the, uh report that's sitting on
192              Superintendent Martin's desk which is, he's the
193              head of the oaf- Officer Professional Standards
194              which is the internal police investigative body,
195              .hh only goes, .h to his desk, .h when an u- s-
196              a:: complaint against an officer has been
197              sustained. .h There's been forty documented
198              cases of torture against .h him and other police
199              detectives underneath him, .h and twenny of them
200              have named him personally. .hh Now, there's been
201              medical testimony, court testimony, .h u::m,
202              there's the Cook County deputy medical examiner
203              has looked at burns on people's bodies, .hhh and
204              have said, yes, these are consistet- consistent
205              with black men's allegations against this man..h
206              Not only that, if they were white suspects this
207              would n::ever, allowed- be [allowed to con[tinue.
208  Audience:                              [x – x – x –   [XXXXXX
209              XXXXXXXXXXXXXXXX . . .
```

In response to the host's invitation, the contributor produces a lengthy utterance in which she constructs an argument in favour of a particular stance on the issue of police brutality. Note that the stance is not just stated, but her argument is supported by various types of evidence (principally, the deputy medical examiner's reports which she cites). Notice also that the audience's applause in line 208 is much more closely coordinated with the completion of her argument than that in the prior extract. The audience begins applauding once it is clear that the speaker is making the point that white suspects would not be subjected to such treatment. She repairs the way this sentence is articulated twice, resulting in some overlap in the onset of applause; but despite that the applause is coordinated to begin in earnest halfway through the last word of the sentence, 'con//tinue.'

We can describe this turn as a whole in terms of a three-stage format. The turn is opened with a position statement (lines 191–197), in which the caller asserts that complaints only go to the internal investigative body of the police when they are actually sustained. This sets up an expectation that the speaker knows of other complaints which have not been sustained, and so are not known about by the named officer, 'Superintendent Martin'. The second stage consists of making a case to support this assertion. The speaker justifies her stance by citing evidence of 'forty documented cases of torture' and the deputy medical examiner's assertion that medical evidence is consistent with the allegations of black victims. Finally, in lines 206–207, she 'rounds off' the argument using a summative assessment: 'if the:y were white suspects this would n::ever . . . be allowed to continue'.

This three-part form tends to be the one taken by the most successful response-generating opinion presentations in this kind of context. In my data of audience participation shows, both on television and radio, it is widely used, and actually comes in two variants: the *progressional* format and the *recursive* format. In the progressional pattern, an opinion presentation goes from a relatively neutral situating component, through an account designed to lead up to an evaluative conclusion, to a final assertion of that evaluation. In the recursive pattern, a position is stated at the beginning, followed by a justificatory or supporting account, then the coda is used to recapitulate the initial position.

These are illustrated using the following two extracts from talk radio, and summarized in Table 3.1.

(4) **Talk Radio [Recursive format]**

1	Host:	Kath calling from Clapham now good morning.
2	Caller:	Good morning Brian. Erm: I (li-) I also agree
3		that thee .hh telethons a:re a form of
4		psychological blackmail no:w. (.) .hhh Be:cause
5		the majority of people I think do know that
6		charities exist, .hh we all have our own
7		charities that we contribute to:, (.) .h we do

```
8          not have open ended pockets where we can keep on
9          doing this. .hh And to sa:y because you have a
10         credit car::d, .hh you just salve your conscience
11         by paying- sending in your number:, .phh I'm
12         sorry but I: think that's making people, (.)
13         appear very erm (.) la:zy.=
14  Host:  =Well it's certainly not blackmail,
```

Here, the caller first situates her stance by taking up a position in agreement with an earlier caller to the show (lines 2–4). She then makes a case for her stance (line 5ff.), offering a justificatory account – again, marked as such through the use of a conjunction, 'Because . . .'. Finally, she produces an evaluative coda to mark the completion of the argument, which summarizes her position: 'I'm sorry but I think that's making people appear very erm, lazy.' Finally, in line 14, we see an indication of the interactional functions of this coda or evaluative summary, as the host coordinates his production of a rebuttal ('Well it's certainly not blackmail') with the caller's rounding off of her argument.

This represents an example of the 'recursive' format. By way of contrast, the following extract shows the 'progressional' format:

(5) **Talk Radio [Progressional format]**
```
1   Host:    It's Ka:y next from: Islington:, good morning.
2   Caller:  Yes guh morning. Um:: (.) I: want to talk about
3            thee- thee report on L.B.C this morning about
4            Diana's visi:t to::, America:? h[.hh
5   Host:                                      [The Princess
6            of Wa:les.
7            (.)
8   Caller:  Princess of Wa:les, yah. .hh E::r th- her stay
9            in a thou:sand pou:nds a night hotel plus V.A.T::,
10           an' on her schedule she's visiting a home- p-
11           place for the homeless. .hhh A:nd there's going
12           to be a ba:::ll, .hh where they're uh- the
13           Americans are clamoring for tickets at a thou:sand
14           pounds a ni- er th- a thou:sand pounds each,=
15  Host:    =[[Mm hm,]
16  Caller:   [[I:    th]ink it's obsce:ne.
17  Host:    .pt Which:, part is obsce:ne.
```

Instead of beginning her opinion presentation by stating a position, the caller here uses a different kind of situating component – a *preface*: 'I want to talk about the report on LBC this morning about Diana's visit to America.' An account of circumstances surrounding the visit is then produced, in a way that will support her eventual statement of a position (e.g., by implying hypocrisy on the part of the Princess and others through a juxtaposition of expensive hotels and tickets for a ball with the problem of homelessness). Finally, the caller explicitly states the position she has been leading up to in the evaluative summary: 'I think it's obsce:ne.'

These formats are summarized schematically in Table 3.1, in which the three argument functions I have mentioned are matched with their associated basic discourse components.

Managing applause

In terms of generating a response (such as applause) from the audience, it is the third part – the rounding off using a position statement or recapitulation – that is the most important. To understand how these work, we can turn to research carried out by Max Atkinson (1984a) and John Heritage and David Greatbatch (1986) on audience reactions to the speech-making of professional politicans. I discuss the key rhetorical devices of *three-part lists* and *contrasts* at greater length in Chapter 8. For now, it is worth mentioning that in their large-scale study of audience responses to the rhetoric of platform speakers at political conferences, Heritage and Greatbatch (1986) found one particular type, which they called *position-taking*, to be 'the most effective single rhetorical format' associated with audience applause. In this device:

> the speaker first describes a state of affairs towards which he or she could be expected to take a strongly evaluative stance. . . . At the end of it, the speaker overtly and unequivocally praises or condemns the state of affairs described.
>
> (Heritage and Greatbatch, 1986: 131)

The speaker's final sentence in the *Oprah Winfrey* detail above, 'if the:y were white suspects this would n::ever ... be allowed to continue', is an example of such a position-taking device. However it also possesses other properties which are related to

Table 3.1 Two Basic Design Formats for Opinion Presentations

Argument functions		Component types	
		Progressional format	Recursive format
Part 1	*Situating the argument*	Preface	Position statement
Part 2	*Making a case*	Accounts and justifications	Accounts and justifications
Part 3	*Rounding off*	Position statement	Recapitulation

the general features of rhetorical devices discussed by Atkinson (1984a), and which play an important role in enabling the audience successfully to coordinate its applause with the 'pay-off' to the speaker's opinion presentation.

As Heritage and Greatbatch (1986: 116) summarize it, rhetorical devices that are effective in generating applause tend to work because of two properties:

> (a) [they] *emphasise* and thus highlight their contents against a surrounding background of speech materials and (b) [they] *project a clear completion point* for the message in question. Atkinson proposes that these two requirements are satisfied by certain conventionalised rhetorical formats – in particular, the contrast (or antithesis) and the three-part list.

The speaker's final sentence 'if the:y were white suspects this would n::ever ... be allowed to continue' has similar projective properties. Its projectability stems from the common rhetorical structure 'if [X], then [Y]'. Gene Lerner (1991) calls this a 'compound unit' because a recipient of the first part 'if [X]' can project what it will take to complete the construction (i.e., 'then [Y]') before that second part occurs. He shows this partly by looking at how people sometimes 'jump in' to provide the second part in their own right. In our extract, the broader context of the discussion also plays a part in enabling the audience to project what it will take for the position-taking statement to be complete. Given that previous audience contributions have condemned police treatment of black people, the phrase 'if they were white suspects' projects a particular kind of position-taking completion: one that contrasts what might happen with white suspects to that which has been said to happen with black suspects. The audience is able to use those features to project the place at which the speaker's summation will be complete, and indeed begins applauding even before the completion of her turn (line 208).

Let us look at another episode involving audience applause. Note that in the turn by the audience contributor referred to as 'Man 3' in the *Oprah Winfrey* extract, the speaker's opinion presentation does not take the form of an uninterrupted rhetorical argument, but is interspersed with questions and challenges from the host. We can observe how these interjections have specific consequences for the rhetorical design of the argument; but also how they furnish additional evidence for the oriented-to effectiveness of the formats and devices described above:

129 Host: Okay. What do you say sir?
130 Man 3: .hhh It's not just a question of individual cops
131 being racist or not. .hh The police department
132 as itself, is a racist institution. (0.5) An'
133 I'll give you an example. In December of this
134 year, (0.5) the London office of Amnesty
135 International issued the first time ever, (.) an
136 accusation against the Sh- uh police department
137 in the US, (.) for using torture against

```
138                    suspects right here the Chicago police
139                    department.
140  Host:            Mm hm.
141  Man 3:           Has been doing this since nineteen seventy two.
142  Host:            Has been doing what.
143  Man 3:           Using electro shock, (0.4) burns, (0.2)
144                    suffocation .hhh and threatened execution on
145                    black prisoners all black prisoners it's
146                    a [racist-
147  Host:              [How do you know that.
148       (0.3)
149  Man 3:           .hhh Cuz there are affidavits, OPS complaints,
150                    (0.8) .hh testimony and depositions (.) in civil
151                    cases going back. The Chicago police department
152                    .hh has promoted him from the ranks, .hhh until
153                    today he's one of the highest ranking officers
154                    in the Chicago police department. .hhh That
155                    sends a message to every cop in the department
156                    that the way to get ahead in Chicago, .hh is to
157                    be racist, violent, an' even to use torture. .h=
158  Audience:        =x[x–XXXXXXXXXXXXXX[XXXXXXXX]XXXXXX . . .
159  Audience:          [WOOO[OOOOOO!        [              ]
160  Audience:              [WOOOoo!         [Woo[hoo!     ]
161  Audience:                               [WOOO! ]
```

Examining how the speaker constructs his argument in the context of the interjections from the host, in lines 142 ('Has been doing wha:t') and 147 ('How do you know that'), we see how different rhetorical devices can be used in the same opinion presentation to make successive attempts to present a recognizably complete argument.

The host's two interjections are of different types. The first, in line 142, appears to be designed to clarify or disambiguate the speaker's immediately prior description, 'Has been doing this since nineteen seventy two:'. The interactional significance of the host's 'Has been doing wha:t' is that it provides the speaker with the opportunity to produce a list of the alleged unlawful practices used by the police department on 'black prisoners=a:ll black prisoners'. This formulation in turn leads into what may well be a first attempt to round off the turn with a recapitulation. That is, 'it's a racist-' (lines 145–6) can be understood as linking back to the position statement with which he began: 'the police department as itsel:f, is a racist institution'.

At this point, then, the speaker seems close to completing a rhetorical argument in the recursive format, which has not been obstructed but actually assisted by the host's interjection. However, the next interjection serves to 'interrupt' his apparent attempt at a summation, and the speaker cuts off before finishing. We do not know whether the host herself recognizes that the speaker is about to move to a summative assessment, and thus interrupts before the audience can applaud. But the talk produced in overlap by the speaker indicates that this may well be what he was intending at that point, which makes the host's intervention timely from her perspective, since otherwise her question is likely to have been competing with audience applause.

It is noticeable that the interruption in line 147 takes the form of a challenge: 'How do you kn<u>ow</u> that.' This turn does not merely seek to clarify a term or reference, but requires the caller to go on to provide further information in support of his stance. Whether this is done supportively, aiming to strengthen the speaker's stance by requiring further justifications, or critically, is unclear. However, the point is that the speaker now has to 'redesign' the completion of his argument.

This turns out to provide further evidence that lay speakers in this setting can rely on the same kinds of rhetorical strategies for managing audience applause as professional orators. After providing further justificatory components, the speaker moves again to a completion, this time culminating in an extremely well-crafted three-part list:

That sends a message tuh <u>every</u> cop in thuh
de<u>part</u>ment that the w<u>ay</u> tuh get ahead in Chi<u>ca</u>go,
.hh is to be <u>ra</u>cist,
(.) <u>vi</u>olent,
(.) an' even to use <u>tor</u>ture.

As in the data discussed by Atkinson (1984a), this list succeeds in generating a highly coordinated response from the audience, not only by virtue of the conventionalized nature of lists of three (see Chapter 8), but also through the speaker's vocal comportment: the first two items in the list are produced with slightly rising intonation, and a tiny gap is left after each part; the final part is produced with a falling intonation, thereby underlining the fact that the list is indeed now completed.

In these ways lay speakers, though they are not coached in public speaking in the same way as professional politicians, can be seen to use similar rhetorical devices to manage the applause of audiences to their points. Thus, while certain aspects of rhetoric may be written into the speeches that politicians give, there is some evidence that persons can 'intuitively' use such devices in order to signal to an audience that they are coming to the completion of an extended, argument-making turn. It is clear that speakers in settings such as the *Oprah Winfrey Show* are often very well-prepared; the speaker in the excerpt above actually brought the Amnesty International report he refers to with him and brandishes it during his speech. But it is equally clear that they are not reading from a script or from idiot boards as many politicians are known to do. Similarly, although there may possibly be elements of their utterances that they have memorized, the above analysis of Man 3's contribution indicates that even when one attempt to rhetorically round off an opinion presentation does not work, the speaker is able to produce a second, and in this case even better-designed rhetorical completion.

Audience participation debate shows provide a public arena in which private citizens can express their opinions on issues in the public domain. A central part of the institutionalized format of such shows involves members of the public being invited by the host to 'have their say' on particular matters of concern. In this sense they are similar to open-line talk radio broadcasts (discussed in Chapter 5). But there are two additional features of the kind of public arena represented by shows such as the one analysed in this chapter. First, they involve a studio audience who themselves become embroiled, often raucously, in the unfolding debate by applauding, jeering and so on (and we see more of this feature in the following chapter). Second, they tend to involve not only lay speakers but 'experts' or the representatives of social institutions, whose talk, as we have seen, can be framed in quite a different way and whose participation therefore is often more closely circumscribed by the mediating actions of the host. These features are among the key elements that shape the nature of the shows' public discourse; elements that become clearer once we focus on the **sequential organization** of that discourse.

Further reading

Carbaugh, D. (1988) *Talking American: Cultural Discourses on 'Donahue'*. Norwood NJ: Ablex.

Haarman, T. (ed.) (2000) *Talk About Shows*. Bologna: CLUEB.

Livingstone, S. and Lunt, P. (1994) *Talk on Television*. London: Routledge.

Thornborrow, J. (2002) *Power Talk*. London: Pearson.

Tolson, A. (ed.) (2001) *Television Talk Shows: Discourse, Performance, Spectacle*. Mahwah, NJ: Lawrence Erlbaum Associates.

Note

1 The show's host, Phil Donahue, is widely credited with inventing the format of the televised audience participation debate during the 1960s.

THE SPECTACLE OF CONFRONTATION

The kind of show discussed in the previous chapter consists of an audience-participation debate on pertinent social issues, pioneered in the US by the long-running *Donahue*, then developed by *Oprah Winfrey* and, in the UK, shows such as *Kilroy*.[1] In the mid-1990s a new variant of this genre emerged, led by the US shows *Ricki Lake* and *Jerry Springer*, and developed for the UK by *Vanessa* and *Trisha*. The topics or themes of talk tend to centre not around questions of wider public concern but 'everyday life dilemmas'. The key speakers are still ordinary members of the public, but this time they appear on the show usually with a bone to pick with each other. The show's discourse routinely revolves around confrontations between ex-lovers, family members, friends who have fallen out, neighbours who are in dispute, and so on. In this sense, such shows create what could be called 'confrontation as a spectacle', in which guests are encouraged to air publicly disputes which, ordinarily, would be confined to the private sphere of everyday life.

Of these, the *Ricki Lake* show was really the first. Like its precursor *Oprah Winfrey* and its competitor *Jerry Springer*, *Ricki Lake* developed its basic format over time. This partly had to do with the sheer number of shows recorded in a typical season, and partly resulted from competition from other shows which sought to 'up the ante' by being more controversial. The earlier, and more innovative shows focused almost entirely on broadcasting revelations and resulting confrontations among friends and family members. Later, in response to *Jerry Springer*'s more extreme controversialism (see Myers, 2001; Lunt and Stenner, 2005), the show often adopted a lighter presentational style. Yet although *Jerry Springer* subsequently gained a wider notoriety, even leading, in the UK, to the emergence of attempts to copy its format (such as *Trisha* or *Vanessa*), it is worth remembering that the format itself, in which ordinary folks confront each other over private life issues and revelations, was pioneered by *Ricki Lake*. At the time of its emergence, this show presented a wholly novel form of televisual discourse, in which audience members, both at home and in the studio, could find themselves 'looking in on' an argument played out between the participants on stage.

The interfacing of the private and the public has long been noted as a key feature of audience participation talk shows in general (Carbaugh, 1988; Livingstone and Lunt, 1994). Indeed, many writers have begun from the idea that audience participation shows can be seen as a means of providing private citizens access to the public sphere represented in large part, in modern society, by broadcasting. For instance, Crittenden (1971), Avery and Ellis (1979) and Verwey (1990) all explicitly addressed the 'democratic functions' of talk radio, examining the degree to which talk radio discussions come to permeate the wider population of the overhearing audience, or evaluating the extent to which different talk radio hosts facilitate open debate between themselves and members of the public (see, however, Wood, 2001).

In this chapter I focus on a different aspect of this private-public interface. I examine the nature of confrontational talk on the *Ricki Lake* show and its variants as a form of public argumentation. Public argumentation is not a new phenomenon in itself: there is a long tradition in democratic societies of debating forums in which large-scale audiences are co-present with the debators. But televised versions of argumentative debate are novel in the sense that, by being broadcast, the debate becomes accessible by a further audience: one that is absent from the debate's physical arena, and is both geographically and temporally 'distributed'. Broadcast forms of public argumentation involve a set of participants (the audience at home) whose very involvement is enabled by virtue of the affordances of the televisual medium. One of the questions that thereby arises is: what forms of argumentative discourse occupy this distinctive public arena?

For the most part, throughout its history as well as in the present, non-fiction television has sought to produce forms of talk that address the 'overhearing' audience more or less directly (Scannell and Cardiff, 1991). This is so even when the talk that is broadcast is ostensibly a conversation between two people face to face in a radio or television studio, such as a news interview (see Chapter 7). What kinds of address formats come into play in contexts such as the confrontational TV talk show, when, as we will see, a routine feature is that guests turn to address each other directly in the course of arguing about matters in their private lives? Specifically, how is confrontational or argumentative talk produced in a setting where there are (a) multiple (i.e. more than two) participants, (b) an array of possible forms of address and 'targetting' for contributions to a confrontation, and, significantly, (c) various kinds of audiences, from the participants in the confrontation, through the host and the studio audience, to the audience at home?

We might imagine that the mere fact that these confrontations are played out in front of a studio audience and broadcast to be heard and observed by a wider audience suffices to make them 'spectacular': that is, a spectacle which is played out in front of, and, like other forms of broadcast talk, specifically for the benefit of, an overhearing audience. But close observation reveals that there are specific characteristics of the structures of talk and of participation in this show that work to facilitate the kind of confrontational talk that occurs, and that play an important role in an audience's ability to hear it *as* spectacular. What is of interest here is not individual audience members' *reactions* to the show as a 'spectacle of confrontation' (on the lines, for instance, of Livingstone and Lunt's (1994) work on TV talk shows), but the indigenous organizational structures through which the show allows itself to be heard and experienced as such. The methods of conversation analysis allow us to look at a number of aspects of this, including the overall structure of the show and the range of different participation dynamics within which the talk is produced.

Framing confrontation talk

The data for this chapter consist of a small, randomly selected set of instalments with predictably provocative titles such as, 'If You Have Something To Say . . . Say It To My Face!' and 'I'm Not Fat . . . I'm All That!'. These shows take similar forms, in which aggrieved guests get a chance to give their account of how they have been the victim of some complainable behaviour – such as being the butt of malicious gossip, or having a mother who so objects to their physical appearance that she refuses to be seen in public with them – before the accused is brought from backstage to join their accuser on a seat centre-stage, and give their side of the story. The host remains standing throughout, positioned within the audience who sit in rows facing the stage. Shortly before the end, an 'expert' (usually some type of pop-psychologist or relationship guru) is brought on and seated in a large armchair to give advice to each pair about what they should do to resolve their problems.

The confrontational talk show has much in common with other audience participation broadcasts as discussed in previous chapters. For instance, it involves a studio audience in live co-presence with the host and the main speakers; the host, as we will see, tends to play a role that fluctuates between mediation and advocacy; and there is some participation by an 'expert'. But the structure of the show also has much in common with a game show. Guest participants are introduced as if contestants, within a discursive structure in which the audience are openly invited to take sides in the dispute-game. This feature is a key factor in the recognizably public character of the show's confrontations.

The shows are divided into segments, and each segment begins with the first guest being introduced by the host. However, first guests are introduced not simply as guests, but as particular *kinds* of occupants of the show's discursive arena. Specifically, they are framed from the outset as the possessors of 'complainable matters'. The standard format is for the host to describe the matter the guest is to complain about, before inviting the guest's own comments. For instance:

(1) **Ricki Lake**
1 Host: This is Erin.
2   (.)

3		.hh Erin now you're having problems
4		with your boyfrien:d Doug's best friend Michelle.
5		(.)
6		What's goin' on.

Here, the host categorizes the guest explicitly and solely as someone who is 'having problems' – in this case with her boyfriend's 'best friend' – before inviting the guest to comment on the matter. This way of categorizing not only invites but entitles the guest to speak (Hester and Fitzgerald, 1999). That is, through being situated as the possessor of a complainable matter – and, for present discursive purposes, nothing more than the possessor of such a matter – the guest's presence at this point in the show is justified.

More than that, however, the introduction projects a sequential space of conditional relevance (see Schegloff, 1991): what is said next is to be heard as a complaint, one that involves another (named but as yet invisible) participant. Note, also, that in an important sense it is the audience (the studio audience and the audience at home) who are being situated as the principal recipient of this next move, the complaint. Though the host does not say 'Tell the audience what's goin' on', the fact that the guest is named in an announcement at the turn's outset ('This is Erin') implicates the audience as principal recipient of the guest's upcoming turn.

Following this introduction, the first guest is framed in close up as they tell the story behind their complaint, prompted by the host. The talk at this point is thus produced in an interview-like framework. However, there are some important differences with the forms of broadcast interview talk previously studied in news interviews (see Chapter 7). One is that the 'interviewer' (that is, the talk show host), does not refrain from *reacting* to the tellings of the interviewee. In fact, she not only produces reactions, but those reactions exhibit a clear *stance* on her part. Consider the following example, in which the host produces an emphatic reaction to the guest's remark about how long the complainable behaviour of her co-guest has been going on:

(2) Ricki Lake

1	Guest :	It's been goin' on fer a year now
2		and I j [us' want-
3→	Host:	[A YEA:R?
4	Guest :	Just a- [just abou:t.
5	Audience:	[° wwuuuhuhuho°
6	Host:	And you've never confronted her on
7		this issue.

One thing to notice here is that the guest appears to accord no especially remarkable status to her revelation that, 'It's been goin' on fer a year now'. That is, she refrains from doing anything that would serve to draw attention to the length of time itself: for example, by emphasizing that length of time through placing stress on the word 'year', or pausing for some kind of reaction following the announcement that the behaviour has been going on 'fer a year'. Rather, without any noticeable pause, she goes on to the next part of the utterance, 'and I jus' want-' before withdrawing from the turn in overlap with the host.

Instead, it is the host herself who draws attention to what could be described as a *particularly* complainable matter. By this I mean that if one can describe some form of bad behaviour as having been going on for 'a year', then it can be said both that the behaviour is particularly bad, and that the victim of it is being particularly victimized. This illustrates how the host monitors the guest's talk for matters which can be picked up in pursuit of controversy or confrontation. But more significantly, in picking up on those matters, she makes them visible *for the audience*, and hence, available as objects for audience (which is to say, public) reaction.

This represents a major difference with work on broadcast news interviews. As we see in Chapter 7, news interviewers tend to refrain from verbally reacting to an interviewee's talk in the course of the interviewee's answers to interviewer questions. The reason for this is that by doing so, the interviewer avoids acting as the primary recipient of the interviewee's talk (even though he or she is both the questioner and, usually, physically co-present with the answerer). That role is thereby preserved for the 'overhearing' audience.

In the present case, by contrast, the host acts precisely to *frame* the audience's role as recipient, providing the studio audience with the opportunity for reactions that are appropriate both in terms of their placement (in this case, in overlap with continuing talk which is moving on from the controversial point) and in terms of their content. Notice, then, that her utterance, 'A YEA:R?', which overlaps the guest's talk, is closely followed by an audible gasp from the audience ('°wwuuuhuhuho°'). Both these actions are designed to do a form of 'negative affiliation' with the speaker: affiliation through an exhibition of dismay at the reported behaviour. This creates a sense in which the host and the audience are heard to be collaboratively aligned against the reported activities of the complained-about guest.

I noted earlier that hosts in these shows often stand, holding their microphone, within the part of the studio occupied by the studio audience. And it is often the case that their reactions to the talk of speakers on the platform are closely coordinated, both temporally and in terms of content (that is, the action they are designed to do), with those of the audience. The host at these points is not only situated within the audience physically or spatially, but also stands *with* the audience in a discursive sense in relation to the confrontations being played out on stage. In later extracts I look at other ways in which the reactions of host and audience to the talk of the platform guests can be closely coordinated in terms of the host's role in actively promoting a confrontational discourse among the participants.

Returning to the overall structure: guest complaints are always produced first in each segment of the show, and are always presented precisely *as* complainables. In the above examples, the complaint is that someone has been talking behind the complainant's back. In other shows, as noted, it may be that the complainant's mother disapproves of their being overweight and refuses to be seen in public with them; or some other, similar kind of matter. Regardless, the complainant always speaks first.

Once the complainant has given their account, the respondent is introduced, typically in the following kind of way:

(3) Ricki Lake
```
1   Host:       ((turns towards studio audience)) Are we ready
2               to meet Michelle gang?
3   Audience:   Ye:[::a::hhh   A:::::hh
4   Audience:      [xx–XXXXXXXXXXXXXXXXXXXXXXX=
5   Host:          [Michelle, come on out
6   Audience:   =[XXXXxxxxxxxxxxxxxxxxxxxxxxx
7   Audience:      [↓ w:ooh BOOOOOOOOOOOO ↑ wooh
```

In this extract the audience both applauds and jeers as the second guest emerges through a door and walks down a short staircase to a seat next to the first guest. Clearly, through the first speaker's telling about the complainable behaviour of these second guests, the latter are already constructed in a negative light. But the very way in which they are announced reinforces this construction, and does so in a way that points up the specifically public nature of the event.

In three important senses, these second guests are presented as someone who has been/is being *revealed*. First, there is the sense that their disagreeable actions, previously confined to the private sphere of the guests' everyday lives, are now being brought to public attention. Second, there is the sense that they are now being physically revealed in order to be called to account; hence the host typically uses formulations such as '[Guest], come on out' or 'Let's bring out [guest] now'. Third, and most significantly, that bringing to account is something that the audience is hearably implicated in. Notice in extract (3) how the host turns slightly towards the audience as she asks them: 'Are we ready to talk to Michelle gang?'.

Looking at the first few moments of the show thus begins to illustrate the important role played by the sequencing of actions in constructing an occasion for the bringing to public account of complainable actions by 'ordinary' people. It is not just that these people have engaged in actions that may readily be condemned, and now they are indeed to be (very publicly) condemned. The organization of the talk – particularly, the way in which the host both introduces, and manages her responses to the talk of, the guests – represents a key factor in the way in which confrontation is framed from the outset as a recognizably *public* spectacle: that is, an event in which the public finds available to it opportunities for involvement both in the revelation and the condemnation of complainable actions. In the next section I turn to look in more detail at how those opportunities for responsive involvement may be actively fashioned by the principal participants.

Participation frameworks and the production of confrontation

The previous section offered a very general account of the way in which confrontation on this show is 'framed', in the sense that participants – both studio guests and audience – are discursively and spatially situated in particular agonistic roles during the opening phases of each segment. But what are the ways in which confrontations are played out within that basic interactional framework? The production of confrontation as a public spectacle is intimately bound up with the organization of talk-in-interaction on a much finer scale.

A key factor involved in this is the range of different participation frameworks that are involved in the talk as each confrontation progresses on from its opening segment. The notion of participation frameworks was introduced by Erving Goffman (1974, 1981) to refer to the way in which any utterance in conversation furnishes a certain range of possibilities for recipients to situate themselves in relation to the speaker. For instance, the way in which an utterance is phrased may enable a hearer to situate themselves as its direct target, an indirect addressee, an overhearer, and so on. However, I will use the term 'participation framework' to refer not just to the ways in which people in different speaker categories address one another – that is, the lexical content of addressing turns – but also to the *sequential* formats in which their talk is produced.

Shows such as *Jerry Springer*, *Trisha* or the *Ricki Lake* show can be seen as forms of multiparty confrontation. It is not just two disputants who are involved in an argument but a whole array of categories of participant. In this sense, there are similarities between these shows and other forms of disputatious interaction involving multiple participants in an institutional setting: principally, professional dispute mediation hearings analysed by Garcia (1991) and panel-based news interview/discussion shows examined by Greatbatch (1992). In all these settings, persons with competing views on an issue are invited by a host or mediator to express and argue over their views, usually in the presence of an audience (whether consisting of other participants, a studio audience, and/or an absent audience of listeners or viewers).

A common theme of Garcia's and Greatbatch's work on these settings is that the turn-taking format itself plays a key role in whether confrontations occur or not, or at least, in the degree of confrontation that is allowed. Briefly, the presence of a central 'mediator' often means that disputants' turns are required structurally (and also normatively) to be addressed to the mediator. This is because disputants can only legitimately speak in response to the mediator's questions. Therefore, there is a systematic bias against the possibility of direct address between the disputants (though of course it may still occur) and this results in an attenuated form of argument.

On the confrontational TV talk show, by contrast, disputants routinely address one another – in fact they may be specifically invited to do so at certain points within their segments – and the host plays a key role not just as questioner, mediator and the target of appeals from one or other of the disputants, but also as an advocate and a key facilitator of alignment and counter-alignment within the dispute. Thus, as we will see, the structures of address within the show's participation frameworks represent an important means by which confrontation may be *accentuated*, rather than attenuated.

At first sight, four principal categories of participant seem to be involved in these shows: host, studio audience, guests, and viewing audience. But in fact there are at least five, since the guests, as noted, play quite different roles, and in a highly structured way. One is always the 'complainant' or 'aggrieved party', while the other is the 'offending party'. There may also be other guests on the platform, usually associated with one or other side in the dispute, and the presence of these participants adds further dimensions to the structures of participation in the show.

Table 4.1 lists the eight basic participation frameworks which routinely come into play:

Table 4.1 Patterns of address in the TV talk show

Basic patterns of address on the TV talk show
1. Host addresses viewing audience (talks to camera).
2. Host addresses studio audience.
3. Studio audience member addresses host.
4. Host addresses platform guest.
5. Platform guest addresses host.
6. Platform guest addresses studio audience.
7. Studio audience member addresses platform guest.
8. Platform guest addresses other platform guest.

Within each of these frames, there may be a great deal more going on than these basic descriptions suggest. For example, within any one of them, the viewing audience may be addressed overtly or covertly; and although each of them has been characterized here as dyadic, there may actually be a wide range of addressees (or 'targets', to use the term adopted by Levinson (1988)) being addressed in a wide variety of ways.

For present purposes I will focus on just two of the frameworks mentioned above: those numbered 4 (host addresses platform guests) and 8 (platform guests address each other). In these two dynamics of talk on the show we find some of the principal ways in which this form of talk is produced, or performed, not only as hearably confrontational, but as confrontational in a hearably public sense.

Between private and public

One of the key themes in previous research on broadcast talk has been the question of how that talk is designed so that its audience(s) may encounter it as produced primarily for them. That is, while a great deal of talk broadcast on radio and television is on one level an interaction between two or more co-present speakers (such as an interviewer and an interviewee), how is it that those speakers produce their talk so that the audience can unproblematically 'overhear' it? As I mentioned earlier, Heritage (1985) suggested that, in the case of news interviews, the fact that interviewers routinely refrain from producing response tokens such as 'mm hm', 'oh' or 'right' during the talk of interviewees represents an important way in which they avoid acting as the primary recipient of the interviewee's answers to their questions, leaving that role open for the listening audience. From a slightly different angle, Montgomery (1986, 1991), looking at the talk of radio DJs, explored a number of ways in which this overtly monologic talk is designed so as to address the audience in subtly differentiated ways both as listeners and as participants.

A common feature of all these studies is that broadcast talk simultaneously exhibits features characteristic of 'private' talk (casual conversation) and expressly 'public' talk (talk directed at a listening audience). It is partly due to its combination of these features that broadcast talk achieves its qualities of 'ordinariness', sociability and accessibility (Scannell, 1996). However, another way of viewing it is that the talk can often be seen as exhibiting *ambivalence* between whether it is designed primarily for the audience or primarily for the co-present participants.

On the *Ricki Lake* show, this ambivalence can play an important part in the spectacular character of the confrontations between guests. I will illustrate that by looking at two quite differently structured examples from the show.

(4) **Ricki Lake [Gisela is Guest 1, Tanisha is Guest 2]**
1   Tanisha: Your first daughter has three, thr:ee fathers,
2   your second one got [two.
3   Gisela: [↑<u>WHAT</u>?
4   Tanisha: An' th<u>e</u>:n- the one-=
5   Gisela: =You don't even know anything a<u>bou</u>t me=
6   Tanisha: =[(   )
7   Gisela: =[<u>I'M NOT</u> preg[nant. I'm not pregnant.
8   Host: =[W<u>ai</u>t.   [Wait.
9   (?):   [[(   )
10 Host: [[Tanisha how does that work, a daughter
11   has three fa:thers?
12 Audience: Ha ha ha . . .

In extract (4) we find a good example of participation framework 8 – guests addressing each other. As a result of the direct address between Gisela and Tanisha – most clearly indexed in the transcript through the repeated use of 'you', but in the video also shown by the bodily orientations of the two disputants who turn to face each other – the talk in the first few lines exhibits the same features as arguments in non-public, non-mediated settings. Remember that there are a number of participant categories involved in the show as an occasion for talk – yet in this particular segment of talk, it is unclear, or ambivalent, what the recipient status of the other participants is. Is this talk designed for the speaking participants alone, for the audience, or somehow for both? In an important sense, it seems, by virtue of the directly addressed exchange of argumentative turns, the audience (both in the studio and at home) is able to 'look in on' a confrontation played out as a spectacle in front of them.

Of course, as in the forms of third-party mediated disputes analysed by Garcia (1991) and Greatbatch (1992), this type of two-party, directly-addressed talk only occurs on certain occasions – even though it is a much more routine, even invited, feature of these talk shows than of other examples such as panel-based interviews. As in those other settings, the host frequently intervenes in the dispute; yet there are notable differences in the kinds of interventions made and in their interactional functions.

The intervention seen in extract (4) illustrates something of this. The host's utterance, 'Tanisha how does that work, a daughter has three fathers?' has very similar features to the case in extract (2). That is, first of all, it picks up on a controversial point which appears in danger of falling below the conversational horizon of relevance. Note that while Gisela has initially reacted with some incredulity to Tanisha's claim that Gisela's daughter has 'three fathers and your second one got two' ('WHAT?'), the argument almost immediately proceeds to a next point apparently having to do with whether Gisela is currently pregnant. (It is not possible to hear what Tanisha says on this issue as her point is loudly overlapped both by Gisela denying that she is pregnant and by the host shouting 'W<u>ai</u>t. Wait.' – hence the empty brackets in line 6.)

The key thing about the host's intervention is not just that it picks up on the apparent absurdity of Tanisha's claim (that is, from a 'common sense' perspective, how could a child have three fathers?), but that it picks up on it in such a way that the joke can be a joke *for the audience*. In order for the audience to take sides by reacting to this claim along with Gisela, a space needs to be provided within the rapid flow of the argument on stage to enable it to do so. This intervention succeeds in providing that space. Thus, again, we find the host standing figuratively 'with' the audience, in actively working to pick up on points of contention in order to further the audience's opportunities to take sides in the dispute being played out on stage.

These remarks give a sense of what I mean when I suggest that these arguments take place in – or constitute – a discursive space that is somehow 'between' the private and the public. Extract (5) offers a slightly different angle on this.

(5) **Ricki Lake [Laurie is Guest 1, Reynold is Guest 2]**

1	Host:	<u>A</u>re you paying child support for this child?
2	Reynold:	I haven't given her money- I've not given her
3		money, in, y'know about th:ree weeks=.h=But I
4		have [re<u>cei</u>pts
5	Laurie:	[TH:REE W:EEKS?

6	Reynold:	I have re<u>cei</u>pts (.) fer- for all the money
7		I <u>have</u> <u>gi</u>ven her. And I've just uh
8		the job I'm working right no:w um I've
9		spoken with them and I told her this about
10		a week ago. before I even knew about this show,
11		that I've spoken with them they've taken
12		forty dollars a week outta each p:ay ch:eck,
13		a:nd they're gonna put it in a check in h:er
14		name sent straight to h:er house.
15	Host:	Alright.
16	Laurie:	OK. We'll see it [when it happens.
17	Host:	[What abo:ut when the
18		child got sick?
19		(.)
20	Laurie:	↑<u>O</u>:h. OH OK, I can tell you [this part.
21	Reynold:	[↓ <u>O</u>:H pss.
22	Laurie:	OK sh<u>e</u> was sick for like three weeks and
23		I took her, <u>I</u> have the d<u>oc</u>tor bills,
24		they were over three hundred dollars.
25		He told me, I ain't givin you no money
26		you shoulda taken her to the health department
27		cos it's fr<u>ee</u>.
28		(0.5)
29	Audience:	O:o[oh
30	Reynold:	[↑ <u>Is</u>n't it? (.) Isn't it fr<u>ee</u>?
31	Audience:	[O:ooh
32	Host:	[REYNOLD. REYNOLD.
33	Reynold:	↑ NO=no=no=no=[no=no:.
34	Host:	[<u>Rey</u>nold, th<u>i</u>s is <u>your</u>
35		<u>chi</u>ld we're talking about. Don't you
36		want the <u>best</u> for y<u>o</u>:ur ch[ild?
37	Reynold:	[Y<u>es</u>. Y<u>es</u>.
38		I d<u>o</u>.
39	Host:	Well, the b<u>est</u> is not fr<u>ee</u>:.

One way in which this extract differs from (4) is that the guests do not address each other. Rather, we find two different participation frameworks in play at the same time. While one of the disputants, Reynold, addresses all his talk at the host and the audience, his girlfriend shifts between directing her talk at the host/audience and directly addressing him. For instance, at the point where she says 'TH:REE W:EEKS?' she turns in her chair to face him.

The extract clearly shows the way in which the host acts not only as mediator, but as facilitator of the disputes being played out on stage. The host works to elicit a story about the defendant (Reynold) from the complainant: 'What about when the child got sick?' Of course, on one level, this turn illustrates a certain level of pre-preparedness about the disputes that occur: that is, it is not just that the disputants are invited to play out their disputes in front of the host and audience, but the host herself evidently already knows a good deal about the key points of contention. This makes it even more clear that the host spends at least some of her time monitoring the talk for those points which can be picked up in order to provide the audience with an opportunity to react.

Some other things are of note about this utterance, 'What about when the child got sick?' First, it seems unclear precisely who the target is: it could be addressed to Reynold, to Laurie, or to both of them. Yet the overall structure of the show's discursive arena, as outlined earlier, enables Laurie to hear it as addressed to her, and to respond to it in the particular way that she does. In this segment, Laurie is the 'first guest' – the complainant – while Reynold's behaviour is the subject of her complaint. The host's turn introduces a fresh complainable matter into the dispute. Whereas both guests potentially know about this issue and so Reynold, conceivably, could go straight into a defence of his behaviour, the host's utterance does not provide enough information for the *audience* to be able to judge that behaviour. This utterance thus needs to be oriented to as an invitation to 'tell the story' rather than to respond to what is already implicitly known by those involved.

Of course, the host may also be using her gaze to select which speaker she expects to respond. This however is a feature that we do not have access to even on the basis of the video-recorded data, since the camera is on the host at the point where she asks about the child. This means that it is impossible to judge which of the participants she may in fact be looking at, since the shot is from a vantage point slightly to one side of where the guests are sitting on the platform. But it is noticeable nevertheless that Laurie responds by *nominating* herself as the speaker able to tell this story ('↑O:h. OH OK, I can tell you this part'), rather than as the speaker who is specifically being *selected* to tell it. There is thus evidence that Laurie hears this not only as an invitation to tell the story, but as an invitation 'properly' aimed at her, even though we cannot say whether gaze direction was also used by the host. This, along with the way the invitation is responded to by Reynold expressing his irritation at 'yet another' issue being brought up ('↓O:H pss'), illustrates how participants themselves orient to and thus preserve the overall structures of participation outlined above.

A second point is that once again we find the host actively involving herself in the audience's reaction against the defendant's villainy. Yet here, in contrast with earlier examples, the audience's reaction (a collective, low-pitched 'Ooooh') *precedes* that of the host. In response to the audience, Reynold himself, maintaining his earlier practice of addressing himself to the audience, speaks ('Isn't it? Isn't it free?'). Note that this utterance could just as well have been addressed directly to Laurie; but the reaction of the audience means that a three-way argument structure comes into play, in which (a) Laurie addresses the audience, (b) the audience then address themselves to Reynold, and (c) Reynold in turn addresses his response to them. This is reinforced on the videotape where it is possible to see that Reynold (somewhat exaggeratedly) orients himself bodily to the audience (that is, frontally) and not to Laurie who is sitting next to him.

It is within this three-way structure that the host now involves herself, as before, in line with the audience. Moreover, her next utterance, 'REYNOLD. REYNOLD', has a similar character to the audience's 'Ooooh' in that both utterance types point to the sense of Reynold's (reported) actions as being 'beyond the pale'. In this way, once more, we observe the spectacular nature of confrontation being produced in the details of a momentary collective alignment of complainant, host and studio audience against the actions of the defendant. While there may be a gross sense in which this pattern of alignment is 'built into' the show as a discursive arena, it is actually produced as relevant for the course of interaction in the local context of turn exchange in the real time unfolding of talk.

The case studies in this and the previous chapter have examined a range of aspects of media talk in the context of studio-based broadcasts which involve hosts, guests who either debate or (in the present chapter) dispute over issues, and studio audiences who in various ways become involved in taking sides in such exchanges. We have seen how the methods of conversation analysis allow us to unfold the nature of interaction, patterns of participation and structures of turn-taking that are at the core of what is distinctive about such broadcast talk. In the following two chapters, I move on to look at similar issues in the different broadcast context of radio phone-in shows.

Further reading

Garcia, A. (1991) Dispute resolution without disputing: How the interactional organisation of mediation hearings minimizes argument. *American Sociological Review*, 56: 818–35.

Greatbatch, D. (1992) On the management of disagreement between news interviewees. In P. Drew and J. Heritage (eds), *Talk At Work*. Cambridge: Cambridge University Press.

Lunt, P. and Stenner, P. (2005) The *Jerry Springer* show as an emotional public sphere. *Media Culture and Society*, 27: 59–81.

Myers, G. (2001) 'I'm out of it: you guys argue': Making an issue of it on the *Jerry Springer Show*. In A. Tolson (ed.), *Television Talk Shows*. Mahwah, NJ: Lawrence Erlbaum Associates.

Note

1 At the time of writing, the *Kilroy* show has been withdrawn from production by the BBC after running for more than ten years following publication of a controversial newspaper article written by its host, Robert Kilroy-Silk, which was widely seen as promulgating racist stereotypes (though this was strenuously denied by Kilroy-Silk himself).

CASE STUDIES PART II: RADIO TALK

5 LANGUAGE, INTERACTION AND POWER ON TALK RADIO

The playwright Bertolt Brecht once wrote that 'the radio would be the finest possible communication apparatus in public life ... if it knew how to receive as well as to transmit, how to let the listener speak as well as hear, how to bring him into a relationship instead of isolating him' (Brecht, 1964 [1932]: 52). Radio phone-ins, or, as I prefer, talk radio shows represent an attempt to accomplish this kind of democratic involvement in broadcasting. Although often castigated for its triviality, and for the intentionally controversial behaviour of some hosts, talk radio – along with its close relation, the television talk show – offers one of the few media environments in which ordinary members of the public are given the opportunity to speak on issues and events in their own voices, as opposed to having their viewpoints represented either in the neutralistic register of broadcast news, or the 'probing' register of current affairs documentary.

There are numerous different types of talk radio show ranging from the 'open line' phone-in where callers are invited to select topics of their own choice; to the single-issue phone-in where callers contribute to a debate on a pre-selected topic, often with a politician or expert in the studio along with the show's host (see Thornborrow, 2001); to various advice-giving shows focusing on relationship issues or other matters involving specialized information. In the next chapter I examine aspects of the advice-giving type of talk radio show; while in the present chapter, my focus is on the open-line phone-in.

Using data drawn from one particular London-based talk radio show in which the host had a reputation for being intentionally argumentative, controversial and frequently rude to his callers, I address two types of issue. First, how do callers seek to present their opinions on the matters about which they are phoning in? In particular, given the well-known argumentativeness of the show's host, are there ways that callers have of strengthening, legitimating or authenticating their viewpoints in anticipation of his potential attacks? The second issue leads on from this: namely what are the ways that the host has of developing an argument with callers' opinions? Here we will come to examine a specific structural feature of open-line talk radio discourse which enables the host to take up a more powerful discursive position than the caller, even though the topic under discussion has been introduced at the caller's initiative.

This takes us back to a matter raised at the end of Chapter 2. Recall that I discussed the relationship between conversation analysis and critical discourse analysis, with particular attention to the question of power relations in talk. I argued that while CDA claims that CA is resistant to linking the organization of talk to wider social issues such as power, this is not actually the case. In the second half of this chapter I return to that issue, providing a practical demonstration of how a CA perspective can be used to describe the operation of power relations in discourse.

Witnessing and the authentication of speakership

In open-line talk radio broadcasts, a form of 'civic news talk' gets produced that is very different from the registers of news produced and broadcast by professional news organizations. Here, people bring to bear their personal opinions or standpoints on the news of the day, making explicit links between newsworthy topics and issues connected to or experienced within their own everyday lives. This suggests an inversion of the standard perspective within media studies on the relationship between audiences and the news. Ian Connell (1980) argued that viewers of television news (and by extension, perhaps, the readers of newspapers and listeners to radio news) are

> hailed as witness of, but not participant in, the struggle and argument over issues ... [This involves] a sense of witnessing (that is, of being present at, but not directly involved in) a 'reality' which is ... made to seem 'out there', separate from and independent of those positioned as witnesses. The relation in which the audience is cast by this visual mode is that of *onlooker*.
>
> (Connell, 1980: 140, 154–5; emphasis in original)

Open-line talk radio shows, and many forms of televised audience participation debates, challenge this sense of the witness as onlooker. In such contexts, lay speakers tend to act as witnesses precisely in the sense of being directly involved in the topics they are discussing. Calling in with their personal opinions on issues, or their personal experience of an issue, callers on talk radio tend to speak not as the abstract experts of professionalized news discourse but (to adopt the distinction made by Livingstone and Lunt, 1994) in the lay speaker's register of immediacy, experience and authenticity.

Harvey Sacks (1992) observed that, in everyday conversation, having witnessed a 'tellable' event entitles a speaker to have an experience associated with the event – for instance, an emotional response. The witness not only has particular rights to tell another about the event, but also to tell of how it emotionally affected them. While the recipient of that story may in some circumstances be able to tell it on to someone else, they not only have to tell it as a story told *to* them – that is, from a second-hand perspective – but also do not possess the entitlement to experience which the witness has by virtue of his or her witnessing.

> For example, you might, on seeing an automobile accident and people lying there, feel awful, cry, have the rest of your day ruined . . . [but] if you call up a friend of yours who is unaffiliated with the event you're reporting, i.e., someone who doesn't turn out to be the cousin of, the aunt of, the person who was killed in the accident, but just somebody you call up and tell about an awful experience, then if they become as disturbed as you, or more, something peculiar is going on, and you might even feel wronged – though that might seem to be an odd thing to feel.
>
> (Sacks, 1992, Vol. 2: 243–4)

In this way, first-hand knowledge such as that of the eye-witness is bound up, in talk, with the authenticity of experience, of emotion, and of the speaker as a legitimate teller of particular kinds of stories. Indeed, Sacks also describes the issue in terms of a recipient 'latch[ing] onto the experience of the [teller] and borrow[ing] it for her own emotions' (1992, Vol. 2: 244).

When we look at talk radio calls, we find that callers regularly use actions associated with making claims to personal knowledge, personal experience, direct perceptual access, or categorial membership in respect of an event or topic under discussion. These can be described as 'witnessing' moves, and they are closely involved in justifying a caller's claim to authentic speakership in the public discourse arena of the talk radio show. To give a rough sense of the frequency of callers' use of such techniques, in a randomly selected sample of 20 calls from a corpus of 130, I found at least one example of a 'witnessing' device in 80 per cent of cases.

These devices can be divided into two broad categories. First, those involving first-hand knowledge, which in turn can be broken down into four sub-types: (1) claims of having been physically present at a scene; (2) claims of having had personal experience of a complained-about event; (3) claims of direct perceptual access (having seen or heard an event); and (4) claims of having physical possession of a topic-relevant item. The second broad category involves the mobilization of collective experience or knowledge: principally, here, callers assert membership of a topic-relevant category in their own right (for instance, pensioners).

The range of actions involved can be illustrated by the following selection of examples. For illustrative convenience, the extracts are taken out of the sequential contexts in which they were produced, though many will reappear subsequently in their sequential context, when I look more closely at the interactional management of witnessing devices.

Category I: First-hand knowledge/experience

In extract (1) the caller emphasizes his physical presence at a demonstration about which the media had produced conflicting accounts (witnessing moves are typed in boldface):

(1) G:26.11.88:3

Caller: **I was actually at the student demonstration** yesterday, and I just wanted to make it clear to your listeners why we were doing what we were doing.

In (2), the caller foregrounds the fact that the problem about which she is calling is one which she personally (along with her family and possibly her whole neighbourhood) is experiencing:

(2) H:2.2.89:4

Caller: **We've got a real problem here** with dogs fouling **our footway**.

In extract (3), the caller's witnessing device involves asserting her personal possession of complained-about materials (charity appeals letters):

(3) H:21.11.88:6

Caller: **I have got three appeals letters here** this week, all asking for donations

while in extracts (4), (5) and (6) callers utilize a technique of asserting their direct perceptual access to an event under discussion:

(4) G:3.2.89:6

Caller: Yes **I've heard it myself.**

(5) G:3.2.89:1

Caller: [The environmental health officer) wants to make sure that those people are not handling the food, raw meat etcetera, which **I have seen** in the borough of Southwark . . .

(6) H:2.2.89:4

Caller: One day **I actually saw** a lady owner allow her dog to do its business right in the middle of my gateway.

Category II: Categorial membership/collective witnessing

Extracts (7) to (11) show callers using one form or another of collective construction in order either to link their personal experience in with other members of a particular category such as pensioners (extracts 7 and 8) or mothers (extract 9); or to suggest that their point is applicable to a wider constituency than merely their own personal experience (extracts 10 and 11):

(7) G:26.11.88:2
Caller: **I'm a pensioner myself** of seventy two

(8) H:21.11.88:9
Caller: A lotta people don't like receiving charity, and now if every working person, and even **every pensioner of which I am one**, was deducted ten pee per week, throughout, you know for ever an' ever, that would do away with a lot of charities . . .

(9) H:2.2.89:4
Caller: **I'm a mother of two small boys** and we've now got to the situation . . .

(10) G:26.11.88:2
Caller: **We had ten pound a week taken from us** in April . . . **We're having a very hard struggle** at the moment.

(11) G:26.11.88:5
Caller: I'm no better off than I was before April. And **I'm not the only one, there's many like me.** I don't grumble, but **when I see the poor old men that fought in the last war** and can't afford to go in and have a pint of beer. **I gave my husband to the last war**, he got killed in the last war, and it makes me bitter . . .

We get a sense, from this series of brief extracts, of the use of witnessing devices of various sorts as a form of legitimation for a contribution to the debate. So far, however, we have only looked at utterances in isolation from their interactional contexts. In every case, the witnessing claim is produced in a specific sequential context, and I next expand two examples (extracts 1 and 2 above) to show how witnessing devices are brought into play in the context of interaction between host and caller.

The first extract is taken from a call made the morning after a large-scale student demonstration in London against a proposed change in government higher education policy. The demonstration, which involved scenes of violence between demonstrators and mounted police, was widely reported in that morning's press, and had been the subject of numerous previous calls to the show.

(12) G:26.11.88:3 [Expansion of Extract 1]
1 Host: Ni:gel from Ha̱ckney.
2   (0.6)

```
3    Caller:   Hello? [Yeh-  ]
4    Host:          [Hello] Nigel.
5    Caller:   Hello.=Yeh my name's Nigel Baker. .h E:r
6→             I was actually at the student pro:test yesterday,
7    Host:     [[Mm.]
8    Caller:   [[An' ] I just wannid tuh make it- (.) cle:ar t'
9              your listeners. .h e:r why we were actually, er
10             doing what we were doing. (.) Uh what was s'pose
11             tuh happen yesterda:y, it wz an org- it was an
12             o:rganised lobby of Parliament by: the National
13             Union of Students.
14   Host:     °M:mm,°=
15   Caller:   =An' the idea was to make, .hh the public of
16             England, an' Great Britain, .h awa:re, .h of:
17             thee loans proposals.
```

As we can see, this comes from the very beginning of the call, and virtually the first thing the caller does, after he is introduced by the host, is to assert his status as a witness of the demonstration that earlier callers had offered opinions on. In line 6, he uses a clear example of a witnessing device in Category I: 'I was actually at the student pro:test yesterday'. Indeed, the whole of this opening utterance from the caller, punctuated only by two continuers from the host (lines 7 and 14), is presented as an 'authentic' account of the event – or more precisely, of the intentions of its organizers. The caller speaks of what was 'supposed' to happen, thereby implying that what did happen (the violent confrontations between police and students) was not what was intended. Perhaps the very fact that the caller, at the start of the call, announces his full name (line 5), when it is customary in this setting for callers to be known only by first names (Hutchby, 1999), adds to this self-presentation as an authentic commentator on the topic. For present purposes, however, it is the arrowed line in which the caller foregrounds his physical presence at the demonstration, that I want to focus on as an instance of a 'witnessing' device.

In extract (13), we see a whole series of witnessing devices brought into play in the course of a caller's presentation of her topic.

(13) **H:2.2.89:4 [Expansion of Extract 2]**
```
1    Host:     And good morning tuh Lin:da frum Ruisl[ip.=
2    Caller:                                          [.hhh
3    Host:     =Good morni[ng.
4    Caller:              [Good mor:ning Brian. .hhh
5→             We've godda real problem he:re with dogs fouling
6              our footway,=
7    Host:     =Oh, so[mething im]portant now.
8    Caller:         [  .phhhh  ]
```

```
9                  (.)
10    Caller:   Pahd↑n:?
11    Host:     Something important this time.=right.=
12→   Caller:   =eYe:s:. (h) Well i' i:s to us: anyway.=
13    Host:     =Yes[:,
14→   Caller:        [I'm:: a- er mother of two small boys, .hh
15→              an:' I've now got tuh the situation where we
16              ca:n't (.) gedout uv our ca::r on the pa:vement
17              si:de e- c- becuz it's so ba::d. .hhhh As I
18              said we've gotta gra:ss verge u-u- s- outside
19              our house, °.hh° an' the local dog owners,= ↑walk
20              their ↓dogs ↑past my ↓house, (.) .h they ↑do:
21              their bizniss, right outside, .hh an' ↓walk
22              a↑wa↓y.
23         (1.0)
24→   Caller:   One da::y, I akchilly sa:w a lady=e-=ow:ner, allow
25              her dog, tuh do its bizniss ↑ri:ght in the middle
26              of my: gateway. .hhh An' when I remonstrated with
27              the la:dy, .h she told me thut her dog 'as got t'do
28              its bizniss somewhe:re, it ↓might ↑as ↓well: be
29              ↑the:re.
30    Host:     M:m[:,
31    Caller:       [.phhh (.) A-e(i)s you c'n imagine I wuz
32              absolutely:=livvid(h),
```

The caller here makes a call in which she expresses outrage at the inconsiderateness of local dog owners who allow their dogs to do their 'business' on the grass verges, with the clear implication that this constitutes a health risk for her two small children. This relates in part to a news story, current at the time, in which it was reported that bacteria from contact with dog faeces (caused for instance by young children falling down while playing) could be transmitted to the face via hands and cause a form of blindness. But it is also an example of the kind of 'bottom up' civic news or neighbourhood politics that frequently gets discussed on open line talk radio (Verwey, 1990).

The caller begins (in line 5) with a different kind of witnessing device to that found in extract (12). Rather than having been an eye-witness of a past event that had been commented on by others, she describes the problem as one which she personally (along with her family) is currently experiencing. Nevertheless, the similarity between the two cases is in the foregrounding of first-hand knowledge of the topic being introduced.

In contrast to the simple 'Mm' with which the host in (12, line 7) responds to the caller's introduction of the topic, here the host offers a hearably sceptical or ironic response: 'Oh, something important now' (see Hutchby, 2001a). As we see in more detail below, the host's scepticism is a factor with which callers frequently have to contend; and in this instance, the caller responds by recapitulating the first-hand nature of the problem. One interpretation might see this as defensive (in that it reduces the issue to a personal one which may indeed not be 'important' in the broader sense, a line taken, for example, in Hutchby, 2001a: 132). But another way of viewing it is to say that the caller re-emphasizes precisely the topic's wider importance by bringing into play, again, her first-hand knowledge/experience. That is, the category 'us' which she uses in line 12 is at least open to being hearable as implicating a broader constituency of 'citizens' or 'mothers with small children'. It is worth noting that immediately after this the caller in fact categorizes herself as 'a mother of two small boys' (line 14). This categorization enables her to describe from another angle her first-hand knowledge of the topic, in the form of a graphic image of she and her children being unable to 'gedout uv our ca::r on the pa:vement si:de *e-* c- becuz it's so ba::d' (lines 15–17).

After a one second pause following her description of the complainable practices of the local dog owners (line 23), the caller utilizes an eye-witness account: 'One da::y, I akchilly sa:w a lady=e-=ow:ner, allow her dog, tuh do its bizniss ↑ri:ght in the middle of my: gateway' (lines 24–26). This then allows her to relate the rudeness of the owner's reaction to her remonstrations, and ultimately to invite the host to sympathize with her ('A-e(i)s you c'n imagine I wuz absolutely:=livvid(h)').

These extracts give a sense of how witnessing devices are brought into play by callers; of the interactional work they can be involved in accomplishing; and of the range of forms they can take. Witnessing devices tend to be used by callers in order to authenticate themselves as legitimate speakers on the subject in question (by having been present at, experienced, seen or heard an event or item, and/or by virtue of belonging to a relevant membership category). They are also brought into play in order to counter the scepticism of the host (or to pre-empt possible scepticism) and therefore to bolster the caller's position.

Having looked at the means by which callers may seek to authenticate themselves as speakers in this environment, it is important now to look in more detail at the other half of the talk radio colloquy – that is, how hosts respond to callers' expressions of opinion. Callers are given the floor at the beginning of calls in order to introduce their issue and express an opinion on it, and in that sense, open-line talk radio shows enable callers to set the agenda for a discussion with the host. However, agendas are not fixed things, nor are they established from one perspective only. In fact, agendas can become the contested arena for disputes focusing on what can relevantly be said within their terms. This leads to a paradox in talk radio disputes. While it may seem that the caller is in a position to control what will count as an acceptable or relevant contribution to their topic, in fact it is the host who tends to end up in that position. The very fact that introducing an agenda is the caller's prerogative on talk radio leads to a situation in which the argumentative initiative can rest with the host, and the caller can relatively easily be put on the defensive. In other words, although the caller may well use 'witnessing' devices to authenticate their views, the host appears to be in a more powerful discursive position. We can use conversation analysis to investigate how that comes about.

Arguments, asymmetries and power

Some years ago in an interview, former talk radio host Brian Hayes complained that social scientists who studied talk radio tended to say little more than that the host was in a position of power over the caller. Hayes was arguing that there was much more to the phenomenon of talk radio than that. And indeed, when I originally recorded Hayes' phone-in as part of my collection of data on media talk, I selected that show precisely because it seemed that the host was concerned to discuss and argue about issues seriously, for the most part, with his callers. (Though admittedly, the entertainment value of confrontation and the frisson of controversy were also major factors in my decision, and in the show's success.)

However, it remains the case that, Hayes' protestations aside, as a listener to talk radio I would often experience a strong sense that the host and the caller were in very different power situations; that the caller was often on the defensive even though he or she had introduced the topic of the call; and that, indeed, the host was in a position to force the caller onto the defensive relatively easily. One kind of account for this stresses the host's 'authority' which derives from his status as a celebrity in the small world of talk radio (Verwey, 1990). Others emphasize that the host controls callers' access to the air, and hence to the conversational floor in their discussions (Moss and Higgins, 1984). Yet such accounts are open to the kind of critique offered by Schegloff (1991), that they merely stipulate the *a priori* terms on which one might *expect* there to be a power relationship between host and caller. They do not demonstrate the existence of that relationship in the details of the interaction itself. Therefore, they fail to describe in adequate, empirical detail how power is an accomplished feature of talk radio encounters on each individual occasion.

Clearly, one way in which this might be shown is by looking for occasions when participants explicitly mention the power relations between themselves. However, in my data of recordings of talk radio calls this does not happen very often. An alternative possibility is that the very ways in which participants design their interaction can have the effect of placing them in a relationship where discourse strategies of greater or lesser power are differentially available to each of them. In this sense, power can be viewed as an 'emergent feature' of oriented-to discourse practices.

To understand this we need to look at the relation between two factors: first, the way that arguments themselves are sequentially organized; and second, the way in which calls on talk radio are organized. The principal sequential unit in an argument is the 'action-opposition' sequence (Eisenberg and Garvey, 1981; Hutchby, 1996; Maynard, 1985), in which actions that can be construed as arguable are opposed, with the opposition itself subsequently open to being construed as an arguable. Within the organization of calls on talk radio, callers are required to begin by setting out their position (Hutchby, 1991). This in turn situates the caller's opening turn as a possible first action in a potential action-opposition sequence. To put it another way, it is the host who has the first opportunity for opposition within each call. This turns out to be a powerful argumentative resource, which is not only linked to a particular kind of asymmetry between hosts and callers, but also has consequences for the shape and trajectory of disputes in the talk radio setting.

The asymmetry between first and second positions in arguments was first remarked on by Sacks in one of his lectures on conversation (1992, Vol. 2 [Lecture 2, Spring 1971]). Sacks proposed that those who go first are in a weaker position than those who get to go second, since the latter can argue with the former's position simply by taking it apart. Going first means having to set your opinion on the line, whereas going second means being able to argue merely by challenging your opponent to expand on or account for his or her claims. While first position arguers are required to build a defence for their stance, those in second position are able to choose if and when they will set out their own argument, as opposed to simply attacking the other's.

It is this which is at the root of the power relationship between host and caller on talk radio, because the asymmetry between first and second positions is one that is built into the overall structure of calls. Callers are expected, and may be constrained, to go first with their line, while the host systematically gets to go second, and thus to contest the caller's line by picking away at its weaknesses. The fact that hosts systematically have the first opportunity for opposition within calls opens to them a collection of argumentative resources which are not available in the same way to callers.

In order to explore some of the uses and consequences of these second position resources, I will concentrate on episodes in which the participants argue about the dispute's agenda itself. I have already remarked that on talk radio, callers' agendas have an interesting status. While it is their role to set up an agenda for discussion, the agenda is not something over which the caller necessarily maintains subsequent control. By being in second position, the host is able to challenge the 'agenda-relatedness' of the caller's remarks: to question whether what the caller says is actually relevant within the terms of his or her own agenda.

One way in which this may be done is through the use of a class of utterances, including 'So?' and 'What's that got to do with it?' which challenge a claim on the grounds of its validity or relevance to the matter in question. However, a significant aspect of such turns is that they need not make clear precisely on what terms the claim is being challenged. They may function purely as second position moves by which the first speaker is required to expand on or account for the challenged claim.

In the following extract the caller is complaining about the number of mailed requests for charitable donations she receives. Notice that in line 7, the host responds simply by saying 'So?'

(14) **H:21.11.88:6:1**
```
1    Caller:   I: have got three appeals letters here this
2              week.(0.4) All a:skin' for donations. (0.2) .hh
3              Two: from tho:se that I: always contribute to
4              anywa:y,
```

5	Host:	Yes?
6	Caller:	.hh But I expect to get a lot mo:re.
7	Host:	So?
8	Caller:	.h Now the point is there is a limi[t to ( )
9	Host:	[What's that
10		got to do- what's that got to do with telethons
11		though.
12	Caller:	hh Because telethons . . . [Continues]

As an argumentative move, this 'So?' achieves two things. First, it challenges the validity or relevance of the caller's complaint within the terms of her own agenda, which in this case is that charities represent a form of 'psychological blackmail'. Second, because it stands alone as a complete turn, 'So?' requires the caller to take the floor again and account for the relevance of her remark.

This floor-returning property is an important argumentative feature of 'So?'. In studies of children's arguments, Goodwin (1990) found that pre-adolescent children tend to use 'So?' frequently. However, Goodwin's data show the item being used in a slightly different way. Two examples follow:

(15) **From Goodwin, 1990**

1	Benita:	I'm eight and a half. I'm almost nine.
2→	Larry:	So, my brother older than you.

(16) **From Goodwin, 1990**

1	Kerry:	Why you wanna bother with him. He's smaller
2		than you.
3→	Earl:	So, he keep mouthing off with me.

The difference here is that 'So' is a preface to a further component in the second speaker's turn, which either (a) offers a counter to the first speaker's claim (in [15]), or (b) provides a reason for the action the first speaker has complained about (in [16]). In these cases, as Goodwin notes, 'So' seems to do the work of denying the importance of the prior action.

By contrast, when 'So?' stands on its own in a turn, as in extract (14) above, it challenges the relevance of the prior speaker's claim in both a more fundamental and a more oppositional sense. In the cases cited by Goodwin (1990), 'So' is used to preface a further component which provides grounds for why the prior speaker's complaint or argument is being rejected: for instance, 'he keep mouthing off with me' in extract (16). The freestanding 'So?' used by the host in extract (14), however, sets up a different relationship between the participants in which it is the first speaker rather than the second who should, in a next turn, account for the relevance of what has just been said.

In this sense, 'So?' functions in a similar way to the other relevance challenge used in extract (14), the host's 'What's that got to do with telethons' (line 10). In the same way that the caller responds to the first challenge by formulating the 'point' of her remarks (line 8), at this second challenge she responds by providing a reason for her claims (line 11). This is illustrated again in the following extract:

(17) **H:21.11.88:11:1**

```
1   Caller:   When you look at e:r the childcare facilities in
2             this country, .hh we're very very low, (.) i-on
3             the league table in Europe of (.) you know if
4             you try to get a child into a nursery it's very
5             difficult in this country. .hh An' in fa:ct it's
6             getting wor::se.
7   Host:     What's that got to do with it.
8   Caller:   .phh Well I think whu- what 'at's gotta d- do
9             with it is . . . ((Continues))
```

Again, the host's challenge (line 7) situates the caller in a position of providing an account for the relevance of his remarks within the terms of the agenda which he himself has introduced.

These turns, then, represent one resource by which the host can rapidly put callers on the defensive about their own agenda. By challenging the agenda-relevance of callers' remarks, the host may take strategic control over the topical field that is locally at work within a dispute.

Another way in which the host may attempt to establish control over the agenda is by selectively *formulating* the gist or upshot of the caller's remarks. Heritage (1985: 100) describes the practice of formulating as 'summarising, glossing, or developing the gist of an informant's earlier statements'. He adds: 'Although it is relatively rare in conversation, it is common in institutionalised, audience-directed interaction,' that is, settings such as courtrooms, classrooms and news interviews, as well as other forms of broadcast talk.

Heritage also notes that in these institutional settings, formulating 'is most commonly undertaken by questioners' (1985: 100). This accords with the common finding in studies of institutional discourse that '[i]nstitutional incumbents (doctors, teachers, interviewers, family social workers, etc.) may strategically direct the talk through such means as their capacity to change topics and their selective formulations, in their "next questions", of the salient points in the prior answers' (Drew and Heritage, 1992b: 49).

Extract (18) shows how formulations can be used in the construction of a dispute. The host here uses two formulations (lines 6, and 8–10) which are linked together to propose a contentious reading of the position being advanced by the caller. The caller has criticised the 'contradictions' of telethons, claiming that their rhetoric of concern in fact promotes a passive altruism which exacerbates the 'separateness' between donors and recipients. He goes on:

(18) H:21.11.88:11:3

```
1      Caller:  . . . but e:r, I- I think we should be working at
2               breaking down that separateness I [think  ] these
3      Host:                                       [Ho:w?]
4               (.)
5      Caller:  these telethons actually increase it.
6→     Host:    Well, what you're saying is that charity does.
7      Caller:  .h Charity do::es, ye[::s   I    mean-   ]
8→     Host:                          [Okay we- so you]'re (.) so
9               you're going back to that original argument we
10              shouldn't have charity.
11     Caller:  Well, no I um: I wouldn't go that fa:r, what I
12              would like to [see is-
13     Host:                  [Well how far are you going then.
14     Caller:  Well I: would- What I would like to see is . . .
```

In line 6, the host proposes that the caller's argument in fact embraces charities in general and not just telethons as one sort of charitable endeavour. This is similar to the 'inferentially elaborative' formulations that Heritage (1985) discusses. Note that although the caller has not made any such generalization himself in his prior talk, he assents to this in the next turn (line 7).

However, it turns out that the caller, by agreeing, provides the host with a resource for *reformulating* the agenda in play here. By linking a second formulation to the first, this time describing the upshot of the caller's position, it is proposed that the caller is going back to an argument which the host had with a previous caller ('that original argument'), whose view had been that 'we shouldn't have charity' (lines 8–10).

The caller in fact rejects this further formulation (line 11). But the point is that the host is able to use the fact that the call is based on what the caller thinks about an issue to construct an argument without having to defend his own view. By relying on his ability to formulate the gist or upshot of the caller's remarks, the host can argumentatively define, and challenge, a supposed underlying agenda in the caller's remarks.

In this sense, the agenda contests which occur within calls begin to reveal significant aspects of the play of power in talk radio disputes. The fact that callers must begin by setting out a topical agenda means that argumentative resources are distributed asymmetrically between host and callers. The host is able to build opposition using basic second position resources. The characteristic feature of these resources is that they require callers to defend or account for their claims, while enabling hosts to argue without constructing a defence for an alternative view. At the same time, as long as the host refrains from setting out his own position, such second position resources are not available to the caller. Distinctive interactional prerogatives are thereby available to the host, by which he can exert a degree of control over the boundaries of an agenda which is ostensibly set by the caller.

Turning the tables

The implication so far has been that the way calls are set up provides the host with a natural incumbency in second position. This does not mean, however, that callers are incapable of offering resistance to the host's challenges. One way of doing this is to adopt the use of second position resources on their own part. But as I have just suggested, particular sequential environments are necessary for this. In particular, the host must have moved or been manoeuvred into adopting first position (that is, indicating an opinion in his own right). On talk radio, the host is able to choose when, or if, he will express his own view on the caller's issue: technically, he is able to conduct a whole call simply by challenging and demanding justifications for the caller's claims. This, however, is very rare. And once the host has abandoned second position, that position then becomes available for the caller.

Extract (19) shows how a caller may succeed in turning the tables in this way. As we will see, in this case the tables are turned only briefly because the host subsequently adopts a strategy for re-establishing himself in second position:

```
(19)  H:2.2.89:3:3
1    Caller:   But I still think a thousand pounds a night at a
2              hotel:, .hhh a:nd the fact that she's going on
3              to visit homeless peop[le,
4    Host:                            [Where should sh- Where
5              should she be staying in New York.
6              (0.2)
7    Caller:   We:ll u-th- at a cheaper place I don't think the
8              money-=.h WE'RE paying that money for her to
9              stay there and I think it's obscene.
10   Host:     Well we're not actually paying the[e the money,
11   Caller:                                       [Well
12             who:'s paying for it.
13   Host:     Well thee:: e:rm I imagine the the:r the money
14             the Royal Family has .h er is paying for it, .h
15             or indeed it may be paid for by somebody else, .h
16             erm but .h y'know if the Princess of Wales lives
17             in: (.) a palace in this country, w-w-why do
18             you think she should not live in something which
19             is comparable, .hh when she's visiting New York?
20   Caller:   Well I should think that she could find
21             something comparable that- that- or- e-it could
22             be found for her that doesn't cost that money.
```

One thing to notice is the way the caller responds to the host's hostile questioning (which has been going on for some while) by suddenly attempting to shift the topical focus of her agenda (line 8). From the question of the price of the hotel suite, she shifts, by means of a self-interruption, to the more emotive issue of the ultimate responsibility of the taxpayer for footing the bill: '.h WE'RE paying that money for her to stay there.'

The host's response to this, in line 10, is significant. By opposing the caller's assertion, he abandons his series of questioning challenges and instead asserts an opinion in his own right. It is this turn which allows the caller to move on to the offensive, and produce a challenge of her own which, in a way characteristic of the second position moves I have been discussing, requires the host to account for his assertion (lines 11–12).

At this stage, then, the local roles of challenger and defender of a position have been inverted. The host, from being in his customary challenger role, has suddenly been swung around into the role of defender. However, this inversion turns out to be only temporary. In the very next turn, the host manages to re-establish the prior state of affairs. He does this by not simply responding to the caller's challenge, but also going on to produce a next challenge-bearing question of his own (lines 16–19). With this move, the host succeeds in doing two things. First, he re-establishes the agenda to which his earlier question, in the second turn of the extract, had been addressed, and which the caller had attempted to shift away from. Second, he re-situates the caller as the respondent to his challenging initiatives, rather than as the initiator of challenge-bearing moves herself.

The asymmetry between first and second positions is not, then, a straightforward, one-way feature of talk radio disputes. Although the organizational structure of calls situates callers in first position initially, they may subsequently find themselves with opportunities to move into the stronger second position. As the previous extract shows, the sequential space for this arises once the host has abandoned the second position strategy of issuing challenges, and made an assertion in his own right. However, the extract also shows that there are strategies available for turning the tables back again; and this suggests that second position itself can become actively contested over a series of turns.

To illustrate this, finally, we can continue with this call, and find that the caller subsequently adopts the host's strategy in order to retake the initiative in the argument. The following extract takes up towards the end of extract (19):

(20) **H:2.2.89:3:3**

20	Caller:	Well I should think that she could find
21		something comparable that- that- or- e-it could
22		be found for her that doesn't cost that money.
23		A[nd] you're only imagining that she's paying=
24	Host:	[But]
25	Caller:	=for herself you don't know ei:ther do you.
26	Host:	E:rm, well . . .

The feature of interest here is in lines 23 to 25. In a similar way to the host in the just prior talk, the caller moves from responding to a challenge, to issuing a question. This requires the host in turn to respond, and further account for his own position that 'she's paying for herself'. In part, the basis for this second challenge lies in the host's long turn in lines 13–19 of extract (19), above, where he responded to the caller's first challenge. That is, the caller is not simply revisiting or revamping the earlier challenge, but developing a new line of attack which relies on the fact that the host's earlier response had been quite vague (see especially lines 13–15 of extract [19]).

To summarize: The call's initial stages situate the caller in first position and furnish the host with the power of second position. But that asymmetry is not an unchanging feature of the context. The more powerful argumentative resources attached to second position may also become available to the caller. Yet this is dependent upon the host expressing an opinion in his own right. Nonetheless, once the opportunity arises, determined and resourceful callers may challenge the host using second position tactics; although second position itself can then become the focus of a discursive struggle.

The interactional pitfalls of 'witnessing'

Returning now to our earlier interest in how callers legitimate their status as speakers in this public environment, the first/second position issue can also have consequences for the effectiveness of certain 'witnessing' devices. In the following, we look at examples in which hosts use second position to test the *limits* of the caller's witnessing; and thereby to suggest that the caller is in fact anything but an authenticated speaker on this issue.

Extract (21) reveals one form of challenge to the caller's claimed status as witness, centring upon a range of claims and counter-claims about direct perceptual access. Here, the caller has been complaining about the behaviour of a Labour MP who has announced that he is to present a political programme on a satellite TV station while still remaining a Member of Parliament (something that is not generally accepted practice):

(21) G:3.2.89:6
```
1     Host:    We::ll e::r, he will still remain a Labour MP: you know
2              he's still Labour MP fuh Grimsby he'll sit on the back
3              benches .h while he is doing his television programme,
4              .h s[o thuh-
5     Caller:     [Well there there have been rumblin's in the g- in
6              the Grimsby constituency for some time now=I think it
7              will come to the fo:re.
```

```
8→   Host:    You know that do you K[en, even tho- even though  ]=
9→   Caller:                         [Yes, I've heard it myself.  ]
10→  Host:    =you live- E:ven though you live in Battersea you
11→           know that there've bin rumblings in Grim[sby about]=
12   Caller:                                          [Well   I::]
13   Host:    =[Austin Mitchell,]
14   Caller:  [I     I::  uh  I ] I'm capable of readin', guh-
15            Geoffrey,
16            (.)
17→  Host:    Yes well I sure you a:re an' y- and you've actually read
18           that there are rumblings there.
19   Caller:  Yes.
```

The issue comes to focus around the 'rumblings' which the caller claims to be witness to in the MP's local constituency party. The host rapidly picks up on the fact that, whereas Grimsby is in the north-eastern part of England, the caller lives some 300 miles away in London. He brings into play an invitation to do witnessing ('You know that do you Ken', line 8) to which the caller responds readily by making a perceptual access witnessing claim ('Yes I've heard it myself', line 9). In the course of the overlap, the host re-starts the second part of his turn three times until, in the clear, he is able make the geographical anomaly explicit ('E:ven though you live in Battersea you know that there've bin rumblings in Grimsby', lines 10–11). Bringing out the apparent anomaly in his direct perception claim leads the caller to resort to a less direct claim in line 14, but nonetheless one that still involves witnessing in the form of an assertion that he has *read* that there are rumblings in Grimsby. This suggests that even when the witnessing device itself is brought into question, callers can find ways of sustaining the claim as a means of legitimating their stance. In this extract the caller does that by making slight alterations in the form of his claim.

The final two extracts reveal more decisive strategies of refutation against a legitimizing witnessing device. In (22), the caller is talking about a product designed to stop dogs 'marking' at the same point on their daily walk. The host takes issue with the notion of 'marking' because 'it means that they never go in a different place':

(22) H:2.2.89:12
```
1    Host:    No I do:n't- I don't believe that,=but you tell me about
2             this- this product? what is it ca:lled and what does
3             it [do:?
4    Caller:  [Yes. (.) It is- it is tru:e, .h er:[m:,
5    Host:                                        [No I don't
6             believe it's tru:e becuz otherwise they'd go duh thuh
7             same place ev'ry time.=Logic is not on your si:de.
8             (.)
```

```
 9→   Caller:   (hn) E:r, well I'm in the tra:de ak(h)chully(h[hh)
10→   Host:                                              [I don't
11→             care what you're in:, logi[c is    ] not on your si:de.
12    Caller:                             [°O:h.°]
```

Notably, the host brings into play a device which, in Livingstone and Lunt's (1994) terms, can be described as a legitimating resource in the 'expert' register of abstract reasoning: namely, logic (line 7: 'Logic is not on your si:de'). After a brief pause (line 8), the caller comes up with a rejoinder using a lay witnessing device – personal experience and first-hand knowledge – which also incorporates elements of abstract expertise, the knowledge base associated with being 'in the tra:de ak(h)chully(hhh)'. While the slight laughter suggests that the caller senses victory at this point, the host comes up with an equally perfect means of discounting of the caller's claim: 'I don't care what you're in:, logic is not on your si:de'. The elegance of this refutation is that, like other second position argumentative moves described earlier, it does not challenge the witnessing claim itself: rather, it challenges the very idea that the witnessing claim has any purchase on the argument it was brought into play to counter.

A slightly less elegant, more mischievous challenge is found in this final example, in which the caller proposes what he takes to be a neat solution to the 'problem' of there being too many charities who therefore do not receive sufficient donations.

(23) H:21.11.88:9
```
 1    Caller:   A lotta peopl:e, .hhh don't like receivin' charity an'
 2              now if, .hh ev'ry wo:rkin' person, (.) .hh an' e- i-
 3→             e:ven ev'ry pensioner uv which I am o:ne, .hh was
 4              deducted (.) ten pee per week, (0.9) throughout,=y'know
 5              fer ever'n ever, (0.9) that e:r- it would do away wi' lot
 6              of charities
```
((11 lines omitted))
```
18→   Host:     u:h is that what you do:? is it give ten pence ev'ry
19              week?
20    Caller:   Well d- if, if ev'rybody wuh duc- d[educted   [(wha?) ]
21    Host:                                        [n-no, no [d's (.)  ] no
22→             n- no d'you do it, bucuz it's easy, y'know anybody c'n do
23              it,
24              (0.8)
25    Caller:   .hh Well, dh- what I do: e:r ev'ry Christmas y'know fuh
26              the bli:nd, an' f' thee .hh Barna:do's, .hh but u-the:n
27              course y- you do get eventu'lly y' find y'self 'bout
28              thirty or forty diff'rent charities comin' through yuh
29              post'n yuh ca:n't d'nate to all of them. .hh [It's] such=
30    Host:                                                  [ b- ]
```

```
31   Caller:   =an expense isn' it when people .hhh [these (      )
32   Host:                                          [We- you don't haf-
33             n-ahold o:n, a m- a moment ago: you were saying we should
34             give to a:ll of them,=now you're saying .h it's too
35             difficult tuh give to them, .h e[r the s:- [the=
36   Caller:                                    [N- no   [the-
37   Host:     =system that you introduced [was still]: charity:,=
38   Caller:                                [it (     )]
39   Host:     =it makes no diff'rence. .hh Thank yih Sidney,
((end call))
```

Note here that when the caller brings into play a witnessing device in line 3, 'e:ven ev'ry pensioner uv which I am o:ne', it seems to function much like the earlier examples as a means of justifying or legitimating his position. In the course of arguing that everyone, even pensioners, should be 'deducted ten pee per week' he could be heard as exhibiting a callousness towards the elderly and less well-off. By asserting his own membership of the category of pensioners, that danger is avoided.

However, later in the call the very same device turns out to provide the host with a resource for undermining the argument being presented (even though the undermining itself involves a wily misinterpretation of the caller's argument). The caller having claimed membership of at least one of the categories that are relevant to his argument ('working people' and 'pensioners'), the host constructs a reading of that argument in which the caller can be taken to task for not actually 'practising what he preaches'. Clearly, there is mischief in the host's twisting of the caller's argument in lines 18–19 (from a proposal of a ten pence tax deduction, it is turned into a voluntary ten pence donation). The point is that the witnessing device itself is turned into a resource for de-legitimating an argument which it seems to have been brought into play precisely to strengthen.

Civic news and discursive asymmetry

Talk radio is a media discourse genre that brings into play the potential for a different sense of news and a different relation between news and news audiences than is generally considered in media sociology. On talk radio, laypersons call in to discuss items 'in the news', but not just news as defined by news gathering organizations. Talk radio offers a context in which people can define as news events as they emerge in or affect their own everyday lives (for instance, 'We've got a real problem here with dogs fouling our footway').

However, those items of what I have called 'civic news' have to be introduced in a specific discourse context, where a variety of institutional and interactional features may come into play. Typically, callers participate as lay speakers who, in a quite literal sense, are calling *in* to talk in an already existing institutional set-up, usually for a very limited length of time, and always as one in a series of such callers-in. The host's voice and presence remain constant throughout the show, while callers' voices vary widely. This asymmetry is reinforced, in the hearing, by the fact that callers' voices are broadcast with telephone quality, with the attendant distortion and extraneous noise, while the host's voice comes across in the richness of full broadcast quality. Thus, there is a palpable sense in which callers speak from a space outside the institutional space represented by the studio, and this is one reason why they may feel it necessary actively to legitimate, or authenticate, themselves as both speakers and the holders of opinions.

The arguments between hosts and callers provide the basis for developing an account of the play of power in this context. I focused on relatively small sequential details of arguments in order to show this. The upshot is that the sequential approach developed within CA has been applied to a question which has concerned critical linguists and discourse analysts – namely how power operates in and through language – by viewing power in terms of the relationships between turns (as actions) in sequences.

The analysis has detailed the relationship between the organization of activities within calls, and the asymmetrical distribution of argument resources. On talk radio, the opening of the call is not only designed to set up an environment in which callers introduce the topic, but by virtue of that it also places the participants on significantly asymmetrical footings with respect to those topics. The fact that callers are required to go first by expressing a point of view on some issue means that hosts systematically get to go second. Going second, I have argued, represents a more powerful position in argumentative discourse than first position. Principally, the host is able to critique or attack the caller's line simply by exhibiting scepticism about its claims, challenging the agenda-relevance of assertions, or taking the argument apart by identifying minor inaccuracies in its details.

However, the fact that hosts may conduct arguments without expressing a counter-opinion or providing explanations and accounts for their own positions does not mean that they never do the latter. The asymmetry I have noted is simply that hosts are in a position to do this whereas callers, by virtue of the organization of the call, are not. At the same time, there are resources available for callers to resist the host's powerful strategies, and sometimes to exercise powerful strategies themselves. Thus, power is not a monolithic feature of talk radio, with the corresponding simplistic claim that the host exercises power over the caller by virtue of his 'control of the mechanics of the radio program' (Moss and Higgins, 1984: 373). Rather, in a detailed way, the power dynamics at work within calls are variable and shifting, instantiated through the details of turn-taking.

Further reading

Avery, R. and Ellis, D. (1979) Talk radio as an interpersonal phenomenon. In G. Gumpert and C. Cathcart (eds), *Inter/Media*. New York: Oxford University Press.

Hutchby, I. (1996) *Confrontation Talk: Arguments, Asymmetries and Power on Talk Radio*. Mahwah, NJ: Lawrence Erlbaum Associates.

Moss, C. and Higgins, P. (1984) Radio voices. *Media, Culture and Society*, 6: 353–75.

Thornborrow, J. (2002) *Power Talk*. London: Pearson.

6 | DISTRIBUTED EXPERTISE: THE DISCOURSE OF ADVICE-GIVING SHOWS

I mentioned in the previous chapter the numerous different types of talk radio show, of which one is the advice-giving type show. This genre of media talk itself comprises a variety of sub-types. For instance, there are shows designed to offer advice and guidance for people experiencing relationship difficulties. These operate along the lines of 'agony aunt' columns in magazines (and sometimes the writers of such columns are also the hosts of the phone-ins – for example, in the UK, Anna Raeburn or Claire Rayner). At the more extreme end of this variety is the American *Good Sex* phone-in hosted by sex therapist Dr Ruth Westheimer (which was actually broadcast on TV though in all other respects it shared the conventions of the radio phone-in). As Bryan Crow (1986) showed in his analysis of this programme, there is a high level of intimacy and delicacy about the topics raised by callers which lends certain characteristics to the talk of the show. In particular, Dr Ruth's matter-of-factness about issues of sexual practice exists in marked contrast to the hesitancy and exaggerated politeness exhibited by callers.

Crow (1986) speculated on the question of what it might be that audience members tuning in to the *Good Sex* show could 'get out of it', given that the topics about which callers tend to call in are highly personalized. Potentially, he suggested, individuals could use the show's discourse to learn about sexual matters in a way that could then be applied to their own relationship circumstances. But as Crow observes, such a speculation takes us beyond the discourse of the show itself and could probably only be tested using survey or interview methods.

The same question, put slightly differently, could be applied to all forms of radio advice phone-ins. For these shows all represent specifically *public* contexts in which private citizens seek advice about matters particular to them, but at the same time they, the individual advice-seeker, are not the only ones privy to the advice being given. The advice is provided in a context where the 'overhearing' audience potentially plays a significant role. Thus, to recast Crow's (1986) question slightly, we can ask: to what extent might the overhearing audience be addressed – and even constructed in various ways as an 'advice recipient' – in the design of the expert's talk? Putting the question this way means that we do not have to move beyond the structural characteristics of the talk to find out about whether the audience is involved in the giving of advice in the phone-in context. We can therefore address the question using the methods of conversation analysis.

In this chapter I explore that question using data from a radio broadcast that provides advice about social security and welfare benefits. Callers address their questions to an expert on welfare matters, who sits in the studio along with the show's (non-expert) host. The structure of interactions on this show takes a standard shape. The show's host begins by announcing the upcoming caller, and after a brief exchange of greetings says something along the lines of 'Go ahead with your question for John' ('John' being the welfare expert). The caller then states their concern in an extended turn, following which the expert takes the floor to provide advice. There may then be some interaction between expert and caller (with occasional contributions from the host). At the end of the call, the host once again comes in to thank the caller and move on to introduce the next caller.

The above is, of course, a highly generalized account of what goes on during these exchanges. The issue to be concerned with is what happens in the details of the talk as individual calls unfold? Are there ways in which, within that general structure, we can observe an orientation to the specifically public nature of the talk: that is, the fact that this form of advice-giving is done in the presence of an 'overhearing audience'? Or, given the comments made earlier in Chapter 1, can we observe the audience themselves being situated not as 'overhearers' but as co-recipients of the advice-giving talk along with the caller? As in most forms of interactive broadcast talk, the audience is hardly ever addressed overtly during these dialogues. But I will show that there are numerous indirect ways in which audience members other than and additional to the caller come to be included in the expert's talk. In short, there are features of both the expert's advice-giving and the host's contributions to the discussions that display an orientation to the significance of the *public* nature of advice-giving on talk radio.

Answering 'more than the question'

The discourse of advice-giving on call-in radio is designed to operate in two distinctive directions: oriented on the one hand towards the specific problem at hand as presented by the caller, and on the other, towards more generalized, broadened versions of that problem as it might be encountered by an abstract 'anyone'. This double orientation is accomplished in part through a general feature of the expert's talk. The expert's responses to caller's advice-seeking questions routinely appear in a two-part format, in which the first part consists of a straightforward answer to the caller's question, while the second part provides an 'auxiliary' response in which subsidiary information or advice was conveyed. I call this the **AAI** (Answer plus Auxiliary Information) format. In short, the expert's responses to callers' questions are designed to be *more than answers* to the actual questions themselves.

This tendency to answer 'more than the question' using the AAI format is a key resource by which the expert handles the tension between the 'personal' and the 'public' dimensions of advice-giving in this communicative set-up. The audience can become situated in the role of advice-recipient at various points as the expert shifts between the particularized and the generalized orientation of his information. However, this also renders the question of who the advice is addressed to ambiguous at certain points, and occasionally problematic, as we will see.

Extract (1) comes from the beginning of one call, immediately following the host's request for the caller to address her question to the expert.

(1) RVS 'Quitting work' [C=Caller, E=Expert, H=Host]

```
1    C:   Erm, my question is that erm, (0.6) what
2         we're considering doing is me going back
3         to wo:rk, after my (.) maternity leave is
4         over, .hhh and my husband givin' up his
5         job an' lookin' a:fter the baby as I earn
6         more than he does. (.). phh What I'd like
7         to kno:w, is (.) can my husband claim
8         unemployment benefit if 'e does that.
9    E:   .hhhh (0.6) Yi- The answer is uw- yes 'e,
10        'e can claim unemployment benefit if 'e
11        satisfies the contribution conditions.
12        .hhh But thuh- the legislation that
13        contro:ls claims from husbands an' wi:ves,
14        o:n'y was changed last year. .h about
15        husbands bein' able to clai::m, .h e:r an'
16        wi:ves bein' able to claim yihknow swappin'
17        the claimant ro:le. .h[h    A]nd, it's quite=
18   C:                          [Mhm,]
19   E:   =difficult to deci:de to be honest, .hh
20        which one (.) can claim and- and u-w- which
21        one you'd be better off with claimin' d'you
22        know what I mean?
23   C:   e[eYes,
24   E:    [.hhh It depends on things li:ke . . . ((Goes
          on to provide details))
```

In lines 1–8, we see that the caller presents a reasonably straightforward question: a request for advice on the matter of whether her husband can claim unemployment benefit if he gives up work to look after their baby. In lines 9–11, this question is answered economically and straightforwardly by the expert: 'The answer is . . . yes, 'e can claim unemployment benefit if 'e satisfies the contribution conditions.' As it stands, this response may work satisfactorily to answer the caller's question; or it may, for instance, occasion a follow-up question such as, 'What are the contribution conditions?'

However, the expert in fact goes on almost without pause to *expand* on his answer, in a second part which provides additional information about 'the legislation that contro:ls claims from husbands an' wi:ves'. The expert's response thus has a two-part form: a straightforward answer, *plus* auxiliary information.

A particular point to note about this example is that, at the outset, the 'answer' part is explicitly described as such: 'The answer is . . . yes'. But we might also note that this way of putting it evidently was not the first selection of the expert. He begins with a cut-off sound, 'Yi-', which may be heard, in context, as an abandoned beginning on the word 'Yes'. By inserting the words, 'The answer is . . .', the expert manages to introduce a contrastive dimension to his response, thereby possibly indicating that the 'answer' alone is not going to prove enough. Furthermore, his turn begins with a marked hesitation: a prolonged inbreath (.hhhh) followed by a pause. Such hesitations at the start of turns commonly work as signs of disjuncture between participants: they may foreshadow disagreements (Pomerantz, 1984a) or otherwise indicate a speaker's 'problem' in coming up with the 'right' response to a prior turn (Pomerantz, 1984b). In short, the expert's hesitation may well be a way of indicating right from the outset that a straightforward 'answer' to the question will not suffice.

The response then proceeds in the direction of overtly prescriptive advice, as we see with extract (2), which comes from the same call a few moments on:

(2) **RVS 'Quitting work'**
1   E: But I: would always say to people if you're
2   gunna do that, .hh yih must go into an
3   advice centre, .h an' sit dow:n with an
4   advice giver in a C.A.B or somethin' like
5   that, .h an' go through the figure work. .h
6   An' go: through whether, it's (.) allowable
7   in your particular case. .hh Because if yuh
8   don't do that an' just go into it b-
9   yihknow, .h e:r because you've 'eard
10   there's been a change in the rules yih
11   can come unstuck.
12   (0.6)
13 E: Okay?
14 C: I: see.

Here, the expert has moved fully into advice-giving mode. He offers advice that is overtly prescriptive: 'yih must go into an ad<u>vi</u>ce centre . . .' (lines 2–3), and also cautionary: 'Because if yuh <u>don</u>'t . . . yih c<u>a</u>n come uns<u>tuck</u>' (lines 7–11).

However, something of particular note about this advice-giving is the way that the expert prefaces his advice about going to an advice centre and going through 'whether it's all<u>ow</u>able in your particular case' with the phrase: 'But <u>I</u>: would always say to people . . .' (line 1). The significance of this lies in what the use of such a phrase may establish for the upcoming advice. For one thing, the 'problem' in question is thereby shown to be one that has a *general* relevance: that is, a relevance not only for the caller at hand but also for any member of an abstract category of 'people'. Second, the advice itself therefore can be treated as having a general relevance: what the expert recommends is hearable as recommended not only for the caller but also for the general class of 'people'.

This way of packaging advice as a 'general prescription' may be a standard practice in professional advice-giving (see, for instance, Heritage and Sefi, 1992), deriving from the fact that advice-givers, as specialists in a domain, routinely encounter a series of different people with similar problems/questions. Packaging advice as a general prescription may be a specific device for 'doing expertise': for exhibiting that 'This advice works for others; it's a good bet for you too'.

In the interactional context of the radio call-in, though, the policy of generalizing the possible relevance of advice can be a strategy by which the expert can structure the design of his talk so as to deal with the special characteristics of his audience. In other words, a way in which he observably orients to the 'public' as well as to the 'personal' dimensions of the context in which he is managing his expertise.

This feature of the expert's talk is altogether more vividly apparent in Extract 3. The way in which the basic AAI format can be used to target information not only upon the caller-at-hand but also upon the wider constituencies of the audience comes out clearly here, since the auxiliary advice offered in the second part of the response is specifically *not* fitted to the requirements of this caller. This leads to trouble in the provision and reception of the advice.

(3) RVS 'Savings'

```
1    C:  I am erm: (0.3) a wido:w, of sixty si:x,
2        (0.6) and erm: (0.3) I f:- have to: apply
3        fuh Social Sec͟urity:, .hhh an' I'm- (.)
4        could you tell me e-how much I:'m allowed
5        in s͟a:vings before I- (.) can cl͟aim from
6        Social Security.
7    E:  e-Yeah. Yi- you can ha:ve (.) ͟up tuh three
8        thousand pounds in sa:vin's,
9    C:  ͟I se[e. ͟I haven'] got anywhere n͟ear that,=
10   E:      [an' still-  ]
```

```
11    E:   =Well: yer okay then. .hh There's only one
12         other figu:re, an' that is when I mentioned
13         earlier on tuh somebuddy about single
14         pay:men:ts,
15    C:   M:m:,=
16    E:   =E:r you ca:n't get single payments, if
17         you've got more than five hundred pounds or
18         e- you ca:n but er, .h[h
19→   C:                        [W- I don't unders-
20         what did you say I'm sorry?
21    E:   Five 'undred pou:nds is the- is the limit
22         fuh people on supplement'ry benefit fuh
23         single payments.
24         (.)
25→   C:   What d'you mea:n [by tha:t.=
26    E:                   [.khmmm
27    E:   =Wul- (0.8) Sorry I've- I:'ve confused you
28         it's my fault. .hh The a- the answer tih
29         you:r question is it's three thousand
30         pounds . . .
```

The caller asks about how much she is allowed in savings, under the regulations, while still being able to claim her Social Security payments. The expert's response again takes the AAI format: a straightforward answer ('You can have up to three thousand pounds', lines 7–8), followed by auxiliary information ('There's only one other figure . . .', lines 10–17). Note that the first part of the response, which comprises the answer that the caller is seeking, is responded to with a display of understanding: 'I see' (line 9). And after this is an exchange which seems to point to the 'adequacy' of the response as it stands: caller says, 'I haven't got anywhere near that [amount]', and expert says, 'Well: yer okay then.'

At this point it would seem that the enquiry is adequately dealt with. But the expert then embarks on producing his auxiliary information. In this case, the auxiliary information explicitly refers to a quite different issue: that of 'single payments', which had been raised in a previous call but which turns out to be entirely irrelevant to this caller's concerns.

This leads to a situation in which the caller, still taking herself to be the intended recipient of the expert's talk, evidently experiences difficulty in following the point of his remarks. In line 18 ('I don't unders- what did you say I'm sorry?'), and again in line 23 ('What d'you mean by tha:t'), she draws attention to the difficulty she is having. As a result, the expert returns to his original, direct response in lines 24–27. And at this point, the stress he lays on the pronoun in 'the answer to you:r question is . . .' carries the strong implication that indeed he had been providing an answer to a question which was (or may have been) someone *else*'s – someone else, that is, in the audience overhearing this interaction.

The routine practice of constructing answers to callers' questions using the two-part AAI format thus allows the expert to display a concern for the possible relevance of his advice for hearers other than the caller-at-hand. Those additional hearers, in this context, are the members of the overhearing audience. One thing that answering 'more than the question' does is to enable the expert to address 'more than the immediate concern'; and, in the context of calls to the radio advice line, to target his advice on 'more than this individual advice-seeker'. In this, one thing that is happening is that the expert is both exhibiting his knowledgeability and expertise; while at the same time exhibiting his sensitivity to the particular context in which he is deploying that expertise: in a nutshell, that this is talk 'for an overhearing audience'.

Involvement by the host

I noted at the beginning that there are four categories of participant involved in expert advice-giving on call in radio: the caller, the expert, the overhearing audience, and the show's host. We have begun to see ways in which the expert can involve not only the caller but members of the audience too as the recipients of advice. A further point of interest concerns the ways that the host, who is not an 'expert' but a professional broadcaster, can also take up an involvement in the provision of advice.

For the majority of the time, the host remains silent during interchanges between the caller and the expert advice-giver. This is one means by which he[1] displays his orientation to his own role in the show as that of 'host' rather than adviser; and correspondingly it is a means by which he orients to the expert's institutional role as 'advice-giver'. Sometimes, however, the host does take turns of his own during advice-giving episodes. These interventions turn out to be closely involved with the move into generalized or audience-oriented modes during the course of calls.

I will look at a few examples of this, beginning with a seemingly quite minor (indeed, hardly noticeable) utterance in line 3 of the following extract:

(4) **RVS 'Disablement benefit'**
```
1        E:   .hh An' if you a:re gettin' (.) several
2             additions at the momen:[t, .h this new=
3→   H:                           [Mmm,
4        E:   =premium, might not come up tuh that
5             standard. .h An' that's of uh yihknow
6             great concern because it could mean that,
7             that .h severely disabled people may lose
8             out. .h But I must keep stressin' all the
9             way through, .h (.) they're on'y proposals,
```

```
10        it's on'y a Green Paper, .hh an:d, if you
11        ar::e, disabled, and in touch with a
12        society, or er .h a disablement group in
13        your area, .h then you must put pressure on
14        that society or group, .h to respond to the
15        reviews . . .
```

Here, we find the expert moving into audience-oriented mode in his talk. There are a number of ways in which this can be seen. First, the use of 'you' becomes ambiguous in the first part of the extract. When the expert says, 'if you a:re gettin' (.) several additions at the momen:t, .h this new premium, might not come up tuh that standard. .h An' that's of uh yihknow great concern because it could mean that, that .h severely disabled people may lose out', it is not clear that he is addressing the caller alone, as against the broader category of 'severely disabled people'. Second, he later more explicitly *selects* a specific constituency within the audience: that is, disabled people who might be 'in touch with a (local) disablement group', as the target for his suggestion to 'put pressure on that . . . group'. Notice that, in saying 'if you ar::e, disabled, and in touch with a society . . .' (beginning in line 10), the expert does not check with the *caller* whether or not she belongs to this category. Previously in the call she has categorized herself as 'in receipt of an invalidity pension' (see extract 5, lines 1–2) but has said nothing about the severity of her disablement nor whether she is active in local pressure groups. It is therefore ambiguous as to who, exactly, is being addressed at this point in the talk. It seems likely that this piece of advice is intended for disabled people 'in general' rather than being specifically tailored to this caller's personal circumstances.

During the course of this turn the host produces the utterance 'Mmm,' in line 3. A principal way that utterances such as 'Mm' (and 'Uh huh', 'Mm hm', etc.) are used in talk-in-interaction is as what Schegloff (1982) called *continuers*. They are resources by which participants display an understanding that an extended turn is underway by a coparticipant and is not yet finished. Thereby, they are also ways of displaying an involvement in understanding a coparticipant's talk. Another way that they function is, of course, as signals of agreement (as abbreviations for 'yes'). Either way, they situate the speaker as an active recipient of the coparticipant's turn. By producing such a token, the host therefore moves into the role normally taken up by the caller (see, for instance, line 15 of extract 3) thereby, at least for the moment, relegating the caller to the role of 'overhearer' along with the rest of the listening audience.

A slightly clearer example, perhaps, is extract (5) where we find the non-expert host beginning to collaborate in the process of 'generalizing' the relevance of advice:

(5) RVS 'Disablement benefit'

```
1    C:   Erm:, (0.4) .h I get thee, (0.2) non-
2         contributory: (.) invalidity pension, (0.4)
```

```
3              .hh an:d also thee, mobility (0.2)
4              allowance, (0.3) .hh an::d er, h .hh I was
5              wondering if there was likely to be any
6              changes in that when thee changes come
7              along.
8        E:    .thhhhh No thee:, thee: Minister 'as said,
9              that benefits fuh disability, er::m are
10             g- are gunna be looked at I think there's a
11             big review goin' on at the moment or 'e's
12             just settin' one up. .hhh Erm, at the
13             moment there's nothin' on those, erm, .hh
14             in terms uh changes. But there are some
15             changes in the supplementary benefit scheme
16             fuh disabled people.
17             (0.5)
18→      H:    But you don't know what they are yet [John.
19       E:                                         [Well
20             no we don't- we know what they a:re we
21             know there's premiums an' things like that
22             but 'e's not told us what the rates are.
```

Again, we see a two-part response to the caller's question in the expert's turn in lines 8–16. The auxiliary information begins here in line 14: 'But there are some changes in the supplementary benefit scheme . . .'. Note that in introducing this auxiliary information, the expert begins once again to move outside the sphere of this caller's immediate concerns. The issue of 'supplementary benefit', while it is presented as *related* to the matter raised by the caller, was not mentioned in the caller's question.

Having introduced the additional information, the expert briefly pauses (line 17). This pause is broken by the host, who elects to topicalize the line of talk about 'supplementary benefit' introduced by the expert. It seems that having introduced this line, the expert realizes that he in fact has no advice to offer on it, since the 'changes in the supplementary benefit scheme' have not yet been finalized. The host infers this uncertainty from the pause in line 17 (and subsequently (lines 19–22) the expert partly confirms that inference by saying 'we know what they a:re . . . but 'e's not told us what the rates are'). However, by topicalizing that line, the host becomes involved in the whole process of generating advice that is at best auxiliary to, and at worst irrelevant for, this caller's concerns; but which *may be* relevant to potential constituencies within the overhearing audience.

This is shown more clearly still in the following extract. Here, the caller has asked a question about her particular entitlement to 'milk tokens'. She has recounted a story in which her postman informed her of her entitlement to this benefit, and she is phoning to check whether he was right.

(6) RVS 'Milk tokens'
```
1       E:   . . . I mean I'll try an' 'ave a quick look
2            but i-if you are entitled to milk tokens
3            you can get the cash back.
4       C:   Ok[ay.
5       E:       [Yeah? .h But e::r I'll 'ave a- I mean u-
6            later on: when we stop fuh the news I'll
7            try an' 'ave a look it up about milk and
8            vitamins an' see 'oo's entitled. .h But I-
9            I ca:n't I mean if the postman said it I-
10           I'll 'ave tuh check it out.=
11      H:   =He's prob'ly got one of those green books
12→          down and e:r f[iled=through.hh Ca- can you=
13      E:                 [ Yea:h (or a list) yeh.
14→     H:   =remember in general how you qualify fo:r
15→          er tokin- tok[ens, fer er, ] milk?
16      E:                [ .hhhhhhh ]
17      E:   Yea:h. Yih-you geddem on two grounds=i- th-
18           there's low income=if yer on supplementary
19           benefit with children you can get milk
20           tokens e:::r fuh children under fi:ve, and,
21           if yer not on supplementary benefit you can
22           qualify on the grounds of low income . . .
```

As the extract begins the expert is indicating that he needs to check whether in her specific case there is an entitlement. At line 11, we find the host once more entering the talk, at first by offering a version of how the postman may have come upon the information he passed to the caller. Following this, he himself addresses a question to the expert: 'Can you remember in general how you qualify fo:r er tokin- tokens, fer er, milk?' Two significant aspects of this question can be mentioned. First, it seeks to address the issue of qualifying for milk tokens 'in general', and thus moves beyond the specific case presented by the caller at hand. Second, as a question it requires the expert to give an answer, and therefore constitutes an invitation to him to talk to that more general issue.

A further thing that is happening as the host becomes involved in these cases is that he and the expert are jointly effecting a shift in the participation status of the caller, from that of principal recipient of sought advice, to that of co-recipient (along with the audience) of auxiliary information only tangentially related to her personal circumstances. Correspondingly, the status of the audience is shifted from that of 'overhearer' to that of 'co-addressee'. This collaboration therefore involves a shift in the overall framework of the call, as the particular concerns of a caller are used as the ostensible basis for informing a wider constituency than the caller alone.

Proxy questioning

The following set of extracts show a much more overt way in which the production of auxiliary advice can result from collaboration between expert and host. Here, the host collaborates with the expert in generalizing the advice by proposing his own auxiliary line of information to be pursued, in a process that I call 'proxy questioning': that is, standing in as a questioner on behalf of matters that the caller may not have thought of, or even of possible interests other than those of the immediate caller.

(7) **RVS 'Quitting work'**

```
1       E:    That's why we say go to an independent
2             advice centre like a C.A.B. .h Because they
3             can give you advi:ce an' say, .h if I were
4             you I would, follow this course of action
5             whereas the D.H.S.S will never do that
6             they'll always sa:y, .hh well it's down
7             to you now yihkno[w, you've got th[ese facts,
8       C:                     [Yeah,          [Sure.
9       C:    That's r[ight.
10→    H:            [Is there not another point John,
11            er when it comes to qualifying for
12            unemployment benefit isn't there a question
13            of, ehow you becam:e unemployed, [.hh and=
14      E:                                     [.hhhh
15      H:    =is there not a delay in getting benefit or
16            a cut in benefit levels if you make
17            yourself unemployed.
18      E:    Yeah. There is a:, a benefit suspension,
19            on unemployment that lasts fo:r guw- eh-
20            six:, six weeks I think it is whe:re if you
21            make yourself voluntarily unemployed, .hh
22            er l- leave work through misconduct or
23            somethin' like that yih get suspended from
24            unemployment benefit. .hhh An' that's
25            exactly the kind of pitfa:ll, that you can
26            fall into which is why I think you- you
27            should go an' get it a:ll sorted out.
```

In lines 1–7 the expert engages in conveying advice which is addressed directly to the caller. The fact that the caller recognizes herself as the addressee is shown in her displays of active recipiency in lines 8 ('Yeah', 'Sure') and 9 ('That's right'). In line 10, however, the host intervenes with a question directed towards the expert, inviting him to speak to additional advice-relevant matters (that is, the possibility of 'a delay in getting benefit or a <u>cut</u> in benefit levels if you <u>ma</u>ke yourself unemployed').

Two things to note about this question are: first, that it is 'non-naive'. That is, the repeated use of the phrase 'Is there not . . .?' sets the question up not so much as a request for information as a request for *confirmation* of a proposal about a state of affairs. There is a similarity here with the standard practice, in settings such as news interviews, of asking questions that are 'non-naive' in that they do not so much request information for the benefit of the questioner as invite the interviewee to talk (often on a prearranged agenda) for the benefit of the audience. In the present advice-giving con-text, such non-naive questions on the part of the host principally operate as invitations to produce expert advice.

Second, the question itself implies a piece of advice: 'Making yourself unemployed can result in delays or cuts in benefit levels.' And here we encounter another means by which the provision of advice can be modulated in this setting, after the expert's answering 'more than the question' and the host 'topicializing' auxiliary lines of advice. The host here is not simply joining in generalizing the advice; rather he is moving more centrally into the sphere of the *provision* of advice, in a particular kind of collaboration with the expert. The advice request in this call has to do with whether the caller's husband can claim unemployment benefit if he gives up work to look after their baby (recall extract 1). In this respect it is notable that the host's utterance in lines 10–17 seeks to convey (albeit indirectly) information about possible difficulties that may be encountered 'when it comes to qu<u>a</u>lifying for unemployment benefit . . . if you <u>ma</u>ke yourself unemployed'. Thus, the host appears to be directing a caveat to the caller, using the expert, as the speaker charged with being the legitimate repository of specialized knowledge here, as 'proxy' for getting that advice across.

In response, the expert unavoidably goes along with this form of proxy advice-giving. But after providing the confirmation that was sought (lines 18–24), he then ties that bit of information in with his own advice that the caller (and, by implication, anyone listening who is in a similar situation) should 'go and get it <u>a</u>:ll sorted out'.

In extract (8), taken from slightly later in the same call, we find the host persisting in his strategy of obliquely offering advice to the caller; while the expert responds by moving the advice-giving more overtly in the generalized direction.

(8) RVS 'Quitting work'

1	E:	. . .that's why it's a r:<u>ea</u>l:: m<u>i</u>nefield in
2		terms uh takin' the dec<u>i</u>sion.
3	H:	Yes because i-i-i- i:s it not <u>poss</u>ible that
4		there is a strong <u>arg</u>ument that m<u>a</u>king
5		yourself unemployed to c<u>a</u>re fo::r .h a
6		baby at h<u>o:</u>me, .h so your wife can then
7		become the w<u>a</u>ge earner is not a- <u>good</u>
8		enough reason fuh bailing out of the job

```
9                you've already got.=
10    E:         =Ri:ght but what I'm, what I'm thinkin' is
11               in anybody's ca:se, (.) if (.) the husband
12               (.) is (.) a mechanic, earnin' ninety
13               pounds a week,
14    H:         (R)ight,=
15    E:         =and the wife, is a professional (.) bank
16               (0.3) cashier or teller or summat like
17               that or a .hh a video operator or summin
18               like that earnin' .hh e:r two 'undred
19               pounds a week, .hh then, a:ll that's gotta
20               be weighed up. in makin' these choices.
```

In lines 3–9 the host asks non-naive questions which make even more explicit reference to the caller's case. In response, the expert more explicitly shifts into the generalizing mode, with phrases like 'in anybody's ca:se' (line 11); and correspondingly by speaking of husbands and wives in terms of general, possible occupational categories such as 'mechanic', 'bank cashier', or 'video operator'.

By means of proxy questioning, then, the expert and the host again collaborate in a particular way to produce advice whose relevance shifts between the caller at hand and a wider, indeed indeterminate constituency made up of any audience members for whom that information may be of use.

Concluding auxiliary advice-giving episodes

The principal focus so far has been on strategies by which advice is generalized 'outwards', towards the 'public' dimensions of advice talk on call-in radio. It is worth pointing out however that, as these excursions into audience-oriented auxiliary advice proceed, a recognition of the 'personal' dimension represented by the caller at hand either remains in play, or at some stage is brought back into play. This point can be illustrated by looking at the closing stages of some of these collaborative excursions into auxiliary advice. As the following extracts show, after a spate of advice designed to target a wider constituency than the caller at hand, the topic of the talk gets brought back explicitly to the concerns with which the call was begun.

In extracts (9) (from the 'disablement benefit' call) and (10) (from the 'milk tokens' call), the host seeks to end the call by inviting the expert to provide specific answers to the callers' questions:

(9) RVS 'Disablement benefit'

```
1     E:         Because it is (.) up fuh grabs I mean it
2                is important that everybody gets their say.
```

```
3     H:    .pt Thee specific a:nswer to Betty's
4           question though is that you can't tell
5           her, [yet until there are some published=
6     E:         [.h khhrm
7     H:    =figures.=
8     E:    =Well I can tell Betty that at the moment
9           her mobility allowance and non-contributory
10          invalidity pension, are not under review in
11          this Green Paper.
12    H:    Er let's go to ((next caller))
```

(10) **RVS 'Milk tokens'**
```
1     E:    . . . a pint a day fer:: each one in the
2           category so it it comes to:: er one
3           pou:::nd seventy five one pound seventy.
4     H:    Righ[t.
5     E:        [E::r no one pound sixty.
6     H:    And ar[e you: de- ] er are you saying=
7     E:          [(  ) a pint.]
8     H:    =that it does sound like Jane is entitled
9           to milk tokens?
10    E:    Yes if she's on supplementary benefit with
11          children under fi:ve then there should be
12          milk tokens payable.=
13    H:    =Oka:y. And get in touch with the D.H.S.S
14          and as:k for the twenty one weeks u-that
15          she's missed, in ca:sh.=It's coming up to
16          news weather and travel time. . .
```

In both cases, an auxiliary advice-giving excursion is concluded by means of the host returning the talk to its originating question. The host names the caller, and asks the expert to state in straightforward terms his advice on their particular case. Following this, situated in his institutional role as 'host' he moves the show on to the next caller (extract 9) or to a scheduled news bulletin (extract 10).

In extract (11), taken from the 'giving up work to look after baby' call, the host ends the excursion by asking the caller herself whether she has found the advice helpful:

(11) **RVS 'Quitting work'**
```
1     E:    That's why you need to 'ave a look at it
2           from an o:verview an' add up the wages,
3           .hh that you're gonna lo:se an- an' an'
4           what 'ave yuh.
```

5   H: D'you find that helpful Margery.
6   C: .h Yes. yi-es I do thank you.

The fact that the caller here is invited to comment on the helpfulness of the advice shows that callers in fact can remain on the line throughout the kinds of auxiliary advice-giving and proxy questioning sequences discussed in previous sections. This in turn suggests that callers may effectively comply with these procedures and the shifts in the participation framework which they involve by remaining silent as the auxiliary advice is conveyed.

These extracts provide a further sense of the modulated character of advice talk on call-in radio: the way in which the talk is designed to address both the specific issue raised by the caller, and more general themes and issues sparked off by the original question. It is not just that callers' questions are used as springboards for informing a wider constituency, so that excursions into auxiliary advice have no limits. Rather, those excursions appear to be 'anchored' in some way to the concerns expressed by the caller, so that part of the work oriented to by the host and the expert involves returning the talk to, and formulating its relevance for, the individual situation of the caller.

This chapter has analysed the management of expertise in advice-giving in a specific, 'public' context: calls to a radio advice line. Instead of being a two-way dialogue between an advice-seeker and an advice-giver, advice talk on call-in radio has a more complex communicative framework in which four categories of participant are involved: the caller (advice-seeker), the expert (advice-giver), the studio host (professional broadcaster) and the 'overhearing' audience. I have considered some ways in which the latter two participant categories (host and audience) can become involved in what might be termed the 'main track' activity of calls: that of providing advice on social welfare matters. With respect to that activity, clearly the two central participants are the caller, who is seeking the advice; and the expert, whose job it is to provide the advice. But as I have shown, there are specific ways in which the basic participation framework of the call can be modulated so that host and audience become situated as participants within the main track advice-giving activity.

The features discussed in this chapter represent systematic ways in which the **recipient design** of talk reveals participants' orientations to the 'institutional' context of their interaction. As noted in previous chapters, for conversation analysis it is not enough simply to assert the relevance of a particular context and then read off its effects in the organization of the discourse. Rather, it is necessary to explicate the ways in which 'the parties, singly and together, select and display in their conduct which of the indefinitely many aspects of context they are making relevant, or invoking, for the immediate moment' (Schegloff, 1987: 219). In other words we need to look for the ways that institutional contexts of interaction are 'joint achievements' brought about by participants, through the details of their interaction, on a moment by moment basis. In this respect, by concentrating on shifts in the address orientation and participation framework within calls, we have discovered something of the joint achievement of the radio advice call-in as a 'public', institutional discourse context.

Further reading

Crisell, A. (1994) *Understanding Radio*. London: Routledge.

Crow, B. (1986) Conversational pragmatics in television talk: The discourse of *Good Sex*. *Media, Culture and Society*, 8: 457–84.

Jefferson, G. and Lee, J.R.E. (1981) The rejection of advice: Managing the problematic convergence of a 'troubles telling' and a 'service encounter'. *Journal of Pragmatics*, 5: 399–422.

Silverman, D. (1996) *Discourses of Counselling*. London: Sage.

Note

1 The host in this chapter's data is, like the expert, male.

CASE STUDIES PART III:
BROADCASTERS AND POLITICIANS

7

NEWS INTERVIEWS: JOURNALISTS AND POLITICIANS ON THE AIR

One of the most significant environments in which broadcasters operate is that of the news. Broadcast news bulletins occupy a major swathe of daily airtime, and have done so since the very earliest days of radio and television. From the point of view of this book, the first important thing about such bulletins is that they are occasions of talk: some of it **monologic**, as when a news reader delivers headlines and leads direct to camera (or microphone in the case of radio); but much of it in the form of social interaction, whether between studio journalist and outside correspondent via live link, between two or more newscasters in the studio, or between broadcast journalists and public figures or other newsworthy actors in the context of a news interview.

Increasingly, the more interactive formats for broadcast news talk are coming to outweigh the monologic contributions of the standard newsreader, or 'anchor'. Key agenda-setting news broadcasts such as BBC radio's *Today* programme or BBC television's *Newsnight* routinely consist of a series of interviews, each prefaced with little more than a brief contextualizing statement from one of the anchors. In the US, long-running high-profile shows such as ABC's *Nightline* have similarly been organized around a series of live interviews. Indeed, even in the case of standard news bulletin broadcasts, recent years have seen a significant growth in the 'dual anchor' format, such that the newsreader's task itself becomes situated within a broader context of interactional talk.

The result of this is that broadcast news messages are increasingly being generated in and through the production of talk-in-interaction. This encourages us to examine news talk not just in terms of its role in the manufacture of news (Cohen and Young, 1973), but also in terms of the structures of interaction in which news talk takes place, and which shape and constrain the very content of news messages (Clayman and Heritage, 2002). As Heritage, Clayman and Zimmerman (1988: 79–80) put it:

The consistent growth in the use of social interaction as a medium through which the news is presented suggests that it has become increasingly unrealistic to analyse the structure and content of news messages independent of the interactional medium within which they are generated. For, although the medium may not be the message, the interactional structures through which broadcast news is conveyed must necessarily contribute to the content and appearance of news messages.

This chapter focuses on one particular aspect of news talk on radio and television: the news interview, which as noted plays a central part in a number of long-running and agenda-setting news programmes. Broadcast news interviews are a specific genre of media talk in which, on the most basic level, journalists and individuals associated with the news of the day – primarily, but not exclusively, politicians and other public figures – engage in question-answer exchanges varying in length from less than a minute to ten minutes or more. However, at another level they are also important arenas in which the mediatization of politics and political issues takes place. Within the formal exchange of question and answer between interviewer and interviewee, a great deal may be going on in terms of the pursuit of competing agendas, as interviewers attempt to pin down politicians in the public interest while politicians attempt to communicate their own 'spin' on the issue.

Beginning from this standpoint, the present chapter is organized around two key questions. First, how do journalists seek to challenge politicians and other figures in the news while maintaining a suitably neutral journalistic stance? Second, the related question of how politicians and other public figures may pursue their own agendas within the interview occasion; in other words the ways that interviewees go along with, evade or challenge the questions put to them by news interviewers.

Aspects of news interview conduct

In Chapter 2 I described news interviews as an example of a formal institutional speech exchange system. In formal systems, 'the institutional character of the inter-action is embodied first and foremost in its *form* – most notably in turn-taking systems which depart substantially from the way in which turn-taking is managed in conversation' (Heritage and Greatbatch, 1991: 95). The basic turn-taking system for news interviews is fairly straightforwardly described as a chain of *question-answer* sequences in which the participants orient to the specialized nature of their talk by restricting themselves to one or other of these turn-types according to their interactional role (that is interviewers ask questions, while interviewees – ideally, at least – answer those questions).

Of course, far more is going on in the question-answer sequences of any interview than this rather barren description implies. For one thing, in line with CA's opposition to the 'container' model of institutional contexts, it should be emphasized that coparticipants are not somehow being caused to produce their talk in such restricted ways by virtue of external constraints emanating from the context. Rather, they actively co-operate to produce the specialized features of that context by consciously organizing their conduct according to their understanding of the normative conventions of the interview. This means that either participant could, if he or she so chose, produce other kinds of turn at any point – though as we see below, in such circumstances that participant may be sanctioned by the other speaker for refusing to co-operate in maintaining the 'interview setting'.

Occasionally the fact that the interview is produced via norms rather than external constraints comes to the surface, as in the following example in which the interviewee begins accusing the interviewer of misrepresenting him in a previous broadcast and demands to know why, while the interviewer overtly requests that the interviewee observe the norms by allowing him to play the 'interviewer' role itself, that is by asking questions (in all data examples in this chapter, interviewers are denoted by IR and interviewees by IE):

(1) Greatbatch, 1988: 421–2

```
1       IE:    despite the fact there were fou:r major factories
2              that you knew about,=despite the fact there was a two
3              hundred and thirty million capital investment programme
4              that you knew about,=.hhh that we dealt in companies you
5              stated and restated toda::y, .hhh despite the fact that
6              ninety one per cent of our companies are still there:,=
7              and only the marginal ones which you knew were sold, .hhh
8              and you e:ven mislead people by suggesting for instance
9              that we owned the Parisian publishing house Brooke.
10→            Why.=
11      IR:    =s-s-s-Sir James I['m so sorry (    ) I'm so s-
12      IE:                      [No,=I'm asking a question now.=
13→     IR:    =It's more conventional in these programmes [fo:r
14      IE:                                                 [Well I
15             don't mind ab[out  convention. = ]I'm asking you why
16→     IR:                 [me to ask questions,]
17             (.)
18      IE:    you distorted those facts.
```

Here, we see that the interviewer appeals to the 'convention' that he should ask the questions, while the interviewee explicitly disregards that convention and persists in attempting to ask a question of his own. Such breakdowns in the normative conduct of the news interview are rare (though we look in more detail at another case later in this chapter), but their occurrence brings to the surface the extent to which the characteristic question-answer structure of the interview is an active accomplishment of the participants rather than a pre-existing factor that constrains their behaviour.

There are some specific features of the news interview question-answer sequence. In many types of question-answer sequence, in ordinary conversation as well as institutional settings such as classroom teaching (McHoul, 1978), there occurs a third position slot in which the questioner acknowledges or evaluates the answer. Thus, in standard information-seeking questions, we may find the sequence *question-answer-acknowledgement*, as in the following example:

(2) **Ordinary conversation**
1   Nancy: How's yer <u>foot</u>.
2   Edna: Oh it's healing beautif'lly.
3→ Nancy: <u>Goo::d</u>.

Similarly, in the kind of knowledge-testing questions asked by teachers we may find the sequence *question-answer-evaluation*, as in:

(3) **Classroom interaction**
1   Teacher: Can you tell me why do you eat all that food.
2   Yes.
3   Pupil: To keep you strong.
4→ Teacher: To keep you strong. Yes. To keep you strong.

In news interviews, by contrast, there is generally no third turn acknowledgement or evaluation; rather, the standard sequence is *question-answer-next question-answer . . .* and so on. (One exception to this question-answer chaining norm, the case of *question-answer-formulation*, is discussed below.) The general avoidance of third-position acknowledgements and evaluations thus acts as one of a number of noteworthy features of the question-answer chaining sequence that is specific to news interviews.

It is also the case that news interviewers refrain from producing verbal reactions *during* an interviewee's turn. In ordinary conversation it is commonplace to find the recipients of lengthy utterances, such as those in which one speaker recounts some 'news' they have to tell, punctuating the talk with utterances such as 'uh huh', 'right', 'yeah', 'oh really?' and so on. Such items do the work of situating their producer as the primary, intended and attentive recipient of the talk being produced by an interlocutor (Schegloff, 1982). Consider the following conversational example, where one speaker recounts some news about having been insulted by a mutual acquaintance, 'Mister R':

(4) **Holt:Xmas 85**
1   Lesley: I'm br<u>oi</u>ling about something hhhheh[h<u>e</u>h .hhhh
2   Joyce: [Wh<u>a</u>::t.
3   Lesley: Well t<u>hat</u> s<u>a</u>:le. (0.2) At- <u>a</u>t (.) the vicarage.

4		(0.6)
5→	Joyce:	Oh ye-:s,
6		(0.6)
7	Lesley:	u (.) ihYour friend 'n mi:ne was the:re
8		(0.2)
9	Joyce:	(h[h hh)
10	Lesley:	[mMister:, R:,
11→	Joyce:	Oh y(h)es, (hm hm)
12		(0.4)
13	Lesley:	And em:. p we (.) really didn't have a lot'v cha:nge
14		that (.) day becuz we'd been to Bath 'n we'd been:
15		Christmas shoppin:g, (0.5) but we thought we'd better
16		go along t'th' sale 'n do what we could, (0.2) we
17		hadn't got a lot (.) of s:e- ready cash t'spe:nd.
18		(0.6)
19	Lesley:	In any case we thought th' things were very
20		expensive.
21→	Joyce:	Oh did you.
22		(0.9)
23	Lesley:	AND uh we were looking round the sta:lls 'n poking
24		about 'n he came up t' me 'n he said Oh: hhello
25		Lesley, (.) still trying to buy something f'nothing,
26	Lesley:	.tch!. hh[hahhhhhhh!
27→	Joyce:	[.hhoohhhh!
28		(0.8)
29→	Joyce:	Oo[: : : [: L e s l e y]
30	Lesley:	[OO:. [ehh heh heh]
31		(0.2)
32	Joyce:	I:s[n 't] [he
33	Lesley:	[What] do y[ou sa:y.
34		(0.3)
35	Joyce:	Oh isn't he drea:dful.
36	Lesley:	eYe::s.
37		(0.6)
38	Joyce:	What'n aw::ful ma:[::n
39	Lesley:	[Ehh heh heh heh
40	Joyce:	Oh honestly. (.) I cannot stand the man it's [just-
41	Lesley:	[I
42		thought well I'm goin t' tell Joyce that,

Four points can be noted about this extract from an ordinary telephone conversation that serve to distinguish its 'news-telling' sharply from the organization of news-telling in interviews. First, the way in which the telling of Lesley's news is introduced as a topic she has been waiting to talk about, and hence potentially represented a reason for her phone call to Joyce in the first place: 'I'm broiling about something,' (line 1). Second, the frequent use of receipt items by Joyce, the story's recipient (arrowed lines). These are designed not only to 'punctuate' the telling but to 'display attention' on Joyce's part. They also act as signals that Joyce is not intending to compete for a turn of her own, but is letting Lesley continue with her telling. Third, the way in which the telling is *responded* to on its completion. In lines 26–30 we find exaggerated displays of 'outrage' in which the two women closely mirror one another in producing, first, sharp intakes of breath (lines 26 and 27), then loud 'Ooo's as they react to the insult ('Mr R' has effectively accused Lesley of bargain hunting in a charity sale). Finally, the way in which the telling is formulated as having been for this particular recipient all along, as Lesley concludes by saying: 'I thought [at the time] well I'm goin t' tell Joyce that' (lines 41–2).

On each of these four dimensions, the production and reception of talk in news interviews is fundamentally different:

1 In news interviews it is not the teller who introduces the news. Newsworthy items are defined by the news organization itself. Moreover, because the conventional format of interviews is organized according to the question-answer sequence, no news can in fact be discussed until the interviewer has asked the first question, thereby 'introducing' the interviewee's topic.
2 Interviewers generally refrain from punctuating the interviewee's talk with items such as 'Mm hm' and 'Oh yes'. The function of such items in conversation is to mark a piece of talk as 'news' *for its recipient*: that is, the person who is being talked to. In broadcast news, the interviewer is not in fact the primary recipient of the interviewee's talk. Although the interviewer may be the direct addressee, the purpose of the interview is to produce talk for the 'overhearing' audience.
3 Interviewers refrain from explicitly *reacting* to the interviewee's talk; especially in the exaggerated kinds of ways exemplified in Extract (4). As noted, interviewers tend to move directly from the interviewee's answer to a next question. In part this has to do with the fact that interviewers orient to an officially 'neutral' stance when talking to interviewees. This is an issue I return to presently.
4 Finally, it is not the case that interviewees display that the talk they produce was designed from the outset for 'this particular hearer'. Despite what Fairclough (1995) describes as the increasing 'conversationalization' of broadcast political discourse, we do not find even modern politicians such as Tony Blair saying things such as, 'I thought, I must tell Jeremy Paxman that' during a *Newsnight* interview.

As a result of these factors, news interviewers and interviewees effectively preserve a sense in which it is the audience, rather than themselves, who are the primary recipients of their talk. As Heritage (1985: 100) summarizes it, the withholding of acknowledgements, evaluations, continuers and other reactions is significant in the design of talk for an overhearing audience for two main reasons:

First, their production would identify prior talk as news for questioners (who are usually fully briefed beforehand or may be required to appear so) rather than the overhearing audience . . . for whom it is, putatively, news. Second, by their production of these receipt objects . . . questioners identify themselves as the primary recipients of the talk they elicit [and] audiences could . . . come to view themselves as literally the overhearers of colloquies that, rather than being produced for them, were being produced and treated as private.

'Neutralism' and challenging questions

A further specific feature of news interview exchanges is related to the key issue of 'neutrality' on the part of journalists. News interviewers may act as questioners, but they also, as Gaye Tuchman (1978) showed in an analysis of news reporting practices, set great store by their professional ethos of neutrality and objectivism. That is, journalists see it as their role to present a 'balanced' account of events and in the process avoid taking up positions that can be heard as partial, either on their own part or in their capacity as representatives of news organizations. However, Steven Clayman (1988) and other conversation analysts have revealed the ways that in the interview, broadcast journalists find means of asking questions that are formally neutral but which nevertheless challenge interviewees.

For this reason, Clayman (1992) stresses that we should prefer the term 'neutralism' over 'neutrality' in discussions of news interview talk. While 'neutrality' implies that the interviewer *is*, somehow, a neutral conduit using questions to extract relevant information from interviewees (an interpretation often favoured by news professionals themselves), 'neutralism' foregrounds the fact that news interviewers actually *achieve* the status of 'being neutral' through a set of specialized discourse practices (see also Greatbatch, 1998).

One such practice is the 'footing shift'. Goffman (1981) used the concept of footing to describe the varying ways in which speakers are able to take up positions of proximity or distance with respect to the sentiments expressed in an utterance. Distinguishing between the *animator* (the producer of the utterance), the *author* (the person whose words are actually being uttered) and the *principal* (the person whose viewpoint, stance, belief, etcetera, the utterance expresses), Goffman noted that at any moment in talk, the animator can exhibit differing degrees of authorship and principalship regarding the words he or she is speaking.

Clayman (1992) adopted this concept to examine how broadcast news interviewers use footing shifts in order to give the appearance of formal neutrality. The following examples illustrate.

(5) **Clayman, 1992: 169**
1   IR: Senator, (0.5) uh: <u>Pre</u>sident Reagan's elected

```
2              thirteen months ago: an enormous landslide. (0.8)
3→             It is s::aid that his programs are in trouble,
4              though he seems to be terribly popular with
5              the American people. (0.6)
6→             It is said by some people at thuh White House
7              we could get those programs through if only we
8              ha:d perhaps more: .hh effective leadership
9              on on thuh hill an' I [suppose] indirectly=
10    IE:                        [hhhheh ]
11    IR:      =that might (0.5) relate t'you as well:. (0.6)
12             Uh what d'you think thuh problem is really.
13→            is=it (0.2) thuh leadership as it might be
14             claimed up on thuh hill, er is it thuh
15             programs themselves.
```

Here, the interviewer begins by stating a statistical fact about President Reagan's election victory (lines 1–2), and at that point he takes up the footing of animator, author and principal. But when he comes to more controversial issues (challenging the effectiveness of the President's programmes and his leadership), he shifts footing so that he is no longer author, and principalship becomes ambivalent (line 3 and line 6). In other words, he *redistributes authorship* for the position that lies behind his eventual question. Note that even when the question gets asked (lines 13–15), after the statement-formulated preamble, the footing shift is sustained: 'the leadership **as it might be claimed** up on the hill . . .'.

The next extract shows how interviewers may repair their turns in order to insert a footing shift which turns the utterance from one in which they begin by expressing an opinion, to one where that opinion is attributed to others.

(6) Clayman, 1992: 171

```
1     IR:      How d'you sum up thuh me:ssage. that this
2              decision is sending to thuh Soviets?
3     IE:      .hhh Well as I started- to say:: it is ay- one
4              of: warning an' opportunity. Thuh warning
5              is (.) you'd better comply: to arms control::
6              agreements if arms control is going to have
7              any chance of succeeding in thuh future.
8              Unilateral compliance by thuh United States
9              just not in thuh works . . .
((Some lines omitted))
10→   IR:      But isn't this- uh::: critics uh on thuh
11             conservative- side of thuh political argument
12             have argued thet this is::. abiding by thuh
```

```
13            treaty is:. unilateral (.) observance (.)
14            uh:: or compliance. (.) by thuh United States.
```

Having begun, in line 10, to ask a question the wording of which heavily implies that he will be both author and principal of the view behind the question (e.g., 'Isn't this [actually unilateral observance by the United States]?'), the interviewer breaks off and then initiates self-repair in order, once again, to redistribute authorship, this time to 'critics . . . on thuh conservative- side'.

Clayman's (1992) argument is that the use of footing shifts enables the interviewer to fulfil two professional tasks simultaneously: to be adversarial, while remaining formally neutral. Interviewers routinely use footing shifts when they want to put forward provocative viewpoints for discussion, when they want to counter an interviewee and put the other side of an argument, or when they want to foster disagreement among interviewees on panel programmes. If they did any of these things while retaining a footing of animator, author and principal, they would inevitably be taking up positions on these issues. With the footing shift, they can avoid this.

Another technique for producing talk that is critical and challenging towards interviewees, and which is also bound up with the production of talk for an overhearing audience, is that of 'formulating' the gist or upshot of the interviewee's remarks, usually in pursuit of some controversial or newsworthy aspect. Heritage (1985: 100) describes the practice of formulating as:

> summarizing, glossing, or developing the gist of an informant's earlier statements. Although it is relatively rare in conversation, it is common in institutionalised, audience-directed interaction [where it] is most commonly undertaken by questioners.

In Heritage's (1985) study of formulations in news interviews, he found that the practice could be used both in a relatively benign, summarizing role ('cooperative recyclings'), and also as a means by which the interviewer seeks to evaluate or criticize the interviewee's remarks ('inferentially elaborative probes'). There are at least two aspects to why formulations are so frequently utilized by interviewers. One is that the practice of summarizing or glossing can act as a means of packaging or repackaging the central point made in an interviewee's turn for the benefit of the overhearing audience. The other is that the same practice can also be used to construct a stronger or more contentious version of the interviewee's stated position. In this, the interviewer can be seen to be challenging the interviewee but, once again, without overtly taking up a position in his or her own right.

Extracts (7) and (8) show examples of the cooperative type of formulation:

(7) WAO: King of Wales
```
1    IR:      Would you be happy to see Prince Charles become King of
2             Wales?
```

3	IE:	heh Well I:(h) cou(h)d(h)n' I- you know I just couldn't
4		care tup<u>pe</u>nce who comes King and who don't like.
5		(0.5)
6→	IR:	You don't think it makes any difference to you.
7	IE:	N<u>o</u>::=Not one bit. (.) Not one bit.

(8) WAO: Common Agricultural Policy

1	IE:	I'm all for having a common agricultural policy, (0.6)
2		but I think it's ab<u>surd</u> to suggest that decisions of
3		(.) im<u>men</u>se economic magnitude .hhh should be taken
4		enti<u>:re</u>ly by .hh (.) the ministers who are (.) most
5		int'rested in one particular segment of the
6		community.=I wouldn't want Ministers d-Defence
7		to take all the decisions on de<u>fen</u>ce and I wouldn't
8		want Ministers of .hhhh of Edu<u>ca</u>tion to take all
9		the decisions on education.=
10→	IR:	=.hhh So you're suggesting there that the <u>fa</u>rm
11		ministers shouldn't decide all this entirely amongst
12		thems<u>e</u>lves that it should be .hhh <u>spread</u> across
13		the board amongst all ministers.
14	IE:	Exactly.=I'm s<u>ay</u>ing that one m<u>u</u>st find some way
15		of (.) of bringing <u>o</u>ther responsibilities (.)
16		particularly those representing the t<u>a</u>x payer
17		and the cons<u>u</u>mer as well as the farmer .hhh much
18		more into the picture.

In each case the interviewer produces a turn (arrowed) which formulates the interviewee's immediately prior answer. The formulations are 'cooperative' in the sense that
they seek to clarify the viewpoint expressed in the answer, possibly for the benefit of the
overhearing audience. In extract (7), IE's 'I just couldn't care tup<u>pe</u>nce who comes King
and who don't like' is expressed in colloquial terms (this being a 'vox pop' in which the
interviewer is asking the views of ordinary people in the street); the IR's formulation
recasts the same view in more 'standard' English: 'You don't think it makes any difference to you'. In (8), IE has given a slightly convoluted answer framed largely in terms of
what he 'wouldn't want' to see. IR's formulation restates that view in terms of what the
IE seems to be arguing *should* happen rather than what should not: that decisions on
agricultural policy should be '<u>spread</u> across the board amongst all ministers'.

These formulations thus seem to be involved in 'packaging' an interviewee's
response in ways that are potentially more easily graspable by an overhearing audience.
A further point to note about them is that in the turn following the formulation,
interviewees respond by agreeing with the interpretation offered. A general feature of
formulations is that they make available in the next turn a slot in which the recipient

can either agree with, disagree with, or otherwise react to the interpretation offered by the formulator. The agreements in these cases add to the sense in which these formulations are 'cooperative'.

A slightly more contentious case is provided in extract (9), in which the interviewee is a woman who has recently won a 'slimmer of the year' competition. At this point she is describing the motivations behind her attempts to lose weight:

(9) WAO: Slimmer of the year

1	IE:	You have a she:ll (1.2) that for so long protects
2		you. (0.7) But sometimes: things creep through the
3		shell and (.) then you become really aware of (.) of
4		'ow awful y'feel. .hhh I never _ever_ felt my age or
5		looked my age,=I was always (.) _old_er,=people always
6		t_oo_k me for older. .hhhh And when I was at college
7		I think I looked a ma:tronly _fifty_. .hh And (.) I
8		was compl_e_tely alone one weekend and I got to this
9		stage where I almost jumped in the river(hh).=I just
10		felt life wasn't worth it any mo:re,=it hadn't
11		an_y_thing to offer (.) .hhhh and if this was living
12		I had had enough.
13→	IR:	You _rea_lly were prepared to commit suicide because
14		you were a b_i_g _fa_tty.
15	IE:	Yes, cuz I- I (.) just didn't see anything in life
16		that I had to look forward to . . .

Once again the formulation constructs and maintains a specific 'reading' of the IE's account, and invites IE to assent to that reading. But while the IE subsequently goes along with the formulation (lines 15–16), it is actually less cooperative than the previous examples in the sense that it reads slightly more into the interviewee's talk and thus proposes a stronger, or upgraded, interpretation. Note, for instance, that while the slimmer refers to never feeling her age and looking a matronly 50, the interviewer formulates this in terms of her being 'a b_i_g _fa_tty'. Second, notice also that her statement that 'I almost jumped in the river(hh)' is re-referenced as being 'prepared to commit suicide'. The slight laughter in the interviewee's utterance, indicated by the h's at the end of 'river(hh)', conveys the impression that she is downgrading the seriousness of this, and possibly even using the phrase as a figurative expression merely to indicate how 'low' she felt at that time. In any case, the phrase 'commit suicide' which appears in the formulation is not present in the interviewee's turn. A third point to note is that the causal connection between the two (being overweight and being 'prepared to commit suicide') is not made explicit in the IE's account, but is made absolutely explicit in the formulation ('You _rea_lly were prepared to commit suicide **because** you were a b_i_g _fa_tty').

Formulations can therefore be used to both simplify and upgrade the version of events presented in an interviewee's turn. This leads to the second major type of formulation, the inferentially elaborative probe, in which interviewers 'restate the interviewee's position by making overt reference to what might be treated as implicated or presupposed by that position' (Heritage, 1985: 110).

The following extract provides two illustrations of this:

(10) TVN: Tea

```
1      IE:     What in fact happened was that in the course of last
2              year, .hh the price went up really very sharply,. hhh
3              and uh the blenders did take advantage of this: uh
4              to obviously to raise their prices to retailers. (0.7)
5              .hhh They haven't been so quick in reducing their
6              prices when the world market prices come down. (0.3)
7              .hh And so this means that price in the sh- the
8              prices in the shops have stayed up .hh really rather
9              higher than we'd like to see them.
10             (0.7)
11→    IR:     So you- you're really accusing them of profiteering.
12     IE:     .hhh No they're in business to make money that's
13             perfectly sensible.=We're also saying that uh: .hh
14             it's not a trade which is competitive as we would
15             like it.=There're four (0.2) blenders which have
16             together eighty five percent of the market .hhh
17             and uh we're not saying that they (.) move in
18             concert or anything like that but we'd like the
19             trade to be a bit more competitive.=
20→    IR:     =But you're giving them: a heavy instruction (.) as
21             it were to (.) to reduce their prices.
22     IE:     .hh What we're saying is we think that prices
23             could come down without the blenders losing their
24             profit margins
```

The interviewee here is the Chairman of the Price Commission, who is being interviewed about the Commission's report on tea prices. Looking at the two arrowed IR turns (lines 11 and 20), what we find is an emergent dispute over what IE can be taken as 'really saying'. In line 11, for instance, the interviewer formulates the long turn in lines 1–9 as 'really accusing [the blenders] of profiteering'. Since the interviewee had not himself used the term 'profiteering', this formulation can be described as inferentially elaborating a claim proposed to be implicit in IE's remarks.

As noted, a central sequential feature of formulations is that they make relevant in the next turn a response in which a recipient either agrees or disagrees with the version being put forward. In this case, IE disagrees with the 'profiteering' formulation (line 12) and quickly moves on to address another issue, lack of competitiveness. In line 20, the interviewer comes back in to formulate these remarks, again using much stronger terms than the interviewee; and once again (in lines 22–24), IE puts forward a weaker version of his argument than the 'heavy instruction . . . to reduce prices' referred to in the formulation.

We thus find a form of dispute in which, while not taking up a position in his own right (and therefore maintaining the professional journalistic stance of objectivity) the news interviewer nonetheless uses his ability to formulate the gist or upshot of the interviewee's remarks to attempt to unpack some underlying agenda proposedly at work in them. Although Heritage (1985) argues that formulations are neutral in the sense that they avoid commenting on or making assessments of the content of a prior turn, he nevertheless acknowledges that formulations can 'make something more of [a topic] than was originally presented in the . . . prior turn' (Heritage, 1985: 101). In other words, formulations are in fact rarely entirely neutral; rather, they act as candidate *re-presentations* of what an interlocutor can be taken as having said, or meant. Such candidate re-presentations are selective, in that they focus on a particular element of the prior talk and preserve that element as the topic for further talk. They can also be driven by an underlying agenda on their producer's part, which in turn can be cooperative, uncooperative or openly argumentative. They open a sequential slot in which the interlocutor may, in the next turn, accept, reject or otherwise respond to the formulation; but whatever the response, the formulation itself reveals its producer not as a neutral conduit but an active interpreter of the preceding talk.

Formulations are more common in forms of institutional interaction than in mundane conversation (Heritage, 1985). But this is not just a matter of statistical frequency. In the examples discussed above, the ability to formulate is bound up with the institutional work being undertaken via the dialogue. In a news interview it is the interviewee's role to answer questions and challenges put to him or her by a professional interviewer, who acts on behalf of the general public interest but whose own view ideally plays no part in the exchange (Clayman, 1988). The practice of formulating enables the interviewer to issue challenges or seek clarifications while 'avoiding the adoption of an overt or official position with respect to the interviewee's statements or arguments' (Heritage, 1985: 114).

Interviewees are therefore 'on the line' in these exchanges: it is their views, opinions and answers that are at the heart of the talk. For this reason, interviewers are structurally positioned to elicit talk that is 'on the record': talk in which it is as clear as possible what the interviewee is 'really saying'. There is also the issue, of course, that interviewers are broadcasters, and may be systematically oriented to the importance of 'clarifying' their interlocutor's talk for the benefit of the overhearing audience. Formulations, as candidate summaries, promptings, focusings, recyclings and the like, are particularly useful in the pursuit of these institutional aims.

Controversy and news interviews

We can now move on to look at how news interviews – particularly political interviews, interviews with political figures – can take on their own 'political' dimensions. By that I mean two things: (1) The ways in which the interview can be 'political' in the sense that both parties (IR and IE) are attempting to pursue their own interests, even if those turn out to be in conflict. (2) The ways in which interviews – or more precisely, what is said in them – become part of the broader political process as the language of an interview is further mediated by press and broadcasting news and projected outwards into the public sphere.

In an important sense, the answers that politicians give to interviewers' questions can be potentially dangerous for the politician. This is because the political interview is not only a mediated phenomenon in its own right – that is, a form of interaction that takes place in the public domain, mediated by radio, TV or newspapers. Sometimes what happens in an interview becomes 'newsworthy' itself, and so takes on a mediatized life of its own. Examples of this are when interviews become confrontational or argumentative; or when the interviewee walks out. This is something I come back to in the final section of this chapter.

Another form of danger that politicians face in media interviews is that of producing a 'gaffe'. This is a statement produced during an interview which may be ill-advised or, to use the language of contemporary media politics, 'off-message', but which the media subsequently pick up on and turn into a reportable phenomenon. In recent times there have been high-profile gaffes such as the statement (actually made in an e-mail but turned nonetheless into a subject of intense media scrutiny) by government communications officer Jo Moore that the events of 11 September 2001 represented 'a good day for burying bad news' – that is, for releasing stories that reflected negatively on the government because they would pass unnoticed in comparison to the magnitude of the terrorist attacks on the World Trade Center. The furore created around this statement led to a press campaign of vilification against Jo Moore and ultimately, following a later incident in which she was incorrectly accused of seeking to 'bury' more bad news, to her resignation.

In other situations, the politician may feel that he or she is choosing their words very carefully – particularly if the issue in question is a controversial one – but the wider media reportage can construct a reading of those words that is quite different from what was originally intended. This is, on the face of it, one good reason why politicians are notoriously *evasive* when it comes to answering interviewers' questions (Harris, 1991). It shows how the talk of political interviews is not just relevant within the interview setting itself – it also takes on a significance in the wider public sphere in which the media operate. The meanings and the upshots of what someone says in a political interview can extend a long way beyond their control (Garton, Montgomery and Tolson, 1991).

News interviews can also generate controversy by virtue of the way they are conducted. For example, on those rare occasions when an interviewee walks out on a live broadcast interview, so that the walking-out therefore goes out on air, that episode becomes newsworthy in itself. As Clayman (1989) has shown, it is generally the news interviewer who takes it as their role to bring interviews to a close. This is partly because interviewers, as the producers of questions, are in overall control not just of which topics can legitimately be raised during the interview (that is, interviewees who wish to raise their own topics have to do special kinds of work to accomplish that, potentially even moving outside the conventions of the interview as we saw with extract 1 earlier in the chapter); but also of what will act as the 'last question' on any given topic. Interviewers also, by virtue of their organizational role as agents of the broadcasting company, need to ensure that the interview is brought to a 'punctual' close: that is, one that falls in line with the time schedule set by the programme's producers.

Thus, when interviewees seek to bring the interview to a close, invariably it is unexpected and, in general, the only avenue open to them to do so is by physically removing themselves from the scene of the interview. Interviewee terminations therefore tend to be far more newsworthy than anything said in interviews themselves, as happened with the following famous example from British television in the 1980s:

(12) **NR: 1982**

```
1       IR:     But why should the public on this issue:: .hh as
2               regards the future of the Royal Navy believe you=a
3               transient .hhh er here toda:y and. hh if I may say
4               so gone tomorro:w politician [rather than] a senior=
5       IE:                                 [(          )]
6       IR:     =officer of many years [experience,]
7→      IE:                            [I'm sorry  ] I'm I'm fed up
8               with this interview really ((standing, removes
9               microphone from tie, throws it down and walks off
10              camera))
11      IR:     Thank you Mister Nott.
```

In this particular instance, a Minister of Defence who has recently announced his intention to retire from politics is subject to an aggressive line of questioning from the interviewer. The extract shows a particularly insulting question, in which the Minister is described as a 'here toda:y and .hh if I may say so gone tomorro:w politician', to which he responds by withdrawing bodily from the interview. As David Greatbatch (1988: 427) points out in a discussion of this case:

The extent to which [it] was deemed to be newsworthy was reflected in its inclusion in BBC Television's review of its news and current affairs coverage in 1982. Moreover, in addition to being widely reported and discussed by newspaper, magazine and broadcast journalists, it was also the subject of a large volume of letters to the major British newspapers and periodicals. All in all, then, the Minister's termination of the interview was generally considered to be far more newsworthy than the interview per se.

Another sort of interest in these cases stems not so much from their role in public controversy, but from the question of what happens when the normative conventions of the news interview as an interactional occasion break down. As remarked earlier, news interviews involve 'specific and significant narrowings and respecifications of the range of options that are operative in conversational interaction' (Heritage, 1989: 34). These narrowings and respecifications are managed ongoingly, and collaboratively, by participants themselves. Significantly, that also goes for *departures* from the news interview conventions, such as when interviewers either adopt a more argumentative line of questioning, or are oriented to by interviewees as moving outside the bounds of formal neutrality.

Both in the US and the UK, there are well-known interviewers who are widely perceived to be adopting an intentionally adversarial style of questioning: for example, Jeremy Paxman or John Humphrys of the BBC, or Dan Rather of CBS. This is not something that is specifically tied to recent trends in broadcasting. As Michael Schudson (1994) shows, in an enlightening history of news interview practices from the mid-nineteenth century onwards, there have always been conflicting views of what the news interview should really be for, as well as different approaches both to the carrying out of interviews by journalists, and to participation in interviews by public figures. Certain interviewers have always seen their job as more about 'pressing for the truth' than 'letting the interviewee get their point across'. ITV's Sir Robin Day, for instance, was well known in Britain for asking questions, live on air, which could cause politicians to walk out on the interview. By the same token, certain interviewees may attempt to avoid answering a particular question, as happened in one recent interview between Jeremy Paxman and then Home Secretary Michael Howard, in which Paxman asked the same question – and Howard avoided answering it – more than 13 times.

Examining these kinds of 'breakdown' in interview conduct is relevant because it tells us more about the very norms and conventions that are relied upon to get standard news interviews done. In other words, by looking at how participants break the rules, we can confirm that those rules are there to be relied on in the first place. To illustrate this I will make some observations on one high-profile American case, a much-discussed 1988 interview between Dan Rather of CBS News and Vice-President George Bush Snr. My reasons for choosing this case in preference to a more recent example are partly pragmatic: there exist recordings and highly detailed transcripts of this nine-minute interview which, as we will see, involved an enormous amount of complex overlapping talk that continued more or less throughout the length of the interview. This factor alone makes the Bush-Rather interview, and its transcript, into a remarkable media phenomenon.

The Bush-Rather case is useful not just because it is so striking, but because there also exists a further collection of studies in which conversation analysts examine the interview in great depth (Clayman and Whalen, 1988/9; Nofsinger, 1988/9; Pomerantz, 1988/9; Schegloff, 1988/9). These studies, which the reader is encouraged to consult, reveal how the publicly perceived 'confrontation' between the two men in fact emerged from a series of departures from the otherwise collaboratively sustained conventions of the interview. Close analysis shows how, while the consistently overlapping talk could potentially be described as orderly in terms of the turn-taking system for ordinary conversation (Sacks, Schegloff and Jefferson, 1974), it was not orderly in terms of the more formal turn-taking system for news interviews.

The cause of the breakdown was that Bush sought to restrict the interview topic to his presidential candidacy while Rather, seeing himself as acting in the public interest, sought to question Bush on his involvement in a secret arms-dealing affair which had recently come to light. Known as the Iran-Contra affair, this involved covert deals brokered by the US secret service to deliver arms to Iran in exchange for the release of American hostages in Lebanon, and the subsequent use of diverted funds from those deals to support right-wing armed forces in Nicaragua (see for instance Lynch and Bogen, 1996). The result is that the entire nine-minute interview descends into what was generally perceived to be an argument (or according to the popular American press, a 'slugfest') characterized by constant interruptions and overlapping talk, ended abruptly by Rather cutting Bush off in mid-sentence.

Let us just look at one example. It shows how the interviewer in this case conducts himself according to one of the established conventions of news interviews: that is, a question may be prefaced with one or more contextualizing statements which serve to 'frame' the question both for the interviewee and for the overhearing audience. However, the interviewee does not observe this convention, instead persistently seeking to 'answer' the statements rather than waiting for the question. Throughout the interview, this led to cycles of interruptive and otherwise overlapping talk in which the interviewer sought to pursue the production of his unasked question while the interviewee pursued the production of his pre-emptive 'answers'.

(12) Rather-Bush: 94–125 [IR is Dan Rather; IE is Vice-President George Bush Snr]

```
1      IE:    . . . I've answered every question put before me.=Now if you
2             have a question, .hh [(what is it.)]
4      IR:                         [I  do  ha]ve one.
5      IE:    Ple[ase ]
6      IR:       [Ah-] I have one. .hh[hh You have  said  that-  if yo]u=
7      IE:                            [Please  fire  away    heh-hah ]
8      IR:    =had know::n, you said tha' if you had known this was
9             an arms for hostag[es sw]ap, .hh that you would've=
10     IE:                      [ Yes ]
```

```
11     IR:    =opposed it. .hhhh You also [said thet-]
12→    IE:                             [E x a c t ]ly
13     IR:    [[that you did NOT KNOW thet y-]
14→    IE:    [[(m-  may-  may I-)   may I      ] answer that.
15            (0.4)
16     IE:    Th[uh right (   )-]
17→    IR:      [That wasn't a] question.=it w[as a statement eh-]
18→    IE:                                   [Yes  it  was  a ]
19→            statement [and I'll   answer  it.  Thuh  President]=
20→    IR:              [Let me ask the question if I may first   ]
21     IE:    =created this program, .h has testified er s:tated
22            publicly, (.) he did not think it was arms fer hostages.
23            .hh [and it was only later thet-  and th  ]at's me=
24     IR:        [That's thuh President Mr Vice President]
25     IE:    =(.hh) [Cuz] I went along with it because ya know why Dan?
26     IR:           [We-]
27     IR:    .hh because I: [worried  when  I  saw  Mister:  .hh=
28     IR:                   [That wasn' thuh question Mr Vice President
29     IE:    =Mister Buckley, (.) uh: heard about Mister Buckley
30            being tor:tured ta death. Later admitted as (a) CIA
31            chief. .hh So if I erred, I erred on thuh side of tryin'
32            tuh get those hostages outta there.
```

To repeat, the two conventions that we need to summarize in order to see what is going on this complex extract are:

1 Interviewers should use statements only in the framework of a question (for example as prefaces).
2 Interviewees should refrain from speaking until a question has been asked (that is treat statements as prefatory to questions).

Note that the extract begins with the IE instructing IR, if he 'ha[s] a question' to 'please fire away' (lines 1–2 and 7). Rather's attempted line of questioning so far has been to establish that Bush, though he denies it, was somehow involved in the covert Iran-Contra arms deals. He begins, in lines 6–11, to form up a question along similar lines using a technique which Pomerantz (1988/9), in her analysis of other parts of the same broadcast, has described: namely to get the IE to agree to two contradictory factual statements, and then ask a question which invites the IE to deal with the contradiction foregrounded in the statements just agreed to. In this, therefore, the IR appears to be observing norm (1) above.

However, in line 14 IE breaches the corresponding norm (2), by interrupting IR's second factual statement (that is 'you also said thet- that you did NOT KNOW . . .', lines 11–13) with an attempt to 'answer' the first ('may I answer that'). Notice how, in the following turns, both parties display their hitherto tacit knowledge of the very norms that are being breached, and on which the properties of this occasion as an 'interview' rely: in line 17 IR says 'That wasn't a question.=it was a statement' and, in line 20, 'Let me ask the question if I may first'; while IE clearly displays that he is moving outside the question-answer turn-taking framework in his intervening utterance: 'Yes it was a statement and I'll answer it' (lines 18–19).

The extract above gives just a glimpse of the way that this interview, in the course of its nine-minute broadcast, came to be widely perceived as a confrontation between the two participants. As Clayman and Whalen (1988/9: 242–3) describe it, media commentary at the time focused on the personalities of the protagonists: Rather being seen as 'combative' and 'volatile', while Bush 'appeared surprisingly forceful and aggressive, and was widely felt to have dispelled his "wimp" image'. However, by the application of CA to the turn-by-turn unfolding of the event, we are able to take a different perspective on the movement between 'interview' and 'confrontation'. This involves determining

> how the participants shaped the encounter from within; [isolating] the specific social practices they employed in its development. Since contributions to inter-action are contingent upon the independent actions of others, they cannot be treated as the straightforward behavioural realisation of preplanned political strategies or psychological predispositions. Whatever prior agendas or predispositions there may have been, the actual course of the encounter must be treated as an emergent and fundamentally *interactional* achievement.
>
> (Clayman and Whalen, 1988/9: 243)

From a conversation analytic perspective, therefore, this encounter and others like it are primarily interesting as deviant cases: ones in which the participants deviate from the normative conventions that underpin broadcast news interviews *as* interviews in the first place. As in other types of deviant case analysis, examining how the interaction changes its shape in the absence of those conventions only serves to reinforce the main point of CA studies: that specific turn-taking practices are crucial factors in the ability of broadcast journalists and public figures to produce news interviews as recognizable occasions for the production of news talk 'on the air'.

Further reading

Clayman, S. and Heritage, J. (2002) *The News Interview*. Cambridge: Cambridge University Press.

Greatbatch, D. (1988) A turn-taking system for British news interviews. *Language in Society*, 17: 401–30.

Greatbatch, D. (1998) Conversation analysis: Neutralism in British news interviews. In A. Bell and P. Garrett (eds), *Approaches to Media Discourse*. Oxford: Blackwell.

Harris, S. (1991) Evasive action: How politicians respond to questions in political interviews. In P. Scannell (ed.), *Broadcast Talk*. London: Sage.

Heritage, J. (1985) Analysing news interviews: Aspects of the production of talk for an overhearing audience. In T. van Dijk (ed.), *Handbook of Discourse Analysis, Volume 3: Discourse and Dialogue*. London: Academic Press.

Schegloff, E.A. (1988/9) From interview to confrontation: Observations on the Bush/Rather encounter. *Research on Language and Social Interaction*, 22: 215–40. (And other articles in the same journal issue.)

8

POLITICAL RHETORIC AND TELEVISED DEBATE

The intertwining of politics and the media in the modern world means that broadcasting, particularly television, is seen by politicians as the key channel through which they can communicate their messages to the electorate. This means that politicians seeking success are groomed, not just in terms of their appearance but also their communicative style, by professional consultants whose role is to increase their appeal across broad constituencies within the populace and maximize their ability to produce media-ready soundbites on key issues – short statements that can be fitted into five- or ten-second slots within the busy schedule of daily broadcast news bulletins. It also means that politicians who, for whatever reason (poor looks or inability to communicate in short, sharp sentences) are categorized as non-telegenic, are increasingly sidelined by the communications directorates of their party in favour of a select few who thus tend to appear with marked regularity in various genres of political broadcasting.

These trends lead to new questions for both the analysis of political rhetoric and the analysis of media talk. As Fairclough (1995: 188) observes:

> Much of contemporary political discourse is mediatised political discourse. Its major genres are no longer just the traditional genres of politics, they are also genres of the media. Traditional political activities and their genres – parliamentary debates, party conferences, international conferences – carry on, but they too are represented in the media. . . . At the same time, genres for political discourse that the media themselves generate are increasingly important for politicians – most notably the political interview, but also, for instance, phone-in programmes.

We have already looked, in the previous chapter, at aspects of mediated political discourse in the news interview. There, one of the key issues was how the interview is produced as a form of talk directed at an 'absent' audience. By way of contrast, the present chapter examines a form of mediatized political discourse that involves politicians in direct address to co-present audiences. I turn to a media-generated political discourse genre which, in the modern environment, is extremely important for politicians, namely the panel debate show. There are numerous forms of political panel debate ranging from the multiparty, moderated interview set-up analysed by Greatbatch (1992); to the orchestrated, 'audience participation' panel debate in which pre-selected members of a studio audience put questions to a small collection of differently affiliated politicians; to late-night discussion formats in which a relatively non-directive interviewer facilitates a debate of sometimes indefinite length between a number of political representatives. Focusing on the second of these three types, I utilize aspects of Max Atkinson's (1984a, 1984b) work on political rhetoric to show how different structures of alignment and counter-alignment are managed between panel members and the studio audience in an episode of one long-running programme, the BBC's flagship *Question Time*.

Question Time is an example of a whole genre of TV shows that are set up to encourage debate and disputation about political issues. These shows differ slightly in their structure and format. In *Question Time*, a panel of participants representing different political parties (plus one 'independent' who tends to be an industrialist, a policy consultant or a journalist) sit around a table, with a regular chairperson who is a professional broadcaster, and take it in turns to answer questions put to them by members of the studio audience, consisting of a 'cross-section' of ordinary citizens. Given that the majority of the panel are representatives of different political positions, they tend to disagree with one another in answering the audience's questions. The audience themselves do not remain uninvolved in this process. Rather, different constituencies within the audience express their collective affiliation and disaffiliation with panel members by clapping, jeering, and so on. We can therefore describe the discourse of *Question Time* as 'alignment-saturated'. By this I mean that most of the discourse of a *Question Time* broadcast is to some degree traceable to the participants' differing political and ideological alignments.

The way that the participants are symbolically juxtaposed or laid out reinforces this alignment-saturatedness. At different times in the show's history that layout has changed slightly. Originally, the Chair sat in the centre of a semicircle facing the audience (and the TV cameras), with panel members to the right of the political spectrum seated on one side of him, and those to the left seated on the other. More recent series have seen the Chair move to a position at the *side* of the table where the panel sit, thus situating himself somewhere 'between' the studio audience and the panel. Within this visual format, the Chair would regularly take the opportunity to leave the table and cross the 'boundary' between panel and audience. At the time of writing, the show has reverted to the older format with the Chair conducting the debate from the centre of the semicircle of participants.

This alignment-saturatedness raises a number of issues for the analysis of the talk that is broadcast by *Question Time*. First of all, alignment centrally involves a process of taking 'sides'. Taking sides is a feature of argument in all sorts of contexts; but an important additional aspect emerges when speakers conduct their disputes in the presence of audiences of whatever kind. One thing speakers in these situations may do is try to recruit the audience to their side. An argument, in other words, need not involve simply an interaction between someone arguing for a position and someone arguing against it. The shifting pattern of alignments found in disputes can expand beyond the ostensible disputants to involve the audience themselves.

But while I have referred to the discourse of *Question Time* as alignment-saturated, that does not mean that a static set of 'alignments' should be understood to pre-exist and determine the course of the talk. The conversation analytic perspective encourages us to describe how alignments are generated, sustained, challenged and changed in the course of talk itself. Therefore, in line with the general approach taken throughout this book, I will focus on how relationships of alignment and counter-alignment are constructed and sustained in 'live' talk within the studio itself, as relayed to the audience at home.

An example of *Question Time* discourse

As the central data I use one extract from a *Question Time* show that was broadcast in the UK in the weeks leading up to a General Election. The debate throughout the show focused on election issues. The key point to note is that the main prediction by pollsters for the outcome of the election at this time was a 'hung parliament', or coalition, with no single party possessing enough parliamentary seats to form a majority government.

However, the interesting thing about this extract is not so much the content of the discussion about election matters. Rather, I focus on this episode because what we see is a particularly noteworthy rhetorical performance from a well-known British Conservative politician, Michael Heseltine, in which he succeeds in managing the structures of alignment at play within the studio (that is, among the other panel participants and the studio audience) to transform a situation in which he is the subject of laughter and ridicule from panel members and the studio audience into one in which he is the recipient of affiliative applause from the studio audience. The ideas of Atkinson (1984a) on the key rhetorical devices utilized by politicans (referred to previously in Chapter 3) can be used to unfold the construction of this performance.

The extract begins in the course of a response to a question from the audience asking the panel their opinions on the possibility of a coalition government. Michael Heseltine's position is that there is nothing positive at all about such a possibility, because it leads to a 'compromise' government. Others have taken issue with this stance, suggesting that compromise is always being struck within parties, so why not between them too? Heseltine responds by asserting that internal divisions within parties are never as extreme as inter-party differences. At this point someone brings up the political episode for which Heseltine is most famous, in which he staged a very public resignation from his cabinet post by walking out of a cabinet meeting and announcing to the press that he had irreconcilable differences with the Prime Minister over a particular political issue (the Westland affair concerning a major manufacturing contract the Government had awarded to an overseas company in preference to a British one). We join the talk as Heseltine responds to this point.

(1) Question Time

```
1    Heseltine:   . . . if somebody wishes to resi:gn from
2                 government that's not a split in the
3                 government that is a distinction
4                 between one member of the cabinet en
5                 the rest of thee, .h eur eurv of the
6                 cabinet [that's not a split.
7    Sissons:            [U-everyone here would call
8                 that a spli[t.
9    Heseltine:             [No they would not. No
10                n[o.=We are talking about fun]damental
11   Audience:    [   °hih hh hh hh    hh°  ]
12   Heseltine:   issues which divi:de the PARty.
13   Sissons:     Like Europe.=
14   Beith:       ='k Europe.
15   (   ):       °Mm.°
16   Heseltine:   Yi-yi Europe [would b]e such an=
17   Audience:                 [hh   hih]
18   Heseltine:   =i[ssue,
19   Audience:      [heh heh HA HA [ha ha ha [ha
20   Heseltine:                   [Europe  [Europe
21                would b[e such an i[ssue,
22   Salmond:            [Or th-     [Or the poll
23                t[ax.
24   Heseltine:    [if it were not, if it were not
25                poss[ible,
26   Smith:           [Or Missis Tha[tcher.
27   Heseltine:                     [to reach, [No:,
28   Audience:                                 [EhHAH
29                HAH HAH [Hah ha
30   Audience:           [x [XXXXXXXXXXXXXXXXXXXXXXXXX=
31   Heseltine:            [It would-
32   Audience:    =XXXXXX(6.0 seconds) x[xx–x
33   Heseltine:                         [Europe would be
34                such an issue, if: it were not possible
35                to reach agreement within the party on
```

36		the matter. .h But within the
37		Conservative Party we have been able
38		to reach agreement on: our view about
39		Europe an' I think it's a very
40		sensible:, (.) compromise between a
41		ra:nge of different views.=.hhh That's
42		qui:te different, .h to sayin:g that
43		whe- one party has agree:d, .h you
44		then have to go out, an' do deal:s,
45		with another party. .hh Because that
46		means that when you're negotiating
47		abroad, you don't know whether you've
48		got a manda:te, .hh when you're
49		negotiating with er .h er industry or
50		with trade unions or whatever power
51		group in society you're dealing wi- .h
52		you don't know that you've got a
53		mandate, an' whAT you DO kno:w, (.) .h
54		is that the party with whom you are in
55		partnership, .h will NOT actually be
56		seeking to support the m:- the: larger
57		party, .h they will be trying to
58		undermi::ne, .h for their narrow
59		advantage, .h whatever the circumstances
60		happen to be. .hh You just imagine. .h
61		You just imagine. .h what was happening
62		if you were having to deal:, .h with
63		the confrontation of public sector
64		unions in the wa:y:, that the Labour
65		Party did when they were in power in
66		the winter of discontent, .h and
67		would have to do if they won this
68		election. .hh If the:y had the backing
69		of the Liberal Party, .hh the Liberal
70		Party would be seeking ev:'ry
71		conceivable wa:y, .h to em:barrass the
72		government that they were in
73		th[eory, in part]nership=
74	Beith:	[°Oh not at a:ll.°]
75	Heseltine:	=wi[th.=.h=Tha's what they would be=
76	Beith:	[Not at all.
77	Heseltine:	=doing.

```
78  Beith:      Try and [put a bitta backbone in[to it.
79  Heseltine:        [Becus-  .h  theh-    [No no
80              you would no[t be putting backbone=
81  Beith:                 [Yeuh we would.
82  Heseltine:  =in[to it.=You:: would] be:: in fact=
83  Beith:         [ We did. hih! .hh ]
84  Heseltine:  =trying to un:dermine their position to
85              get advantage fuh the Liberal Party.=.h
86              WHY:? .h Because you might well kno:w, .h
87              that there could be an early general
88              election in which you'd have to stand
89              up an' be counted.=.h=You wouldn't be-
90              wanted to be associated, .hh with the
91              government that you were supporting
92              which was becoming unpopular.=.h=So
93              you would [rat on them.
94  Audience:             [x-x-xx-XXXXXXX [XXXXXXX]=
95  Heseltine:                            [That's what ]=
96              =[you would do:.]
97  Audience:   =[XXXXXXXX]XXXX(4.5 seconds)XX . . .
```

We can make some initial observations on the patterns of alignment in play in this extract. At the beginning, the central alignment structure pits Heseltine against all the other participants (including the Chair), plus a large constituency in the audience. For instance, in lines 7–8, Sissons (chairing the debate) responds to Heseltine's assertion that 'if somebody wishes to resi:gn from government that's not a split in the government' by invoking a general consensus against that position: 'everyone here would call that a split.' Heseltine disagrees ('No they would not. No no'), and counters by attempting to invoke an alternative consensus on the relevancies of the topic under dispute: 'We are talking about fundamental issues which divi:de the PARty'.

But this in turn is responded to in a way that perfectly embodies the consensus against Heseltine. For one thing, he is presented with a *three-part list* of candidate 'fundamental issues' dividing his party: Europe (lines 13–14), the Poll Tax (line 22), and Mrs Thatcher (line 26). Lists of three act as rhetorical devices which convey 'completeness' in respect of an issue; which as it were 'cover the ground' on that issue (Atkinson, 1984a). This list of fundamental divisions thus proposes that the Conservative party is not just split, but is fundamentally split. Atkinson's (1984a) work also indicates that three-part lists are rhetorically effective in generating applause when speakers are addressing large-scale audiences.

For instance, consider the following extracts from party conference speeches by ex-British Prime Minister Margaret Thatcher. In each case, a point is made by listing three items, after the third of which we see the audience applauding loudly:

(2) **Conservative Party Conference**

```
1  Thatcher:  This week has demonstrated (0.4) that we are a
2             party united in
3             purpose                                      1
4             (0.4)
5             strategy                                     2
6             (0.2)
7             and reso[lve                                 3
8  Audience:          [Hear [hear
9                           [x-xxXXXXXXXXXXXXXXXXXXXXXXXXXXxx-x
                     |              (8 seconds)                    |
```

(3) **Conservative Party Conference**

```
1  Thatcher:  Soviet Marxism is
2             ideologically,                               1
3             politically                                  2
4             and morally bankru[pt                        3
5  Audience:                      [xxXXXXXXXXXXXXXXXXXXXXXXXxx-x
                     |                   (9 seconds)                 |
```

(4) **Conservative Party Conference**

```
1  Thatcher:  There's no government anywhere that is tackling
2             the problem with more
3             vigour,                                      1
4             imagination                                  2
5             and determination                            3
6             than this conservative government
7  Audience:  Hear  [hear
8  Audience:        [x-xxXXXXXXXXXXXXXXXXXXXXXXXXXXxx-x
                     |             (8 seconds)                |
```

In each case, the audience's applause is coordinated very closely with the production of the third part in the list. In fact, in the first two extracts it is noticeable that the onset of applause overlaps slightly with the final syllable of the third list part.

It is not just politicians of Margaret Thatcher's era who are prone to use three-part lists. More recently, in a speech by British Prime Minister Tony Blair on military strikes against Afghanistan, he too uses a list of three factors which summarize 'the dangers of inaction':

(5) **Blair Oct 2001**

```
Blair:      The world understands that whilst of course there are dangers in acting
            as we are, the dangers of inaction are far, far greater:
```

the threat of further such outrages	1
the threats to our economies	2
the threat to the stability of the world	3

Indeed, throughout their victorious election campaign in 1997, the British Labour Party made extensive use of a slogan which simply consisted of a list of three (repeated) items: 'Education, education, education'.

Extract (5) also shows that lists can be used in combination with the other major rhetorical device discussed by Atkinson (1984a): the *contrast* (in this case, between 'dangers in acting as we are' and 'dangers of inaction'). Heritage and Greatbatch (1986: 116) argue that rhetorical devices which are effective in generating applause tend to work because of two properties:

> (a) [they] *emphasise* and thus highlight their contents against a surrounding background of speech materials and (b) [they] *project a clear completion point* for the message in question. Atkinson proposes that these two requirements are satisfied by certain conventionalised rhetorical formats – in particular, the contrast (or antithesis) and the three-part list.

Following this up, Heritage and Greatbatch (1986) conducted a statistical analysis of a large corpus of 476 recorded broadcast political speeches and found that, either singly or in combination, three-part lists accounted for some 12.6 per cent of all 'applause events' in their data base, while contrasts accounted for no fewer than 33.2 per cent (p. 139).

The reason for this success is, as Heritage and Greatbatch (1986) say, that three-part lists and contrasts are particularly effective at projecting their own completion. In other words, as they are being built, they signal when they are likely to end. The devices themselves provide the audience with a cue when to clap and thus allow collective displays of affiliation. With three-part lists this seems to be because of a conventionalized expectation in ordinary conversation that lists are most effectively done in tripartite form.

Gail Jefferson (1990) showed that when people produce lists in conversation, they tend to do so using three parts. The following extracts come from Jefferson's (1990) study of the interactional properties of listing, and all occurred in everyday conversation, either on the telephone or in face-to-face interaction.

(6) **Jefferson 1990: 64**

1	Sydney:	While you've been talking to me I mended,	
2		two nightshirts,	1
3		a pillow case?	2
4		enna pair'v pants	3

(7) **Jefferson 1990: 64**

1	Maybelle:	I think if you

2	exercise it	1
3	an' work at it	2
4	'n studied it	3
5	you do become clairvoyant.	

More interestingly, in these next extracts speakers have produced two parts of a list, but either have exhausted the relevant items which could be used to extend the list, or cannot find an appropriate word with which to complete it. In each case they use an item such as 'or something', 'things like that', and so on, to complete the lists as a three-part unit.

(8) Jefferson 1990: 66

1	Heather:	And they had like a concession stand at a fair	
2		where you can buy	
3		coke	1
4		and popcorn	2
5		and that type of thing.	3

(9) Jefferson 1990: 66

1	Sy:	Take up m:Metacal er,	1
2		Carnation Slender	2
3		er something like that.	3

These extracts tell us something very interesting about three-part lists. Note that in each case the third part is not actually another item like the two that went before. Instead, it is a general term, such as 'and that type of thing'. Where a specific third component does not come to mind, speakers can use a general term in order to end up with a three-part list. By using these 'generalised list completers' (Jefferson 1990) speakers in extracts (8) and (9) are displaying their sensitivity to a norm of conversation that runs something like: 'if doing a list, try to do it in three parts'.

This means that in ordinary conversation, when one speaker is producing a list, a co-participant can anticipate that when the third item is produced, then the list is likely to be complete. As Jefferson shows, coparticipants recurrently treat the end of the third part of a list as a legitimate place to start taking their next turn.

(10) Jefferson 1990: 74

1	Matt:	The good actors are all dyin out.
2	Tony:	They're all- they're all
3		dyin out [yeah.
4	Matt:	[Tyrone Po:wuh. Clark Gable, Gary Cooper,
5	Tony:	Now all of 'em are dyin.

Here, Matt's list of good actors who are 'dying out' – 'Tyrone Po:wuh. Clark Gable,

Gary Cooper,' – could easily have been extended. Thus, Tony's decision to start talking when he does displays his understanding that Matt's list could be treated as complete upon the provision of a third item.

Just as third items in conversation are conventionally taken to be possible utterance completion points, so too are they treated as completion points in speeches. An audience can see that a politician is making a list, and their tacit sensitivity to conventions of everyday conversation enables them to anticipate that it is likely to be completed not after two points, and not after four, but after three. Each individual member of the audience can therefore predict the end of a specific point and is thereby provided with a resource, intrinsic to the speech, through which their behaviour can be coordinated with the other audience members to provide a collective response.

Returning to the *Question Time* extract, one interesting point to note in the light of these features of three-part lists is that this one is produced collaboratively among the members of the panel, each of them (except Sissons, the Chair) representing different political alignments from Heseltine:

(1) Question Time [Detail]

```
13   Sissons:    Like Europe.=                                              1
14   Beith:      ='k Europe.
15   (     ):    °Mm.°
16   Heseltine:  Yi-yi Europe [would b]e such an=
17   Audience:                [hh   hih]
18   Heseltine:  =i[ssue,
19   Audience:     [heh heh HA HA [ha ha ha [ha
20   Heseltine:                   [Europe  [Europe
21               would b[e such an i[ssue,
22   Salmond:           [Or th-    [Or the poll                             2
23               t[ax.
24   Heseltine:  [if it were not, if it were not
25               poss[ible,
26   Smith:          [Or Missis Tha[tcher.                                  3
27   Heseltine:                    [to reach, [No:,
28   Audience:                                [EhHAH
29               HAH HAH [Hah ha
30   Audience:           [x[XXXXXXXXXXXXXXXXXXXXXXXXXXX=
```

In lines 13 and 14, Sissons and Beith almost simultaneously propose 'Europe'; in line 22, Salmond suggests 'the Poll Tax'; and in line 26 Smith contributes 'Mrs Thatcher'. Hence it is not just the three-part construction of the list proposing the extreme level of division within the party, but also the way in which each of the other participants around the table contributes to its production, that embodies the consensus against Heseltine.

Nevertheless, the collaboratively produced three-part list works in a similar way to other such lists in political rhetoric, as the audience uses its structure to cue a loud burst of laughter and applause that lasts for some six seconds (lines 28–32). Note that there has already been some laughter within the audience following the first part of what turns out to be the three-part list ('Europe') (see line 19). Potentially, this represents certain audience members orienting to one possible interpretation of Heseltine's utterance in lines 16–18: 'Europe would be such an issue.' On its own, this is hearable as a concession that, indeed 'Europe' represents a fundamental division within the party: a matter that, at the time, the media were keen to establish while the party itself was strenuously denying. Therefore Heseltine could be heard as admitting that, in fact, the media were right.

However, it turns out that Heseltine's utterance is designed as a first clause in a *rebuttal* to the 'Europe' claim. As he goes on to say: '<u>E</u>urope would be such an issue, <u>if</u>: it were not possible to reach agreement within the party on the <u>ma</u>tter. .h But with<u>in</u> the Conservative Party we h<u>a</u>ve been able to reach agreement <u>o</u>n: our view about Europe' (lines 34–39). But Heseltine has to struggle to complete this rather lengthy rebuttal because his initial attempts are interrupted by the other panel members contributing their items to the three-part list of divisive issues (lines 22–23 and 26).

Thus, although the first signs of audience laughter in line 19 can be seen as responding to a potential back-down under pressure by Heseltine, the much longer and larger-scale burst of laughter and applause comes in at the end of a three-part list, and can be seen as responsive to the way in which that list, produced collaboratively, rhetorically 'covers the ground' in terms of fundamental issues that divide the Conservative party.

Heseltine, who has actually been attempting since line 16 to rebut the suggestion that 'Europe' represents a divisive issue within his party, now abandons that attempt (line 31) until the applause has died down. He then, in a long turn running from line 33 to line 75, produces his rebuttal, turning it in the process into an attack on the Liberal party and what he takes to be their coalitionist parliamentary strategy. As might be expected, at this point the Liberal MP Alan Beith attempts to rebut Heseltine's accusatory suggestions (at lines 74, 76, 78, 81 and 83). But it is notable that Heseltine, having established himself in occupation of the floor, is able to persist in his point, eventually ending by winning a burst of affiliative applause from members of the audience (line 94).

In gross terms, then, it is possible to trace a trajectory of alignment and counter-alignment here in which Heseltine transforms a situation in which he is collectively aligned against into one in which he has succeeded in building an alignment structure for his own position. As noted, a major way in which he does this is by shifting the topical line away from the question of splits in his own (Conservative) party, and towards an attack on another party (the Liberals). By this means Heseltine successfully exploits the partisan nature of the studio audience, enabling his own supporters to affiliate collectively with his criticisms of Liberal party politics.

However, as I have already remarked, it is not just the audience but the panel too who can be described as 'alignment-saturated' in the context of the *Question Time* show.

This, of course, is what lies behind Beith's hearing of the attacks on the Liberal Democrats as something to which he should respond; an issue I return to in more depth later. What interests me here is the interplay between the alignments of the panel and those of the audience; in particular, the way that certain patterns of alignment and counter-alignment are constructed on particular topics in the ongoing course of actual *Question Time* discourse. There is a sequence in our extract in which that play and its local handling can be closely examined. This is the little sequence between lines 74 and 96, in which three particular things take place: (1) Liberal politician Beith attempts to counter Heseltine's accusations against his party; (2) Heseltine deals with that attempt; and (3) Heseltine's argument wins applause from the audience. In what follows I explore this sequence in some detail, using it to raise a variety of issues to do with the local, practical negotiation of alignments and the management of applause in this form of broadcast talk.

'Recompletion' and the management of applause

We can approach these issues by exploring the use made by Heseltine of a device described by Atkinson (1984b), in his work on the public oratory of politicians, as 'recompletion'. This device has a number of interactional properties that are of value to Heseltine in his negotiation of alignment structures in the episode. In analysing these properties I will show how the strategy of recompletion is employed by Heseltine as a means for building an argument on the basis of locally emergent features of the talk.

Let us look again at what happens in lines 69–77 of the target extract, attending particularly to Heseltine's final sentence:

```
(1)  Question Time [Detail]
69   Heseltine:        . . . hh the Liberal
70                      Party would be seeking ev:'ry
71                      conceivable wa:y, .h to em:barrass the
72                      government that they were in
73                      th[eory, in   part]nership=
74   Beith:            [°Oh not at a:ll.°]
75   Heseltine:    =wi[th.=.h=Tha's what they would be=
76   Beith:            [Not at all.
77   Heseltine:    =doing.
```

Two features are of note about this fragment. First, Heseltine makes a hearably complete point in lines 69–75: 'the Liberal Party would be seeking ev:'ry conceivable wa:y, .h to em:barrass the government that they were in theory, in partnership with.' Second, he then 'recompletes' that point immediately afterwards: 'Tha's what they would be doing.' Part at least of the way in which the point made in the first instance is hearably complete comes from the fact that it is packaged as a syntactically complete sentence. Bound up with that is its terminal intonation contour, indicated by the full-stop after 'in partnership with'. And part at least of the way that the recompletion works as a *re-completion* stems from the fact that it adds nothing in the strictly informational sense to what was said before. Rather, what it does is to underline and emphasize that a particular point was, in fact, intended in the prior sentence.

This use of recompletion to recapitulate a point that has just been made is common in the rhetorical discourse of politicians during speeches made to audiences, as Atkinson (1984b) has shown (see also Heritage and Greatbatch, 1986). In these rhetorical contexts, recompletion may be used to foreground an 'applause-relevant' place in the speech; that is, to signal to the audience that the speaker has made a point for which he or she is inviting or expecting applause. Frequently this device is used when the point has not been made in a particularly effective way first time round.

Extracts (11) and (12) provide examples. In both cases, the speaker uses a standard rhetorical device for eliciting applause: the contrast (Atkinson, 1984b: 391–8). Contrast structures facilitate applause by providing a framework in which a specific point can be emphasized (by being contrasted with an alternative), and by setting up projectable completion points (that is, following the second part of the projected contrast) at which the collective activity of applauding can be coordinated (Heritage and Great-batch, 1986: 111–17). In these two cases, for some reason, the audience appears to find difficulty locating the 'right' place to applaud following the contrast. This results in a gap, after which the speaker 'recompletes' the point:

(11) Party Conference Speech

```
1     Pardoe:   . . . an' which will GUARANTEE: (0.5) what is
2               perhaps the most important thing that can be
3               guaranteed, (1.0) that NO ONE IN BRITAIN CAN
4               EVER AGAI:N BE BETTER OFF BY NOT WORKING
5               THAN WORKING.
6→              (0.7)
7→              THAT'S THE FIrst thing to guarantee.
8     Audience: x-xx-xxxxxxxxxxxx (5.0 seconds) xxxxxxx-x-x
```

(12) Party Conference Speech

```
1     Heath:    In my: view it is right that the government
2               should consider these matters and take them
3               into account. (1.0) What is entah:rly
4               unacceptable (0.8) is the view:: that
5               pah:rliament never can (0.6) and never
6               should (0.6) appro:ve any legislation (0.8)
7               nor should a government pursue any policy
8               (0.8) unless first of aw:l the trade unions
```

```
9                     themselves (.) approve of it.
10→                   (0.5)
11→                   THAT is entah:rly unacceptable.=
12    Audience:       =Hear [hear
13    Audience:            [x-xxXXXXXXXXXXXXX(8.0 seconds)XXXxx
```

In extract (11) the contrast is between people being better off by 'not working' than by 'working'; while in extract (12), what is 'acceptable' is contrasted with something that is 'entah:rly unacceptable'. In both cases, the silences that emerge following these contrastive devices seem to indicate difficulty on the audience's part in appropriately following or grasping the point. Hence, the recompletion is used to recapitulate and rhetorically underline that point. Note that in both cases, the attempt is successful in gaining the audience's applause.

One rhetorical use of recompletions, then, is to 'pursue' a response that for some reason has not been forthcoming. But the same device can also be used for very different interactional purposes in a different sequential environment: namely *after* the onset of applause by the audience. Extract (13) is an example from a speech at a mass demonstration:

(13) Demo Speech
```
1     Foot:           THERE'S NO:: (0.3) DESPAI:R (0.3) IN THIS:::
2                     (.) GREAT (.) DEMONSTRATION. (.) THERE IS A
3                     DETERMINATION TO DESTROY: THEM AN' THEIR
4                     POL[ICIES
5     Audience:          [Yeh::[::::::::::::[:::::::::::::::::::::::::::
6→    Audience:               [x-xxXX [XXXXXXXXXXXXXXXXXXXXXXXXXXXXX
7→    Foot:                            [THAT'S WHAT WE'RE HERE FOR
```

Here, Foot's 'THAT'S WHAT WE'RE HERE FOR' manifests the same basic properties as the other recompletions: that is, it recapitulates the point contained in the prior sentences, and it uses the word 'That' at the start of the sentence to point out the fact that the point is being recapitulated. But unlike extracts (11) and (12), this recompletion is actually produced in overlap with an ongoing response from the audience. Atkinson (1984b) argues that this kind of 'post-response-initiation' recompletion is used in such a context to add strength to the point being made, by proposing, in effect, that the point was not completed when the audience began its response. Hence the suggestion is that the audience began applauding 'early', an early response in this context being 'hearable as a display of greater than usual affiliation for what the speaker is saying' (Atkinson, 1984b: 398).

To summarize, the recompletion format displays flexibility in the sequential and interactional contexts in which it can be rhetorically effective. We have so far looked at two of its uses. First, to pursue a response when applause is late, by retrospectively flagging the applaudable message; and second, to propose the heightened enthusiasm of a response in progress, by suggesting that applause has come too early.

Returning once again to the *Question Time* data extract, I want to draw out some different, though related, rhetorical uses of recompletion made by Michael Heseltine in his dispute with Alan Beith. As with the examples so far cited, though in a little more detail, I want to look at what the device accomplishes interactionally at these moments in the talk; its role in Heseltine's work of local alignment-building.

Alignment structures and the design of talk

I will look at the specific alignment structures being constructed in the talk by concentrating on how person reference forms are used to establish particular identities and identity relationships among the participants. There are two instances of recompletion in the target extract. I have already noted the first, in line 75:

(1) Question Time [Detail]

```
69      Heseltine:                      . . .hh the Liberal
70                      Party would be seeking ev:'ry
71                      conceivable wa:y,. h to em:barrass the
72                      government that they were in
73                      th[eory,   in   part]nership=
74      Beith:           [°Oh not at a:ll.°]
75→     Heseltine:     =wi[th.=.h=Tha's what they would be=
76      Beith:              [Not at all.
77      Heseltine:     =doing.
```

The second occurs slightly later in the extract (line 95):

(1) Question Time [Detail]

```
89      Heseltine:                      . . . You wouldn't be-
90                      wanted to be associated, .hh with the
91                      government that you were supporting
92                      which was becoming unpopular.=.h=So
93                      you would [rat on them.
94      Audience:                [x-x-xx-XXXXXXX[XXXXXXX]=
95→     Heseltine:                              [That's what ]=
96→                     =[you would do:.]
97      Audience:       =[XXXXXXXX]XXXX(4.5 seconds)XX . . .
```

At first glance, this case looks almost identical to the first. In fact, there are both similarities and significant differences between these recompletions. Of the similarities, first of all, both of them take a similar linguistic form: 'That's what (X) would do/be doing.' Again, then, as in the earlier examples, there is a recapitulation of the point just made, indexed by a sentence-initial 'That'. Second, each one is produced in a similar sequential context; that is, after the onset of a response to the prior talk (that is, lines 74 and 94). On this second dimension, they are at least formally related to the case discussed earlier, in extract (13), where a recompletion was used rhetorically to heighten the enthusiasm of an audience's applause.

However, the more significant relationship between these cases for my purposes stems from the fundamental differences between them. These differences in the details of the utterances' design reveal how recompletion is used by Heseltine in his work of locally constructing disputatious alignments among himself, Beith, and the studio audience. I want to note two in particular. First of all, it is noticeable that only the later recompletion, in line 95, comes after the onset of audience applause. In the earlier case, line 75, it is not the audience but the Liberal politician Beith whose response comes in just before Heseltine's recompletion (line 74). And while the applause may be hearable as affiliative, in a similar way to extract (13), Beith's interjections are clearly *dis*affiliative, which lends that example a quite different complexion to extract (13).

Relatedly, each recompletion has a different pronominal format: line 75 is addressed in the third person ('Tha's what **they** would be doing') while line 95 uses the second person pronoun ('That's what **you** would do'). In fact, these pronominal formats are at the heart of Heseltine's alignment building in this stretch of talk. Each one is related closely to the nature of the responses that occur just prior to each recompletion, and especially to the sources of those responses.

In this, the key factor is that in our target extract, there are more than two principal categories of participants. This makes the *Question Time* data different from the other extracts cited so far, in which only two principal categories were relevant: the platform speaker and the 'mass' audience. In each of the cases in the *Question Time* extract, the recompletions come after the onset of a response from a *third* party, and not the party that is ostensibly addressed. At the same time, the dynamics of address – in the sense of who it is that is situated as third party to Heseltine's talk – shift significantly in the course of the extract. It is Heseltine's live sensitivity to these shifting dynamics that underpins his success in building the alignment structures that we observe in this stretch of talk.

To trace this in more detail, we need to observe what happens *between* the two recompletions in lines 75 and 95. As a result, we will see that each recompletion serves a quite different interactional function: the first I will describe as an 'occluding' function, and the second as a 'recruiting' function. Here is a fuller data segment including the two recompletions:

(1) **Question Time [Detail]**
```
69   Heseltine:                    . . . .hh the Liberal
70              Party would be seeking ev:'ry
71              conceivable wa:y, .h to em:barrass the
```

```
72              government that they were in
73              th[eory,  in   part]nership=
74  Beith:        [°Oh not at a:ll.°]
75  Heseltine:  =wi[th.=.h=Tha's what they would be=
76  Beith:         [Not at all.
77  Heseltine:  =doing.
78  Beith:      Try and [put a bitta backbone in[to it.
79  Heseltine:        [Becus-  .h  theh-    [No no
80              you would no[t be putting backbone=
81  Beith:                  [Yeuh we would.
82  Heseltine:  =in[to it.=You:: would] be:: in fact=
83  Beith:        [ We did. hih! .hh  ]
84  Heseltine:  =trying to un:dermine their position to
85              get advantage fuh the Liberal Party.=.h
86              WHY:? .h Because you might well kno:w, .h
87              that there could be an early general
88              election in which you'd have to stand
89              up an' be counted.=.h=You wouldn't be-
90              wanted to be associated, .hh with the
91              government that you were supporting
92              which was becoming unpopular.=.h=So
93              you would [rat on them.
94  Audience:          [x-x-xx-XXXXXXX[XXXXXXX]=
95  Heseltine:                        [That's what ]=
96              =[you would do:.]
97  Audience:   =[XXXXXXXX ]XXXX(4.5 seconds)XX . . .
```

Beith objects twice, in lines 74 and 76, to Heseltine's characterization of how the Liberal Democrats would behave under coalition with the Conservative party's main rivals, Labour. As Stephen Levinson (1988) points out, in the panel debate show context accusations or attacks, particularly party-political ones, are prone to be heard as 'indirectly targetted' by those representatives on the panel who stand for the viewpoint being attacked. Because of the structural characteristics – or speech exchange system – of the panel debate (described by Greatbatch, 1992) in which the chairperson plays a central role in inviting the different participants to speak and regulating the length and number of turns they are allowed to take, direct forms of address (e.g. 'you', 'your party', 'your position') are rarely used. Far more common are indirect forms of address (e.g. 'the Liberal party', 'Mr Smith's view'). As Levinson (1988: 211) suggests:

> Perhaps the occurrence of such utterances is in general typical of chaired meetings, where the chairman may be formally addressed but others intended – as in the parliamentary manner of 'Now, Mr Speaker, the Right Honorable Member for

Tewksbury North seems to be quite unaware of the 1957 Act'. In any case, in such political panels, simply by an identification of participants with political parties [which I refer to as 'alignment saturation' – IH], accusations of political incompetence (etc.) can readily pick out a representative of a political party as a non-addressed recipient, or *indirect target*. Typically, the non-addressed target immediately responds . . .

In Levinson's data, such immediate responses by the indirectly addressed target sometimes resulted in them gaining a turn in which they could respond to the perceived accusations. In our data extract, however, there is a strong sense in which Beith's responses are 'occluded' or blocked out by Heseltine using the strategy of recompletion (line 75/77). Note that Heseltine's talk up to that point had been directed at the audience; at the point where Beith starts to respond, Heseltine has been saying: 'the Liberal Party would be seeking ev:'ry conceivable wa:y, .h to em:barrass the government that **they** were in theory, in partnership with' (lines 69–75). The occlusion is accomplished in the way that the recompletion maintains the audience as direct recipient: 'Tha's what **they** would be doing', thereby working to ignore the fact that Beith has interjected.

Beith, however, persists in disagreeing, asserting, in line 78, that his party would merely 'Try and put a bitta backbone into' the Labour Party. In line 79, Heseltine's initial strategy is to continue blocking Beith's objections out of his talk, by overlapping this turn with an attempt to keep the audience as his direct target: 'Becus- theh-' (where 'theh' is hearable as a truncated version of 'they', mirroring his previous third person reference to the Liberals).

But at the end of line 79, Heseltine, hearing that Beith has now turned from merely objecting and begun to advance a competing version of events ('Try and put a bitta backbone into it'), begins to take issue with him directly ('No no you would not be putting backbone into it'). This, then, is a key point, at which the participation framework of the talk has shifted. The studio audience has moved from being the ostensible recipient of Heseltine's talk to being overhearer (albeit 'ratified', in the sense of Goffman, 1981) of a dispute between Heseltine and Beith.

Nonetheless, it is the audience who respond just prior to the second recompletion, in line 94. And now, in a quite different way from the 'occluding' function of the first recompletion, Heseltine uses recompletion to 'recruit' the response of the audience to his side. Note the second person address of Heseltine's talk as the audience begins its applause: '**You** wouldn't be- wanted to be associated, .hh with the government that **you** were supporting which was becoming unpopular . . . so **you** would rat on them', and the *continued* second person form as the recompletion is done in overlap with that applause: 'That's what **you** would do:'. Thus, the recompletion succeeds in emphasizing the affiliative nature of the applause (in a similar way to extract 13); but at the same time offers the powerful impression that Heseltine and the applauding audience are mutually aligned in opposition to Beith and his party.

In these ways, recompletion is used as a resource within the local sequential contexts of the talk to build an alignment structure *in situ*. It may be true that, given the alignment-saturated nature of *Question Time* discourse, such an alignment structure is in some sense already 'in play' by virtue of the combative set-up of the show. But those alignments only really become observable in the ways that they are (to adopt a phrase coined by Heritage, 1984) 'talked into being' in the course of the show. By focusing on the local participatory contexts of the talk in this extract, we see how Heseltine's manipulations of the device in terms of its pronominal format and associated forms of address show a close sensitivity to the details both of how third-party responses emerge, and which third party they are emanating from. In this way, Heseltine exploits the shifting participation framework and associated sequential contexts to construct a discursive alignment structure in which he and 'his constituency' in the audience are pitted against the Liberal Democrats in the person of Beith.

Question Time is just one example of a whole genre of radio and television debate shows that politicians increasingly treat as important arenas for selling themselves and their political parties to the general populace. Although the discourse of such shows is therefore politically aligned to an often exaggerated degree, those political alignments are not 'natural' features of the setting but active achievements of the participants. This chapter has revealed how even in one small debate on one episode of the show, the amount of discursive and rhetorical work that goes into accomplishing such align-ments can be considerable. Politicians agreeing to enter the broadcast arena of the show cannot rely on automatic audience affiliation; neither can they predict how other panellists might respond to what they say on any given issue. What conversation analy-sis enables us to do is to put their behaviour in such a context under the microscope, opening up to scrutiny, by focusing the lens on the sequential organization of talk, the practical and skilful means by which they construct alignments in the light of others' responses.

Further reading

Atkinson, J.M. (1984a) *Our Masters' Voices: The Language and Body Language of Politics*. London: Methuen.

Atkinson, J.M. (1984b) Public speaking and audience response: Some techniques for inviting applause. In J.M. Atkinson and J. Heritage (eds), *Structures of Social Action: Studies in Conversation Analysis*. Cambridge: Cambridge University Press.

Greatbatch, D. (1992) On the management of disagreement between news interviewees. In P. Drew and J. Heritage (eds), *Talk At Work*. Cambridge: Cambridge University Press.

Tolson, A. (ed.) (2001) *Television Talk Shows: Discourse, Performance, Spectacle*. Mahwah, NJ: Lawrence Erlbaum Associates.

POSTSCRIPT

9

MEDIA TALK AND CONVERSATION
ANALYSIS: SOME CONCLUDING REMARKS

I will draw this book to a close with some remarks that can be applied to all of the case studies contained in it. These chapters have collectively sought to delineate the field of broadcast talk studies, with a particular concern for the contribution of conversation analysis. As I began by saying, the aim has not been to provide an exhaustive analysis of all the forms of media talk available to audiences. Instead I have focused on particular genres in which the methods of CA prove most fruitful. Principally that means genres of media talk where relatively unscripted or spontaneous talk-in-interaction tends to be found: interviews, phone-ins, audience participation talk shows, live political debates and so on. In each of these areas, we have seen how the conceptual and methodological tools of CA provide a means by which to analyse the specific communicative properties of broadcast talk: a form of talk that can be described as both 'in public' and 'for the public'.

We saw in Chapter 1 that talk on radio and television is characterized by conditions of production and reception that are highly specialized. As Scannell (1991b: 3) put it: 'the places from which broadcasting speaks and in which it is heard are completely separate from each other.' In large part, the main audience for any stretch of broadcast talk is distributed, physically, geographically, and often temporally. There may be co-present audiences in the studio setting, and that collection of recipients may act as a 'mass' audience in the traditional sense (Atkinson, 1984a). But even then there is a further layer of recipients who are not only physically absent but individually distributed. One of the key problematics animating much of the work discussed in this book is: Given these conditions of production and reception, how is broadcast talk itself mediated and distributed to its various recipient constituencies? Conversation analysis shows how this mediation and distribution is the active work of broadcast talkers, whether lay or professional, accomplished in and through the design of turns and sequences of talk.

Conversation analysis focuses on both the nature of turn-taking and the nature of social actions undertaken by means of utterances and sequences. These are, in fact, two sides of the same coin, since utterances are treated as sensitive to their sequential context and sequences are themselves constituted by turns that are sequentially sensitive to one another. We have seen how many of the specific properties of broadcast talk – principally, its relationship to ordinary conversation, its institutional character, and its orientation to the overhearing audience – are traceable in the design of individual turns and sequences.

In Chapter 2, we saw that institutional forms of talk such as media talk could be characterized according to the relative formality or informality of their constitutive turn-taking systems. For example, in the case of news interviews a particular type of question-answer structure provides the oriented-to means by which the institution of the broadcast interview is produced and sustained by participants; but also the means by which interviewers can be adversarial within the constraints of journalistic neutralism. In the case of radio phone-ins, by contrast, we have seen how a much more informal system of turn exchange nevertheless yields observable features of institutionality and of an orientation to the public, broadcast nature of the talk. In the case of the audience participation TV debate show, we saw how structures of turn-taking and utterance design could also reveal ambivalence in the nature of broadcast talk. On the one hand, during confrontations being played out face-to-face on the platform in shows such as *Ricki Lake* or *Jerry Springer* it is not immediately clear to what extent the speakers exhibit a mutual orientation to the relevance of an overhearing audience. On the other hand, the design of the host's turns in particular reveal an orientation to framing that talk in terms of the involvement of an audience (both absent and co-present).

A starting point for the analysis of broadcast talk using CA methods is therefore found in the general study of institutional talk-in-interaction. However, we have also seen very clearly how radio and television talk has a specific character which serves to differentiate it from the vast majority of institutional forms of discourse and which therefore provides a specialized set of questions to which CA researchers have been drawn to address themselves. These questions pose challenges for the application of CA methodology, as well as for our understanding of the properties of media talk itself.

One feature of particular relevance for CA stems from the fact that the primary recipients for any stretch of broadcast talk – the audience – are absent from the site of its production. While there are a number of shows in which a studio audience is co-present with the broadcasters, it is equally common for the only other parties co-present in the studio to be the production crew. And even when a show is produced in the presence of a studio audience, the audience of viewers and listeners remains a principal recipient toward whom the talk is oriented. The question of how broadcast talk is designed for recipiency by an absent, 'overhearing' audience has been central to many of these chapters.

A second, related issue concerns broadcast talk and its relationship with CA's distinctive perspective on the analysability of talk: that is, the focus on the sequential organization of talk-in-interaction, in which analysis concentrates on turn-taking and associated structural phenomena. The issue here is that one of broadcast talk's specific properties is its 'one-way' character. With a few exceptions, such as radio phone-ins or shows that offer the opportunity for viewers to e-mail or send in text messages via mobile phone, there is no opportunity for immediate interaction between those producing the talk (broadcasters) and those receiving it (audiences). The talk is projected out toward its intended recipients without any 'next turn proof procedure' by means of which recipiency can be acknowledged. Given such conditions, how do the communicative properties of broadcast talk actually work? Throughout these chapters we have explored aspects of how the producers of broadcast talk manage or accomplish communication in that mediated and distributed context.

The question for analysis has therefore been twofold. First, how can the tools and techniques of CA be used to discover the kinds of talk people encounter when watching and listening to radio and television? Second, what can its analysis tell us about the communicative properties of those media? The first of these, the focus on the specific characteristics of broadcast talk as a form of talk in its own right, seems to be a distinctively CA-type question; whereas the focus on communicative properties of media per se seems more closely related to traditional concerns in media sociology, as outlined in Chapter 1. Yet in establishing the specificity of broadcast talk studies in the preceding chapters, we have hopefully seen that the two questions cannot in fact be pulled apart in this way. The study of broadcast talk *as* talk-in-interaction raises fundamental issues for both research communities, offering a strong basis for understanding the media as a significant arena of contemporary discourse practices, as well as emphasizing the central importance of discourse practices to any meaningful study of the media.

CA reveals something that is absolutely fundamental to broadcasting, but that remains invisible to conventional approaches within media studies: the interactional dynamics of the live talk that forms the basis of programmes as they are broadcast. If we think about it, what is it that any of us watching any of these genres of media talk actually observes? At one very basic but crucial level it can be described as a form of social interaction involving various categories of speakers and recipients in patterns of alignment and collaboration which are not fixed but always unfolding within the course of the talk that is being broadcast. In order to analyse that unfolding, it is necessary to move 'inside' the broadcast talk itself. As Heritage *et al.* (1988: 79–80) argued:

[I]t has become increasingly unrealistic to analyse the structure and content of [media] messages independent of the interactional medium within which they are generated. For, although the medium may not be the message, the interactional structures through which broadcast [talk] is conveyed must necessarily contribute to [its] content and appearance.

In short, the different genres of media talk have their own frameworks of participation and dynamics of address that operate within, and necessarily shape, the 'message' that reaches the audience at home.

All this has particular implications for how we might best study the products of broadcasting. I have argued that it is inadequate to view broadcast talk in the simplistic sense of media analyses that focus on the mediation of 'messages' between the 'encoding' institutions of broadcasting and the 'decoding' or receiving audience at home. As Scannell (1991b: 10) observed, media studies continues to be dominated by such a model, mapped on to which is 'a text-reader theory, derived from literary studies of written "texts", to account for the relationship between the products of radio and television and their audiences'. As he points out: 'The combined effect of these positions is to make it well-nigh impossible to discover talk as an object of study in relation to broadcasting' (ibid.).

Concentrating on talk itself, on the other hand, leads us to treat as the focus of our interest the particular dynamics of live interaction in the studio. In the foregoing one thing we have repeatedly seen is that conversational resources that are used in other interactional arenas come to be used in specialized ways in the arena of media talk. This reveals what can be called the *underlying interactional matrix* of media messages. By looking at how the talk itself is organized, we gain insight into the very interactional production of the mediated public sphere.

The upshot is that if we want to understand the cultural impacts of talk-based shows like the ones analysed in these chapters, it is all the more important to study the phenomenon itself: that is, the structures of turn-taking, opinion formulation, dispute and alignment-building that actually constitute the show in question. These structures are instantiated in, and made sense of through, talk. To be sure, such talk is broadcast, and so consumed by a wider audience than the one involved in its production. But it is first and foremost in terms of the underlying interactional matrix that viewers encounter, and are able to make sense of, the phenomena of broadcasting.

We can further deepen our understanding of this question using the concept of *affordances* (Hutchby, 2001b). New communications technologies often bring about new possibilities for communicative action and interaction. The affordances of such technologies – the possibilities, enablements and constraints that they make available – are realized in the interplay between technological forms and our practical uses and applications of such forms. Scannell (2002: 16) argues that the concept of affordances helps us to understand some of the uses of broadcasting technology:

> Radio and television were, originally, live-to-air communicative technologies and recording devices in each case came later. In each case sound and video recording were sought for not in order to replace live broadcasting but to give it greater flexibility, more communicative affordances. Instant replays are one such affordance out of the repertoire of what can be done with recording devices for television (this article is another!). By virtue of the double process of broadcasting

live and simultaneously recording this process, new communicative possibilities, hitherto impossible, are afforded viewers.

This, then, offers an additional approach to one of the key themes of this book: the distinctive nature of mediation afforded by broadcasting. As Scannell puts it, broadcasting has brought about a situation in which 'public events now occur, simultaneously, in two different places: the place of the event itself and that in which it is watched and heard. Broadcasting mediates *between* these two sites' (Scannell, 1996: 76).

This perspective in turn opens on to ways in which the analytic approach described in this book might offer opportunities for linkages and new directions involving other aspects of 'media talk'. Talk on radio and television can in fact be described in terms of a broader category of *mediated and distributed talk-in-interaction*. These chapters have each shown key aspects of how talk on radio and television is both mediated, via the technology of broadcasting, and distributed, in the sense that its 'overhearing' audiences exist in multiple spaces both geographically and temporally. But broadcast talk is not the only possible form of mediated and distributed talk-in-interaction. Other forms of technologically enabled interaction can be brought to mind, raising in their turn further possibilities for considering the nature of talk's mediation and distribution.

The telephone, for instance, is a technology that for over a century has allowed people to speak with the intimacy of face-to-face conversation without being physically co-present. Conversation analysts have investigated the nature of talk and recipiency on the telephone in some detail (Hopper, 1992; Hutchby, 2001b). The advent of mobile telephony yields further possibilities for extending that research (Hutchby and Barnett, 2005). The internet also enables new and distinctive forms of distributed interaction. Here newsgroups and internet 'chat' domains have grown up as spaces in which participants can interact (albeit largely through a textual rather than a verbal medium) while being geographically distributed.

Studies of online interaction have brought into play temporality as a dimension of additional relevance. Newsgroup interaction tends to be asynchronous, in the sense that participants leave messages that can be retrieved at any time by others (Baym, 1995, 1996); in this, there is a similarity to voicemail (itself an extension of telephone technology), albeit on a 'mass' scale. Internet relay chat, on the other hand, is synchronous in the sense that participants need to be online at the same time in order to contribute to the discussion (Hutchby, 2001b; Garcia and Jacobs, 1999).

Temporality is also key to broadcasting, especially on television. This is because broadcasting, even in its most conventional forms, enables something quite remarkable: the ability of viewers and listeners to have immediate experience of an event that is occurring elsewhere (as, for instance, in sports broadcasts) or that occurred at another time (as in recorded broadcasts). To return to the above quoted remarks from Scannell (2002), these two phenomena are brought together in a unique way in the technology of the action replay, as audiences watch again an event that occurred moments previously, while the occasion in which that event is embedded (a football match, say) continues 'live' and is returned to once the action replay is over (Marriott, 1996).

The three technological forms I have mentioned – broadcasting, telephony and the internet – while each involved in different ways in the production of distributed inter-action, are also interrelated on a number of levels. For instance, the earliest forms of broadcasting, on wireless radio, drew in significant ways on the technological innov-ations of early telephony. In fact one of the early uses of the telephone system as conceived by its major developers was as a means to broadcast concert music – in other words, an early version of what later became the wireless radio (Hopper, 1992; Grint and Woolgar, 1995). Similarly, the later development of television itself grew out of the technology of radio. The internet too represents a development of telephone technol-ogy combined with that of the digital computer. Digitization itself is now, in turn, affecting the structure and organization of telephony and of television broadcasting.

Both the telephone and the internet also play increasingly complex and integral roles *within* broadcasting. The telephone has traditionally had a major part to play in radio and television broadcasting in the shape of the phone-in (Hutchby, 1996; Verwey, 1990), while being central to major broadcasting phenomena such as the telethon, quiz shows (where befuddled contestants may be given the opportunity to 'phone a friend'[1]) and broadcast news where it is used both in interviewing (more often on radio than on television) and in relaying reports from foreign correspondents. The internet, because of the comparative recency of its rise to popularity, has a less well-defined presence within broadcasting; yet it seems clear that internet technology is key to the ongoing development of interactive and digital television services. One major area in which it is already having a considerable impact is that of journalism and news reporting, both in terms of the 'breaking' and subsequent dissemination of news (Allan, 2005) and in terms of resources for conducting detailed research on the evolution of news stories (Montgomery, 2005). On all these dimensions, there are a whole range of ways of further investigating the impacts of the convergence of technologies on the nature of mediation in broadcasting, and analysing the relationships between affordances of technologies and practices of mediated discourse.

Further reading

Hutchby, I. (2001) *Conversation and Technology: From the Telephone to the Internet.* Cambridge: Polity.

Moores, S. (2003) The doubling of place. In N. Couldry and A. McCarthy (eds), *Media/Space: Place, Scale and Culture in a Media Age.* London: Routledge.

Robins, K. (1996) Cyberspace and the world we live in. In J. Dovey (ed.), *Fractal Dreams: New Media in Social Context.* London: Lawrence and Wishart.

Scannell, P. (1995) For a phenomenology of radio and television. *Journal of Communication*, 45: 4–19.
Scannell, P. (1996) *Radio, Television and Modern Life*. Oxford: Blackwell.

Note

1 This phrase is associated with the popular television quiz show *Who Wants to Be a Millionaire?* At the time of writing, the show's popularity in the UK is such that the question 'Can I phone a friend?' has passed into everyday usage as an idiom used in situations of doubt or perplexity.

GLOSSARY

AAI: The Answer-plus-Auxiliary-Information format often used by expert advice-givers on radio phone-ins such as the one discussed in Chapter 6. It involves answering 'more than the question' by providing additional information to that originally requested. It may in fact be more widely used by advice-givers outside the broadcast context; but in the case of radio and TV talk, it offers a means by which advice can be generalized so as to be potentially relevant to members of the **overhearing audience** other than the caller.

communicative ethos: A term used to describe a distinctive approach to communicative procedures and policies. In the case of broadcasting, the term is associated with an evolving approach to audience engagement, traced through historical studies described in Chapter 1, by which early broadcasters moved from a more patrician to a more democratic mode of audience address.

conversation analysis: An approach to the study of talk in social interaction originating in the work of Harvey Sacks in the mid- to late-1960s. Its distinctive characteristics include an insistence on working only with recordings and transcriptions of speech examples from natural situations in everyday life, and a focus on the **sequential organization** of **talk-in-interaction**. It has been applied both to the study of ordinary conversation and to forms of **institutional discourse** including radio and television talk.

co-presence: A term referring to forms of social interaction where the participants occupy the same space. Following the ideas of Erving Goffman, people in co-presence can be engaged in collaborative or 'focused' activities (such as having a conversation) or 'unfocused' activities (such as simply being together in a doctor's waiting room). Communications technologies also enable interaction to take place in situations other than co-presence: for instance, via the telephone.

cultural dope: A term associated with the work of sociologist Harold Garfinkel. It refers to the idea that human beings are the puppets of social forces beyond their understanding, a view that Garfinkel fundamentally challenged. The 'cultural dope' is a model of the social actor relied upon in the sociological notion that humans are 'socialized' by institutional forces. For Garfinkel it is not the case that humans are 'acted upon' by such forces; rather, humans are competent and knowledgeable agents who play an active part in their own societal membership. In the context of media talk, the 'cultural dope' viewpoint can be associated with certain approaches to **media effects**, which in turn are challenged by approaches drawing from **conversation analysis** (themselves influenced by Garfinkel's ideas).

dialogic: Deriving from 'dialogue', meaning an exchange between two speakers, this term nevertheless has multiple layers of meaning. At one level it is associated with the work of Russian linguist Mikhail Bakhtin, who argued that all forms of language are 'dialogic' in the sense that any utterance takes into account the speaker's knowledge of and expectations about his or her recipient (cf. **recipient design**). In the context of this book, it is used in a more basic sense to refer to forms of broadcasting that involve interaction between two or more speakers, by contrast with **monologic** forms where one speaker addresses the **overhearing audience** directly.

distributed recipients: Another way of referring to the **overhearing audience** for radio and television talk. It seeks to emphasize the sense in which those to whom broadcast talk is directed are separated from the broadcaster by space and time.

genre: A way of referring to specific types of broadcasting that have defining characteristics. For instance, the 'radio phone-in genre' would involve, at a minimum, the studio presence of a host and the provision of designated phone numbers by which audience members could make a call and talk to the host on air. There may be **sub-genres** within any genre; for example, the radio phone-in includes 'open-line' discussion shows, advice-giving shows, competition slots, and so on.

institutional discourse: Used to refer to forms of talk that take place in settings such as workplaces, organizations and so forth. It is frequently characterized by a relationship between ordinary laypersons and professionals, as for example in doctor-patient interaction. But in other types of workplace setting, the talk may be more readily specialized by virtue of being directed towards carrying out certain work-relevant tasks. On the most general level, institutional discourse is contrasted with ordinary conversation, often for comparative purposes as in **conversation analysis**.

interpersonal communication: Used in various areas of communication studies to refer to talk between peers. It is often contrasted with **institutional discourse**, though the latter can also be said to include (specialized) forms of interpersonal communication. More generally, the term is used in the sense of 'one-to-one' conversation in contrast with **mass communication** (thought to be a form of 'one-to-many').

mass communication: Communication that reaches large numbers of people, whether they are in **co-presence** as in political rallies, large-scale lectures, speeches and so forth; or **distributed recipients** as in the case of the press and broadcasting (the 'mass media'). In the latter case, the term may be somewhat misleading since the audiences for radio, television and newspaper output do not necessarily hear, watch or read that output simultaneously (especially since the advent of video-recorders and the like) and are therefore not a 'mass' in the same sense as a co-present collective. Nevertheless, the term is used at various points in this book by contrast with **interpersonal communication**.

media effects: A term referring to the idea that the contents of media output have measurable consequences in terms of human behaviour. For instance, watching more violence on television is said to make people more violent, or less sensitive to the consequences of violence. Many ideas about media effects have entered popular consciousness, probably because the media's own reporting of traumatic events such as child murders or serial killings are often couched within the language of 'effects'. But the approach is out of vogue within media studies, and from the point of view of this book, is fundamentally flawed by its **cultural dope** model of the audience.

monologic: See **dialogic**.

next-turn proof procedure: In **conversation analysis**, this refers to the way in which the **recipient** of a turn at talk displays, in the next turn, their understanding of what the prior turn was about. By the same token, it provides a way in which the analyst of that exchange can examine, in the **sequential organization** of talk, the participants' own understandings of their interaction. This is key to the conversation analytic perspective, in which it is thought more important to try and explicate the ways that the participants in any interaction display their understanding of what they are doing than to begin from theoretically-driven assumptions about what might be going on.

overhearing audience: A term sometimes used to refer to the audience for radio and television talk. While convenient, it is not entirely accurate since the audience are not technically 'overhearers' (i.e. eavesdroppers). Rather, as various chapters of this book show, the audience can be characterized as being addressed in various ways by broadcast talk. Hence the term **distributed recipients** may be more appropriate.

parasocial interaction: A term used in an important article called 'Mass communication and parasocial interaction' by Donald Horton and Richard Wohl (see Chapter 1). It refers to the way in which broadcasters give the impression that they are addressing the individual audience member directly (e.g. through direct gaze to the camera lens). In Horton and Wohl's account, this could lead to false impressions in audiences, particularly in the early days of television, leading some to conclude that they were actually somehow acquainted with the TV personality. The modern equivalent can be found in the occasional tendency of 'stalker fans' to become obsessed with their chosen celebrity, feeling rejected (sometimes murderously) if their attempts at communication are rebuffed.

proxy questioning: A form of questioning used in phone-in advice broadcasts whereby the host, who tends to be a non-expert, assists the expert advice-giver (and possibly also the caller) by 'prompting' the expert to provide further information while giving the impression that he or she (the host) in fact knows that information but is refraining from stating it. The host's question thus acts as a 'proxy' for the expert while maintaining the host's own neutral or non-expert role.

recipient: In conversation analysis, a way of referring to the person or persons to whom an utterance is directed. It is preferred to 'hearer' or 'addressee' because these terms imply a more passive role. In **talk-in-interaction**, a recipient is not simply the person who hears a turn or is addressed by it. The role of recipient involves showing, by way of a response, that one understands oneself to have been the intended target of the prior speaker's turn. This in part is what makes the question of how broadcasters address the **overhearing audience** in their talk such a complex one, since the audience cannot display their active recipiency by virtue of a **next-turn proof procedure**.

recipient design: A term used in **conversation analysis** to describe the way that utterances display their speaker's understanding of and expectations about the mutual knowledge that exists between themselves and their **recipient**(s). For example, in conversation people tend to adopt the most minimal available ways of referring to other people, preferring (if possible) simple recognitionals such as 'Uncle John' over more complex equivalents like 'That 58 year old man we both know who also happens to be the younger brother of my father'. In media talk, recipient design is complex due to the indeterminate nature of the **overhearing audience**, but various chapters of this book describe ways in which broadcasters orient to expectations and understandings about their audiences.

sequential organization: A fundamental term within **conversation analysis**, it refers to the particular, rule-bound ways that turns in **talk-in-interaction** are linked together. It can be usefully contrasted with the 'serial organization' of turns. Taking turns in a serial manner implies that one turn merely follows another. For conversation analysts, talk is organized differently from this. Sequential organization means that one turn can have specific *consequences* for the next turn that should follow: for instance, asking a question makes it relevant that the **recipient** should produce an answer, and failure to do so may mean that they can be held to account for 'ignoring' you (for example). Sequential organization is therefore at the heart of coherence, intelligibility and normative order in talk-in-interaction.

speech exchange system: In **conversation analysis**, a term used to describe the set of normative procedures that people utilize to regulate the distribution of opportunities to speak in given settings. They vary from the informal, such as ordinary conversation, in which who speaks, what they say and how long a turn they have are all freely variable, to the highly formal such as wedding ceremonies, in which each of these aspects is to a degree pre-ordained. Speech exchange systems may also be referred to as **turn-taking systems**.

sub-genre: See **genre**.

talk-in-interaction: The object of study in **conversation analysis**. This term is preferred over 'conversation' because conversation analysts do not study only conversation itself. Rather, they study any form of talk which involves interaction between two or more participants.

turn-taking system: See **speech exchange system**.

turn-type pre-allocation: A term used to describe certain formal types of **speech exchange system**. It refers to the way in which some social settings involve a linkage between the social role a speaker takes up and the type of turn he or she is thereby enabled to take. For example, in a courtroom trial the witness is required to restrict themselves to answering questions put by attorneys, who in turn are allowed only to ask questions (not, for instance, to make statements, except during their introductions and summings up). In media talk the closest to this is perhaps the news interview, where the roles of interviewer and interviewee carry with them the requirement, respectively, to produce questions and answers.

REFERENCES

Adorno, T. and Horkheimer, M. (1972) *The Dialectic of Enlightenment*. New York: Seabury Press.

Allan, S. (2005) News on the web: The emerging forms and practices of online journalism. In S. Allan (ed.), *Journalism: Critical Issues*. Maidenhead: Open University Press.

Atkinson, J.M. (1984a) *Our Masters' Voices: The Language and Body Language of Politics*. London: Methuen.

Atkinson, J.M. (1984b) Public speaking and audience response: Some techniques for inviting applause. In J.M. Atkinson and J. Heritage (eds), *Structures of Social Action: Studies in Conversation Analysis*. Cambridge: Cambridge University Press.

Atkinson, J.M. and Drew, P. (1979) *Order in Court: The Organisation of Verbal Interaction in Judicial Settings*. London: Macmillan.

Atkinson, J.M. and Heritage, J. (eds) (1984) *Structures of Social Action: Studies in Conversation Analysis*. Cambridge: Cambridge University Press.

Atkinson, P. and Silverman, D. (1997) Kundera's *Immortality*: The interview society and the invention of the self. *Qualitative Inquiry*, 3: 304–25.

Austin, J.L. (1962) *How to Do Things with Words*. Oxford: Oxford University Press.

Avery, R. and Ellis, D. (1979) Talk radio as an interpersonal phenomenon. In G. Gumpert and C. Cathcart (eds), *Inter/Media*. New York: Oxford University Press.

Barbour, R. and Kitzinger, J. (eds) (1999) *Developing Focus Group Research*. London: Sage.

Barker, M. and Petley, J. (eds) (1997) *Ill Effects: The Media/Violence Debate*. London: Routledge.

Baym, N. (1995) From practice to culture on UseNet. In S.L. Star (ed.), *The Cultures of Computing*. Oxford: Blackwell.

Baym, N. (1996) Agreements and disagreements in a computer-mediated discussion. *Research on Language and Social Interaction*, 29: 315–45.

Bell, A. and Garrett, P. (eds) (1998) *Approaches to Media Discourse*. Oxford: Blackwell.

Blumler, J. and Katz, E. (1974) *The Uses of Mass Communication: Current Perspectives in Gratifications Research*. London: Sage.

Boden, D. and Zimmerman, D. (eds) (1991) *Talk and Social Structure*. Cambridge: Polity.

Brecht, B. (1964 [1932]) The radio as an apparatus of communication. In J. Willett (ed. and trans.), *Brecht on Theatre: The Development of an Aesthetic*. London: Methuen.

Brundson, C. and Morley, D. (1978) *Everyday Television: 'Nationwide'*. London: BFI.

Cage, J. (1960 [1952]) *4'33"*. Edition Peters 6777. London: Henmar Press.

Camporesi, V. (1994) The BBC and American broadcasting, 1922–55. *Media, Culture and Society*, 16: 625–40.

Carbaugh, D. (1988) *Talking American: Cultural Discourses on 'Donahue'*. Norwood NJ: Ablex.

Cardiff, D. and Scannell, P. (1986) 'Good luck war workers!' Class, politics and entertainment in wartime broadcasting. In T. Bennett, C. Mercer and J. Woollacott (eds), *Popular Culture and Social Relations*. Milton Keynes: Open University Press.

Chomsky, N. (1965) *Aspects of the Theory of Syntax*. The Hague: Mouton.

Clark, H. and Haviland, S. (1977) Comprehension and the given-new contract. In R.O. Freedle (ed.), *Discourse Production and Comprehension*. Hillsdale, NJ: Erlbaum.

Clayman, S. (1988) Displaying neutrality in television news interviews. *Social Problems*, 35: 474–92.

Clayman, S. (1989) The production of punctuality: Social interaction, temporal organisation and social structure. *American Journal of Sociology*, 95: 659–91.

Clayman, S. (1990) From talk to text: Newspaper accounts of reporter-source interactions. *Media, Culture and Society*, 12: 79–103.

Clayman, S. (1992) Footing in the achievement of neutrality: The case of news interview discourse. In P. Drew and J. Heritage (eds), *Talk At Work*. Cambridge: Cambridge University Press.

Clayman, S. and Heritage, J. (2002) *The News Interview*. Cambridge: Cambridge University Press.

Clayman, S. and Whalen, J. (1988/9) When the medium becomes the message: The case of the Rather-Bush encounter. *Research on Language and Social Interaction*, 22: 241–72.

Cobley, P. (1994) Throwing out the baby: Populism and active audience theory. *Media, Culture and Society*, 16: 677–87.

Cohen, S. and Young, J. (1973) *The Manufacture of News*. London: Constable.

Connell, I. (1980) Television news and the social contract. In S. Hall, D. Hobson, A. Lowe and P. Willis (eds), *Culture, Media, Language*. London: Hutchison.

Coulter, J. (1982) Remarks on the conceptualisation of social structure. *Philosophy of the Social Sciences*, 12: 33–46.

Crisell, A. (1994) *Understanding Radio*. London: Routledge.

Crow, B. (1986) Conversational pragmatics in television talk: The discourse of *Good Sex*. *Media, Culture and Society*, 8: 457–84.

Crittenden, J. (1971) Democratic functions of the open mike forum. *Public Opinion Quarterly*, 35: 200–210.

Drew, P. (1992) Contested evidence in courtroom cross-examination: The case of a trial for rape. In P. Drew and J. Heritage (eds), *Talk At Work: Interaction in Institutional Settings*. Cambridge: Cambridge University Press.

Drew, P. and Heritage, J. (eds) (1992a) *Talk At Work: Interaction in Institutional Settings*. Cambridge: Cambridge University Press.

Drew, P. and Heritage, J. (1992b) Analysing talk at work: An introduction. In P. Drew and J. Heritage (eds), *Talk At Work: Interaction in Institutional Settings*. Cambridge: Cambridge University Press.

Eisenberg, A. and Garvey, C. (1981) Children's use of verbal strategies in resolving conflicts. *Discourse Processes*, 4: 149–70.

Eysenck, H. and Nias, D.K.B. (1978) *Sex, Violence and the Media*. London: Temple Smith.

Fairclough, N. (1995) *Media Discourse*. London: Edward Arnold.

Ferrara, W.K. (1994) *Therapeutic Ways with Words*. Oxford: Oxford University Press.

Frankel, R. (1984) From sentence to sequence: Understanding the medical encounter through microinteractional analysis. *Discourse Processes*, 7: 135–70.

Frankel, R. (1990) Talking in interviews: A dispreference for patient-initiated questions in physician-patient encounters. In G. Psathas (ed.) *Interaction Competence*. Washington DC: University Press of America.

Garcia, A. (1991) Dispute resolution without disputing: How the interactional organisation of mediation hearings minimizes argument. *American Sociological Review*, 56: 818–35.

Garcia, A.C. and Jacobs, J.B. (1999) The eyes of the beholder: Understanding the turn-taking system in quasi-synchronous computer-mediated communication. *Research on Language and Social Interaction*, 32: 337–67.

Garfinkel, H. (1967) *Studies in Ethnomethodology*. New York: Prentice Hall.

Garton, G., Montgomery, M. and Tolson, A. (1991) Ideology, scripts and metaphors in the public sphere of a general election. In P. Scannell (ed.), *Broadcast Talk*. London: Sage.

Goffman, E. (1961) *Encounters*. New York: Bobbs-Merrill.

Goffman, E. (1974) *Frame Analysis*. New York: Harper and Row.

Goffman, E. (1981) *Forms of Talk*. Oxford: Blackwell.

Goodwin, M.H. (1990) *He-Said-She-Said: Talk as Social Organisation Among Black Children*. Bloomington, IA: Indiana University Press.

Gramsci, A. (1971) *Selections from the Prison Notebooks*. London: Lawrence and Wishart.

Greatbatch, D. (1988) A turn-taking system for British news interviews. *Language in Society*, 17: 401–30.

Greatbatch, D. (1992) On the management of disagreement between news interviewees. In P. Drew and J. Heritage (eds), *Talk At Work*. Cambridge: Cambridge University Press.

Greatbatch, D. (1998) Conversation analysis: Neutralism in British news interviews. In A. Bell and P. Garrett (eds), *Approaches to Media Discourse*. Oxford: Blackwell.

Grint, K. and Woolgar, S. (1995) *The Machine At Work*. Cambridge: Polity.

Haarman, T. (ed.) (2000) *Talk About Shows*. Bologna: CLUEB.

Hall, S. (1980) Encoding/decoding. In S. Hall, D. Hobson, A. Lowe and P. Willis (eds), *Culture, Media, Language*. London: Hutchison.

Hall, S., Hobson, D., Lowe A. and Willis, P. (eds) (1980) *Culture, Media, Language*. London: Hutchison.

Harris, S. (1991) Evasive action: How politicians respond to questions in political interviews. In P. Scannell (ed.), *Broadcast Talk*. London: Sage.

Heath, C. (1992) The delivery and reception of diagnosis in the general practice consultation. In P. Drew and J. Heritage (eds), *Talk At Work*. Cambridge: Cambridge University Press.

Heritage, J. (1984) *Garfinkel and Ethnomethodology*. Cambridge: Polity.

Heritage, J. (1985) Analysing news interviews: Aspects of the production of talk for an overhearing audience. In van Dijk, T. (ed.), *Handbook of Discourse Analysis, Volume 3: Discourse and Dialogue*. London: Academic Press.

Heritage, J. (1989) Current developments in conversation analysis. In D. Roger and P. Bull (eds), *Conversation*. Clevedon: Multilingual Matters.

Heritage, J., Clayman, S. and Zimmerman, D. (1988) Discourse and message analysis: The micro-structure of mass media messages. In R.P. Hawkins, J. M. Wiemann and S. Pingree (eds), *Advancing Communication Science: Merging Mass and Interpersonal Processes*. London: Sage.

Heritage, J. and Greatbatch, D. (1986) Generating applause: A study of rhetoric and response at party political conferences. *American Journal of Sociology*, 19: 110–57.

Heritage, J. and Greatbatch, D. (1991) On the institutional character of institutional talk: The case of news interviews. In D. Boden and D. Zimmerman (eds), *Talk and Social Structure*. Cambridge: Polity.

Heritage, J. and Sefi, S. (1992) Dilemmas of advice: Aspects of the delivery and reception of advice in interactions between health visitors and first time mothers. In P. Drew and J. Heritage (eds), *Talk At Work*. Cambridge: Cambridge University Press.

Hester, S. and Fitzgerald, R. (1999) Category, predicate and task: Some organisational features in a radio talk show. In P. Jalbert (ed.), *Media Studies: Ethnomethodological Approaches*. Washington DC: University Press of America.

Hobson, D. (1980) Housewives and the mass media. In S. Hall, D. Hobson, A. Lowe and P. Willis (eds), *Culture, Media, Language*. London: Hutchison.

Hopper, R. (1992) *Telephone Conversation*. Bloomington, IA: Indiana University Press.

Horton, D. and Wohl, R.R. (1956) Mass communication and para-social interaction: Observations on intimacy at a distance. *Psychiatry*, 19: 215–29.

Houtkoop-Steenstra, H. (1991) Opening sequences in Dutch telephone conversation. In D. Boden and D. Zimmerman (eds), *Talk and Social Structure*. Cambridge: Polity.

Hutchby, I. (1991) The organisation of talk on talk radio. In P. Scannell (ed.), *Broadcast Talk*. London: Sage.

Hutchby, I. (1992) Confrontation talk: aspects of 'interruption' in argument sequences on talk radio. *Text*, 12: 343–71.

Hutchby, I. (1995) Aspects of recipient design in expert advice-giving on call-in radio. *Discourse Processes*, 19: 219–38.

Hutchby, I. (1996) *Confrontation Talk: Arguments, Asymmetries and Power on Talk Radio*. Mahwah, NJ: Lawrence Erlbaum Associates.

Hutchby, I. (1999) Frame attunement and footing in the organisation of talk radio openings. *Journal of Sociolinguistics*, 3: 41–64.

Hutchby, I. (2001a) 'Oh', irony and sequential ambiguity in arguments. *Discourse and Society*, 12: 123–41.

Hutchby, I. (2001b) *Conversation and Technology: From the Telephone to the Internet*. Cambridge: Polity.

Hutchby, I. and Barnett, S. (2005) Aspects of the sequential organisation of mobile phone conversation. *Discourse Studies*, 7: 147–71.

Hutchby, I. and Wooffitt, R. (1998) *Conversation Analysis*. Cambridge: Polity.

Jefferson, G. (1978) Sequential aspects of storytelling in conversation. In J. Schenkein (ed.), *Studies in the Organisation of Conversational Interaction*. New York: Academic Press.

Jefferson, G. (1990) List construction as a task and resource. In G. Psathas (ed.), *Interaction Competence*. Washington, DC: University Press of America.

Jefferson, G. and Lee, J.R.E. (1981) The rejection of advice: Managing the problematic convergence of a 'troubles telling' and a 'service encounter'. *Journal of Pragmatics*, 5: 399–422. (Reprinted in P. Drew and J. Heritage (eds), *Talk at Work*. Cambridge: Cambridge University Press, 1992.)

Jefferson, G., Sacks, H. and Schegloff, E.A. (1987) Notes on laughter in pursuit of intimacy. In G. Button and J.R.E. Lee (eds), *Talk and Social Organisation*. Clevedon: Multilingual Matters.

Lazarsfeld, P. and Merton, R. (1948) Mass communication, popular taste and organised social action. In L. Bryson (ed.), *The Communication of Ideas*. New York: Harper.

Lerner, G. (1991) On the syntax of sentences in progress. *Language in Society*, 20: 441–58.

Lerner, G. (ed.) (2004) *Conversation Analysis: Studies from the First Generation*. Amsterdam: John Benjamins.

Levinson, S. (1983) *Pragmatics*. Cambridge: Cambridge University Press.

Levinson, S. (1988) Putting linguistics on a proper footing: Explorations in Goffman's concepts of participation. In P. Drew and A.J. Wootton (eds), *Erving Goffman: Exploring the Interaction Order*. Cambridge: Polity.

Lindstrom, A. (1994) Identification and recognition in Swedish telephone conversation openings. *Language in Society*, 23: 231–52.

Livingstone, S. and Lunt, P. (1994) *Talk on Television*. London: Routledge.

Lunt, P. and Stenner, P. (2005) The *Jerry Springer* show as an emotional public sphere. *Media Culture and Society*, 27: 59–81.

Lynch, M. and Bogen, D. (1996) *The Spectacle of History: Speech, Text and Memory at the Iran-Contra Hearings*. London: Duke University Press.

MacCabe, C. (1985) *Theoretical Essays: Film, Linguistics, Literature*. Manchester: Manchester University Press.

Marriott, S. (1996) Time and time again: 'Live' television commentary and the construction of replay talk. *Media Culture and Society* 18: 69–86.

Matheson, D. (2005) *Media Discourses*. Maidenhead: Open University Press.

Maynard, D. (1985) How children start arguments. *Language in Society*, 14: 1–30.

McHoul, A. (1978) The organisation of turns at formal talk in the classroom. *Language in Society*, 19: 183–213.

Mehan, H. (1979) *Learning Lessons: Social Organisation in the Classroom*. Cambridge, MA: Harvard University Press.

Moerman, M. (1988) *Talking Culture: Ethnography and Conversation Analysis*. Philadelphia, PA: University of Pennsylvania Press.

Montgomery, M. (1986) DJ talk. *Media Culture and Society*, 8: 421–40.

Montgomery, M. (1991) 'Our Tune': a study of a discourse genre. In P. Scannell (ed.) *Broadcast Talk*. London: Sage.

Montgomery, M. (2005) Talking war: How journalism responded to the events of 9/11. In S. Allan (ed.), *Journalism: Critical Issues*. Maidenhead: Open University Press.

Morley, D. (1980) *The 'Nationwide' Audience: Structure and Decoding*. London: BFI.

Moss, C. and Higgins, P. (1984) Radio voices. *Media, Culture and Society*, 6: 353–75.

Moores, S. (1993) *Interpreting Audiences*. London: Sage.

Moores, S. (2003) The doubling of place. In N. Couldry and A. McCarthy (eds), *Media/Space: Place, Scale and Culture in a Media Age*. London: Routledge.

Munson, W. (1993) *All talk: The Talk Show in Media Culture*. Philadelphia, PA: Temple University Press.

Myers, G. (2001) 'I'm out of it: you guys argue': Making an issue of it on the *Jerry Springer Show*. In A. Tolson (ed.), *Television Talk Shows*. Mahwah, NJ: Lawrence Erlbaum Associates.

Nightingale, V. (1996) *Studying Audiences*. London: Routledge.

Nofsinger, R. (1988/9) 'Let's talk about the record': Contending over topic redirection in the Rather/Bush interview. *Research on Language and Social Interaction*, 22: 273–92.

Parkin, F. (1972) *Class Inequality and Political Order*. London: Paladin.

Pomerantz, A. (1984a) Agreeing and disagreeing with assessments: Some features of preferred/dispreferred turn-shapes. In J.M. Atkinson and J. Heritage (eds), *Structures of Social Action: Studies in Conversation Analysis*. Cambridge: Cambridge University Press.

Pomerantz, A. (1984b) Pursuing a response. In J.M. Atkinson and J. Heritage (eds), *Structures of Social Action: Studies in Conversation Analysis*. Cambridge: Cambridge University Press.

Pomerantz, A. (1988/9) Constructing skepticism: Four devices used to engender the audience's skepticism. *Research on Language and Social Interaction*, 22: 293–314.

Priest, P.J. (1995) *Public Intimacies: Talk Show Participants and Tell-all TV*. Cresskill, NJ: Hampton Press.

Robins, K. (1996) Cyberspace and the world we live in. In J. Dovey (ed.) *Fractal Dreams: New Media in Social Context*. London: Lawrence and Wishart.

Ross, K. and Nightingale, V. (2003) *Media Audiences: New Perspectives*. Maidenhead: Open University Press.

Sacks, H. (1972a) An initial investigation of the usability of conversational data for doing sociology. In D. Sudnow (ed.), *Studies in Social Interaction*. New York: Free Press.

Sacks, H. (1972b) On the analysability of stories by children. In J. Gumperz and D. Hymes (eds), *Directions in Sociolinguistics*. New York: Holt, Rinehart and Winston.

Sacks, H. (1975) Everyone has to lie. In B. Blount and M. Sanchez (eds), *Sociocultural Dimensions of Language Use*. New York: Academic Press.

Sacks, H. (1984) Notes on methodology. In J.M. Atkinson and J. Heritage (eds), *Structures of Social Action: Studies in Conversation Analysis*. Cambridge: Cambridge University Press.

Sacks, H. (1992) *Lectures on Conversation* (2 Vols. ed. G. Jefferson). Oxford: Blackwell.

Sacks, H. and Schegloff, E.A. (1979) Two preferences in the organisation of reference to persons in conversation and their interaction. In G. Psathas (ed.), *Everyday Language: Studies in Ethnomethodology*. Hillsdale, NJ: Erlbaum.

Sacks, H., Schegloff, E.A. and Jefferson, G. (1974) A simplest systematics for the organisation of turn-taking for conversation. *Language*, 50: 696–735.

Saussure, F. de (1984 [1915]) *Course in General Linguistics*. London: Fontana.

Scannell, P. (ed.) (1986) *Broadcast Talk*: Special Issue of *Media, Culture and Society*, Vol.8 No. 4. London: Sage.

Scannell, P. (1988a) The communicative ethos of broadcasting. Paper presented at the International Television Studies Conference. London: BFI.

Scannell, P. (1988b) Radio times: The temporal arrangements of broadcasting in the modern world. In P. Drummond and R. Patterson (eds), *Television and its Audience: International Research Perspectives*. London: BFI.

Scannell, P. (1989) Public service broadcasting and modern public life. *Media, Culture and Society*, 11: 135–66.

Scannell, P. (ed.) (1991a) *Broadcast Talk*. London: Sage.

Scannell, P. (1991b) Introduction: The relevance of talk. In P. Scannell (ed.), *Broadcast Talk*. London: Sage.

Scannell, P. (1995) For a phenomenology of radio and television. *Journal of Communication*, 45: 4–19.

Scannell, P. (1996) *Radio, Television and Modern Life*. Oxford: Blackwell.

Scannell, P. (2002) The meaning of live. Paper presented at the International Seminar on Broadcast Talk. Glasgow: Ross Priory, University of Strathclyde.

Scannell, P. and Cardiff, D. (1991) *A Social History of British Broadcasting* (Vol.1). Oxford: Blackwell.

Schegloff, E.A. (1979) Identification and recognition in telephone conversation openings. In G. Psathas (ed.), *Everyday Language*. Hillsdale, NJ: Lawrence Erlbaum Associates.

Schegloff, E.A. (1982) Discourse as an interactional achievement: Some uses of 'uh huh' and other things that come between sentences. In D. Tannen (ed.), *Analysing Discourse: Text and Talk*. Washington, DC: Georgetown University Press.

Schegloff, E.A. (1986) The routine as achievement. *Human Studies*, 9: 111–52.

Schegloff, E.A. (1987) Between micro and macro: Contexts and other connections. In J. Alexander, B. Giesen, R. Munch and N. Smelser (eds), *The Micro-Macro Link*. Berkeley and Los Angeles: University of California Press.

Schegloff, E.A. (1988) Presequences and indirection: Applying speech act theory to ordinary conversation. *Journal of Pragmatics*, 12: 55–62.

Schegloff, E.A. (1988/9) From interview to confrontation: Observations on the Bush/Rather encounter. *Research on Language and Social Interaction*, 22: 215–40.

Schegloff, E.A. (1991) Reflections on talk and social structure. In D. Boden and D. Zimmerman (eds), *Talk and Social Structure*. Cambridge: Polity.

Schegloff, E.A., Jefferson, G. and Sacks, H. (1977) The preference for self-correction in the organisation of repair in conversation. *Language*, 53: 361–82.

Schegloff, E.A. and Sacks, H. (1973) Opening up closings. *Semiotica*, 7: 289–327.

Schudson, M. (1994) Question authority: A history of the news interview in American journalism, 1860s–1930s. *Media, Culture and Society*, 16: 565–88.

Seaman, W.R. (1992) Active audience theory: Pointless populism. *Media, Culture and Society*, 14(2): 301–11.

Shattuc, J. (1997) *The Talking Cure: TV Talk Shows and Women*. London: Routledge.

Silverman, D. (1996) *Discourses of Counselling*. London: Sage.

Terasaki, A. (2004) Pre-announcement sequences in conversation. In G. Lerner (ed.), *Conversation Analysis: Studies from the First Generation*. Amsterdam: John Benjamins.

Thompson, J.B. (1984) *Studies in the Theory of Ideology*. Cambridge: Polity.

Thornborrow, J. (ed.) (1997a) *Broadcast Talk*: Special Issue of *Text*, Vol. 17 No. 2. Amsterdam: Mouton de Gruyter.

Thornborrow, J. (1997b) Having their say: The function of stories in talk show discourse. *Text*, 17: 241–62.

Thornborrow, J. (2001) Authenticating talk: Building public identities in audience participation broadcasting. *Discourse Studies*, 3: 459–80.

Thornborrow, J. (2002) *Power Talk*. London: Pearson.

Thornborrow, J. and Fitzgerald, R. (2002) From problematic object to routine 'add-on': Dealing with e-mails in radio phone-ins. *Discourse Studies*, 4: 201–24.

Thornborrow, J. and van Leeuwen, T. (eds) (2001) *Authenticity in Media Discourse*: Special Issue of *Discourse Studies*, Vol. 3 No. 4. London: Sage.

Tolson, A. (ed.) (2001) *Television Talk Shows: Discourse, Performance, Spectacle*. Mahwah, NJ: Lawrence Erlbaum Associates.

Tuchman, G. (1978) *Making News: A Study in the Construction of Reality*. New York: Free Press.

Verwey, N. (1990) *Radio Call-ins and Covert Politics*. Avebury: Gower.

Wittgenstein, L. (1953) *Philosophical Investigations*. Oxford: Blackwell.

Wood, H. (2001) 'No *you* rioted': The pursuit of conflict in the management of 'lay' and 'expert' discourses on *Kilroy*. In A. Tolson (ed.), *Television Talk Shows*. Mahwah, NJ: Lawrence Erlbaum Associates.

INDEX